DO Y

THE SAINTS
?

Compiled and edited by
ADELINE KUZAN

POCKET REFERENCE BOOKS

A POCKET REFERENCE BOOK

Pocket Reference Books Publishing Ltd.
Premier House
Hinton Road
Bournemouth
Dorset BH1 2EF

First Published 1996

Typesetting	Gary Tomlinson PrintRelate (Bournemouth, Dorset) (01202) 897659
Cover Design	Van Renselar Bonney Design Associates West Wickham, Kent BR4 9QH
Printing and Binding:	RPM Reprographics Units 2-3 Spur Road Quarry Lane, Chichester West Sussex PO19 2PR Tel. 01243 787077 Fax. 01243 780012 Modem 01243 536482 E-Mail: rpm@argonet.co.uk

ISBN 1 899437 90 8

Contents   Pages

ALL POCKET REFERENCE BOOKS INCLUDE A
FREE FULL PAGE ADVERTISEMENT ON THE
INSIDE FRONT COVER FOR A WELL-KNOWN CHARITY
SELECTED BY THE COMPILER

THE HISTORY OF THE CHARITY IS INCLUDED ON
THE INSIDE BACK COVER

The Publishers cannot be held responsible for any omissions or
information which is incorrect.
A very wide range of sources has been used by the compiler and the
editor, and the content of this Pocket Reference Book is dependent
upon the accuracy of those sources.

INTRODUCTION

Few people in this hurried and harassed age have the time to wade through bulky publications. It is to provide a compact, easily-read reference I offer this compilation of Do You Know The Saints?

Together with the 'outstanding', lesser-known saints have been included from differing countries, ranks and conditions of life. Chosen to appeal not only to those who have made a study of hagiography but also to those who perhaps know nothing of the lives of saints.

To the many saints who have been mentioned and to the great many more who sadly have had to be omitted, "ora pro nobis".

ADELINE KUZAN

WHAT DO YOU KNOW ABOUT THE SAINTS?
TRY THESE TEASERS

1 Who lived as a recluse in a hut at the bottom of her garden?

2 Do you know of the particularly grisly death devised for Saint Erasmus?

3 Which pope was summoned to the Pincian Palace, went in alone; leaving his clergy at the door, and was seen no more?

4 Who wrote the famous "Spiritual Exercises?"

5 He is usually represented in his chancellor's robes, often wearing a scholar's cap. He is patron saint of lawyers. Who is he?

6 Who was seen daily walking through the streets of his town carrying his straw bed upon his shoulders?

7 Colleges at both Oxford and Cambridge are dedicated to this saint.

8 Upon whose request did Attila the Hun spare the city of Troyes?

9 Who lived on a pillar for 68 years?

10 Who was the first of the apostles to be martyred?

The answers will be found in the following pages.

A LEGEND OF HEAVEN

The angels had ceased from their singing
Strange whispers were filling the air;
The Saints seemed perturbed over something
And gathered in groups here and there.
Strange people were walking through heaven
With shadowy garments and face.
Saint Paul to Saints Thomas and Andrew –
"Who let those queer folks in this place?"
But no one could answer this question;
He set out to look for his mate;
For surely St Peter could tell him,
He'd know if they passed through the gate.
But Simon knew nothing about it,
So off they both went to explore,
And hunted in vain through the heavens,
Until, at the very last door,
They heard such a terrible racket
Both looked at each other and stopped.
Says Paul, "What can Joseph be doing?"
For this was his carpenter shop.
Then opening the door kind of slowly,
Sure, what do you think did they see –
A hole in the flag-stones of heaven,
And Joseph down on his knees;
Till, spying a ladder descending,
They saw the whole mystery unfold –
He'd built a back door-way to heaven
To rescue the poor suffering souls.
St Peter got mad as a hatter,
"Old man, this has all got to stop,
Or else you'll get put out of Heaven;
We'll close up your carpenter shop."
St Joseph got up from the ladder
And drew himself up full of pride –
"If you dare to put me out of heaven,
I'll take with me, Mary, my bride;
And since she's truly God's Mother
She'll take with her Jesus, her Son,
And then there'll be no Heaven.
Says Peter – "Joseph, you've won."

January 1
SAINT FULGENTIUS
Bishop and Confessor – AD 533

Saint Fulgentius was descendant of a noble family of Carthage. Born 468, his virtuous conduct and mild carriage caused him to be beloved and admired wherever his name was known.

He was chosen as lieutenant-governor and general receiver of taxes of Byzacena. He later joined the monastery in Byzacena delighting in the austere and penitential way of life, saying, "He who has inspired me with the will to serve Him, can also furnish me with the courage and strength to carry it through." Fulgentius having now obtained all he wished for in this world gave his estates to his mother, and built a spacious monastery in Byzacena. Not wanting to live with others he retired to a cell and lived alone near the seashore. His modesty, meekness and humility gained him the affections of all.

The following feasts are also celebrated today:
St Almachius or **Telemachus** whose death, c400 put an end to the cruel shows in the area. He protested against gladiatorial fights and was killed by the people: **St Clarus**, Abbot: **St Concordius**, martyr about 178: **St Eugendus**, Abbot: **St Fanchea**, virgin, 585: **St Felix** of Bourges, Bishop 580: **St Odiolo** or **Olon** sixth Abbot of Cluny, 1049: **St William**, Abbot of St Benignus (**William of Dijon**), 1031.

January 2
SAINT MACARIUS OF ALEXANDRIA
Hermit – AD 394

Saint Macarius was a citizen of Alexandria and a confectioner. Whilst still a young man he left his home to live alone in the deserts of upper Egypt, praying, fasting and meditating.

Still aiming for greater sanctity, he moved to lower Egypt to a desert called the Cells, this name being given to it on account of the multitude of hermit-cells with which it abounded. Each hermit, or anchoret, had here his separate cell, which he made his continued abode, except on Saturday and Sunday, when all assembled in one church to celebrate the divine mysteries. If anyone was absent, he was concluded to be sick, and was visited by the rest.

When a stranger came to live among them, each offered his cell, being ready to build another for himself. Their cells were not within sight of each other. A profound silence reigned throughout the whole desert.

A memorable instance of the great self-denial professed and observed by these holy hermits is recorded; a present was made of a newly gathered bunch of grapes to St Macarius who took them to a neighbouring hermit who was sick. The sick monk passed the bunch of grapes to another, who passed them in like manner to all the cells in the desert and was eventually brought back to Macarius, who exceedingly rejoiced at the self-denial of his hermit brethren but still could not bring himself to eat the grapes.

The following feasts are also celebrated today:

St Adelhard or Adelard, Abbot 827, first cousin to Charlemagne. He forsook the Court and retired to a monastery in his twentieth year: **St Aspasius**, Bishop, about 560: **St Munchin**, 640, Patron of the Diocese of Limerick, described as "the Wise": **St Vincencianus**, Hermit, about 672.

January 3
SAINT GENEVIEVE
Virgin – AD 512

St Genevieve was born about the year 422, at Nanterre, a small village four miles from Paris. At the age of seven, in the presence of St Germanus, Bishop of Auxerre, her parents and people of the village, she consecrated her life to God.

About fifteen years of age, she became a nun and entered a convent in Paris. From then on she would only eat twice a week, barley bread with a few beans. Her prayers were almost continual, and generally attended with a large flow of tears.

The first design of the magnificent church built by King Clovis in Paris and dedicated to SS Peter and Paul is attributed to Genevieve. Upon the report of the march of Attila with his army of Huns, the Parisians were preparing to abandon their city, but Genevieve persuaded them to stay, fasting, watching and praying. She assured the people of Paris of the protection of heaven and their deliverance.

She died, aged eighty-nine, in the same year as King Clovis.

The tombs of St Genevieve and King Clovis are together and can be seen in the subterranean church, or vault, in the church of SS Peter and Paul, Paris. The miracles which were performed there from the time of her burial rendered this church famous all over France, so that at length it began to be known only by her name.

The following feasts are also celebrated today:

St Antherus, Pope for only one month and ten days: **St Bertilia**, virgin, 705: **St Florentius**, Bishop of Vienne, martyred about 275: **St Gordius**, martyr: **St Peter Balsam**, Martyr, 311: **St Theopemptus**, Bishop and martyr, towards the end of the third century.

January 4
SAINT TITUS
Disciple of St Paul – Bishop

St Titus was employed by St Paul as his secretary and interpreter. He was a very dear and close friend of St Paul's and is mentioned in Paul's epistles.

Titus was made bishop of the island of Crete. He finished a laborious and holy life by a happy death in Crete. His body was venerated in the cathedral of Gortyna. The cathedral was destroyed by the Saracens in 823 and the relics were lost. Only the head of Titus was conveyed to Venice and is now in the Ducal basilic of St Mark.

The following feasts are also celebrated today
St Ferriolus, Bishop of Uzès: **St Gregory**, Bishop of Langres: **St Pharaildis**, virgin, of Flanders: **St Rigobert**, or **Robert**, Archbishop of Rheims, 745.

January 5
SAINT SIMEON STYLITES

St Simeon was a son of a poor shepherd in Cilicia, on the borders of Syria. Only thirteen years of age he went to a monastery near his home and lay before the gates for several days, without eating or drinking, begging to be admitted. The holy abbot called Timothy, took him in and gave him the duties of the lowest servant. Although still very young he practised all the austerities of the monks and was noted for his charity and humility.

From the monastery of Heliodorus, Simeon went to the hermitage at the foot of Mount Thelanissa. Here he passed the forty days of Lent in total abstinence, after the example of Christ. He actually passed twenty-six Lents in this manner, spending the first part of Lent in praising God standing; growing weaker, he continued his prayer sitting, and towards the end, finding his spirits almost quite exhausted, not able to support himself in any position, he would lie on the ground.

Crowds of people, troubled in mind and body, would seek him asking for his blessing. Many sick would recover after touching him. To escape, Simeon built many pillars upon which he would live for years at a time. Thus he became known as Simeon Stylites, from the Greek word "stylos" which signifies a pillar. His pillars three feet in diameter on the top, made it impossible for him to lie down extended upon it, neither would it allow a seat. He spoke to the crowds gathered below twice a day. His garments were skins of beasts and he wore an iron collar around his neck.

Princes and queens of the Arabians came to his pillar to receive his blessing. The emperors Theodosius and Leo often consulted him.

He always looked upon and treated himself as the outcast of the world, and the worst of sinners. He died in prayer, bowed on his pillar in the sixty-ninth year of his life. His body was buried in Antioch attended by bishops, royalty and the whole country.

The following feasts are also celebrated today:

St Æmiliana, virgin, aunt to St Gregory the Great: **St Gerlac**, hermit, who lived seven years in the hollow of a tree: **St Syncletica**, virgin, who consecrated herself early to God and retired to a lonely monument, where many women resorted to her for spiritual advice, owing to the fame of her sanctity. She foretold her own death, which took place about 409, when she was eighty, after terrible sufferings, borne with exemplary patience: **St Telesphorus**, the eighth Pope, an early Bishop of Rome, who kept the Easter festival on Sunday.

January 6
The following feasts are celebrated today

St Erminold, Abbot and martyr, famous for his charity to the poor: **St Guarinus: St Melanius: St Peter Thomas**, Bishop, Archbishop and Patriarch of Constantinople 1366: **St Wiltrudis**, widow, c986.

January 7
SAINT CANUTE
King and Martyr – AD 1086

Saint Canute, King of Denmark, was the illegitimate son of Swein Estrithson (the nephew of King Cnut of England). Canute succeeded his brother Harold to the throne of Denmark in 1081 to become Canute IV.

Six years earlier he had made his first attempt to win the crown of England from William the Conqueror, but he succeeded only in invading York before he was defeated.

In 1085 Canute prepared a second attack on England. The planned invasion had to be abandoned, however, when Canute faced a widespread rebellion led by his brother Olaf. Canute fled to Odense and was finally captured in the church of St Alban.

The rebels killed him as he knelt at the altar, along with 18 of his followers.

Canute came to be regarded as a martyr and veneration toward him increased by the miracles reported at his tomb. In art he is usually represented as a Scandinavian king (often barefoot) with his royal insignia and the sword or dagger with which he was killed.

The following feasts are also celebrated today:

St Aldric, Bishop of Le Mans, born 800 died 856. He lived at the Court of Charlemagne in his youth and later was confessor to his son Louis. Aldric took part in the Councils of Paris and Tours, and was a bishop for twenty-four years: **St Kentigerna**, widow: **St Lucian**, priest and martyr, 312, who, after being racked for his loyalty to the faith after nine years in prison died at Nicomedia: **St Reinold**, martyr: **St Tillo**, Confessor, eighth century: **St Valentinus**, Bishop.

January 8
(two saints with the same name)
SAINT SEVERNUS
Abbot, Apostle in Austria – 5th century
SAINT SEVERNUS
Bishop of Septempeda – 6th century

The following feasts are also celebrated today:

St Albert, Archbishop (?) of Cashel in the eighth century and principal patron of that diocese: **St Apollinaris** the Apologist: **St Atticus**, Bishop of Constantinople: **St Baldwin** martyr about the year 670: **St Erhard**, Bishop late in the seventh century: **St Frodobertus or Frobert**, Abbot of Troyes: **St Garibaldus**, Bishop of Raisbon, about 762: **St Gudule**, virgin, Patroness of Brussels: **St Lucian**, martyr: **St Patiens**, Bishop of Metz: **St Pega**, virgin, early in the eighth century: **St Wulsin or Vulsin**, Bishop of Sherborne, 1005.

January 9
The following feasts are celebrated today:

St Adrian, Abbot of Canterbury, Confessor, an African by birth, appointed by Pope Vitalian to succeed St Deusdedit. He laboured for thirty-nine years in England, founding many schools: **St Brihtwald**, Archbishop of Canterbury in the eighth century: **St Felan**, Abbot: **Saints Julian** and **Basilissa**, a devout couple said to have been forced to marry by the parents of Julian, died at Antioch early in the fourth century: **St Marciana**, virgin and martyr in the second century: **St Paschasia**, virgin and martyr about 178: **St Peter of Sebaste**: **St Waningus** or **Vaneng**, 683.

He who does not think much of himself is greater than he who believes himself to be.

January 10
SAINT WILLIAM,
Confessor, Archbishop of Bourges – AD 1209

William Berruyer, of the illustrious family of the ancient counts of Nevers, learned from his infancy to despise the folly and emptiness of the riches and grandeur of the world.

On the death of Henry de Sully, Archbishop of Bourges, the clergy of that church requested his brother Eudo, Bishop of Paris, to come and assist them in the election of a pastor. Wanting to choose some abbot of the Cistercian order, then renowned for holy men, they put on the altar the names of three.

Eudo, drew first the name of the abbot William. This news overwhelmed William with grief. He left his dear solitude with many tears. He redoubled all his austerities, saying it was now up to him to do penance for others as well as for himself. He always wore a hair-shirt under his religious habit, and never added, nor diminished, anything in his clothes either winter or summer. He never ate meat, though he had it at his table for strangers.

He died on the morning of the 10 January 1209. His body was interred in his cathedral; and being honoured by many miracles, was taken up in 1217; and in the year following he was canonized by Pope Honorius III. His relics were kept with great veneration till 1562, when they were burnt, and scattered by the Huguenots.

The following feasts are also celebrated today:
St Agatho, Pope, surnamed the Wonderworker; he was originally in Palermo and was over one hundred years old when he succeeded Pope Domnus. He died in Rome 681: **St John Camillus Bonus,** Confessor in the seventh century, Bishop of Milan: **St Marcian**, priest and Confessor in the fifth century: **St Peter Urseolus** or **Orseolo,** Confessor 987: **St Sethrida or Sæthryth**, virgin, about 660.

January 11
SAINT THEODOSIUS
The Cenobiarch – AD 529

St Theodosius was born at Mogariassus, called in latter ages Marissa, in Cappadocia in 423. During his youth he set out for Jerusalem, but went purposely out of his way to visit the famous St Simeon Stylites on his pillar, who foretold him several circumstances of his life and gave him instructions for his behaviour in each. Having visited the holy places in Jerusalem, he began to consider dedicating himself to God in a religious state.

A pious lady having built a church on the high road to Bethlehem, asked Theodosius to take charge of it. After a short time he left to live in a cave at the top of a neighbouring desert mountain and spent his time in fasting and prayer. Many desired to serve God under his direction: he at first determined only to admit six or seven, but was soon obliged to receive a greater number and at length came to a resolution never to reject any that seemed sincere.

The first lesson which he taught his monks was the continual remembrance of death; to imprint this more deeply in their minds, he had a great grave or pit dug, which might serve for the common burial-place of the whole community, that by the presence of this memorial of death, and by continually meditating on that object, they might more perfectly learn to die.

At the great feast of Easter one year, they had nothing to eat; they had not even bread for the mass; the saint bid them trust in God and He would provide; which was soon remarkably verified by the arrival of mules loaded with provisions.

St Theodosius, drawing great numbers to him who desired to serve God under his direction found his cave was too little for them all, therefore he built a monastery at a place called Cathismus, not far from Bethlehem, a small distance from his cave and it was soon filled with holy monks. The monastery itself was like a city of saints in the midst of a desert, and it reigned in silence, charity and peace.

During the last year of his life he was afflicted with a painful illness which he bore with heroic patience. He died in the one hundred and fifth year of his life. He was buried in his first cell called the Cave of the Magi, because the wise men who came to adore Christ soon after his birth were said to have lodged in it.

The following feasts are also celebrated today:

St Egwin, third Bishop of Worcester, Confessor, died December 30, 717, founder of the Abbey of Evesham: **St Hyginus**, Pope for four years (about 138-142), a Greek by birth, buried on the Vatican Hill near the tomb of St Peter: **St Leucius**, Bishop of Brindisi, Confessor: **St Palæmon**, hermit: **St Salvius** or **Sauve**, Bishop of Amiens, 625: **St Vitalis**, Monk of Gaza martyred on this date at Tybury, 1584.

January 12
SAINT BENEDICT BISCOP
Commonly called Bennet – AD 690

St Benedict was nobly descended and one of the great officers of the court of Oswi, the religious king of the Northumbers. At the age of twenty-five, he made a journey to Rome and at his return devoted himself wholly to the studies of the scriptures and other holy exercises.

Some time later our saint travelled a second time to Rome and after he went to the great monastery of Lerins he took the monastic habit and spent two years in the most exact observance of the rule. After this he returned once again to Rome where he received an order of Pope Vitalian to accompany St Theodorus, Archbishop of Canterbury, and St Adrian, to England.

St Bennet stayed about two years in Kent, giving himself up to religious exercises and sacred studies.

When he returned to Northumberland, St Bennet built a monastery, founded on the mouth of the river Were. When the monastery was built, St Bennet went over to France and brought back with him skilful masons, who built the church for this monastery of stone, for till that time stone buildings were very rare in Britain, even the church of Lindisfarne was of wood. St Bennet also brought over glaziers from France, for the art of making glass was then unknown in Britain.

His first monastery was dedicated to St Peter. Later he built another monastery at a place called Girwy, now Jarrow, on the Tyne, six miles away from the former, and this latter was called St Paul's. These two monasteries were almost looked upon as one and St Bennet governed them both.

The last three years of his life was spent paralysed and confined to bed. In art he is portrayed by the River Tyne, together with his two monasteries. Patron saint of painters and musicians.

The following feasts are also celebrated today:
St Arcadius, martyred under Valerius or Diocletian, with terrible brutality: **St Aelred**, 1167, Abbot. He was master of the household of King David of Scotland. Eventually he joined the strict Cistercian Order at Rievaulx or Rydal in Yorkshire, where later he became Abbot: **St Cæsaria**, virgin: **St Tatiana**, virgin and martyr: **St Tigrius** and **Eutropius**, martyrs: **St Victorianus**, Abbot.

January 13
SAINT HILARY
Bishop and Doctor – AD 368

St Hilary was born at Poitiers and his family was one of the most illustrious in Gaul. Brought up in idolatry, he ardently set about learning about God and after some researches into the nature of the Supreme Being, quickly was convinced that there can be only one God, and that the same is eternal, unchangeable, all-powerful, the first cause and author of all things. He had the greatest veneration for truth, sparing no pains in its pursuit, and dreading no danger in its defence. He was an excellent orator and poet.

He was married before his conversion to the faith, and his wife, by whom he had a daughter named Apra, or Abram, was still living when he was chosen Bishop of Poitiers, about the year 353.

He fearlessly championed Catholic orthodoxy against the prevalent heresy of Arianism. Banished as a trouble-maker, he was exiled to Phrygia by Constantius in 356. Exile, however, did not silence him. Hilary's arguments against Arianism were so effective that the Arians appealed to the emperor to end his exile and allow him to go back to Gaul. There was general rejoicing on his return to Poitiers in 360.

He was named a Doctor of the Church in 1851, and his feast-day has traditionally been used to mark the beginning of Hilary term in Chancery and at some universities.

In art he is often depicted with a child in a cradle at his feet, and he is known as the helper of backward children. Patron saint of backward children, invoked against snakes.

The following feasts are also celebrated today:
St Agrecius, Bishop of Trier or Trève for twenty years: **St Potitus**, martyr: **St Veronica of Milan** whose honest peasant father never sold a horse without telling the buyer its faults rather than its good points.

January 14
SAINT KENTIGERN
Bishop of Strathclyde, Apostle of Cumbria – AD 603

Little is known of Kentigern's life though in Scottish folklore he is a potent figure around whom many legends have grown.

According to legend, Kentigern was the illegitimate grandson of a British prince, possibly Urien. His pregnant mother, a princess named Thenew, was thrown from a cliff when her pregnancy was discovered, found alive at the bottom and was placed in a coracle and left to drift on the Firth of Forth. She was taken in by St Serf at Culross who gave the baby the pet name Mungo ('dear friend').

Serf raised Mungo, who grew up to become a hermit in Glasghu (modern Glasgow) in the traditions of Irish monasticism, known for his holiness. He founded a monastery there at Cathures and was consecrated first bishop of Strathclyde in c543. He met St David at Menevia and founded a monastery at Llanelwy.

Another legend claims that he exchanged pastoral staffs with the elderly St Columba, who was believed to have paid him a visit in c584. He died an old man in Glasgow, and his relics are claimed by the cathedral of St Mungo there.

One of the most famous anecdotes associated with Kentigern tells how he came to the aid of an unfaithful queen, who had given the king's ring to a lover. The outraged king had thrown the ring into the sea and challenged her to find it within three days or face dire consequences.

Kentigern comforted her, and one of his monks miraculously caught a salmon, inside which the ring was found unharmed.

Along with his mother Thenew, he is regarded as the patron saint of Glasgow. The legend of the ring and the salmon forms the basis of the heraldic arms of Glasgow.

The following feasts are also celebrated today:
St Barbasymas (or **Barbashemin**) **and Companions**, martyred for refusing to worship fire and water: **St Datius**, Bishop of Milan: **St Felix** of Nola: **St Hilary**: **St Macrina the Elder**, widow: **St Sabas**, Archbishop of Servia.

January 15
SAINT PAUL
The First Hermit – AD 342

This saint was a native of the Lower Thebais in Egypt, and had lost both his parents when he was fifteen years of age; nevertheless he was proficient in Greek and Egyptian learning, was mild and modest and feared God from his earliest youth. The bloody persecution of Decius disturbed the peace of the church in 250.

During these times of danger, Paul kept himself concealed in the house of another; but finding that a brother-in-law was inclined to betray him, he fled into the deserts. There he found many spacious caverns in a rock, which were said to have been the retreat of money-coiners in the days of Cleopatra, Queen of Egypt. He chose for his dwelling a cave in this place, near which was a palm-tree and a clear spring. The former by its leaves gave him clothing and by its fruit gave him food, and the latter supplied him with water for his drink.

Paul was twenty-two years old when he entered the desert. His first intention was to enjoy the liberty of serving God till the persecution should cease. Learning the spiritual advantages of holy solitude, he resolved to return no more among men, or concern himself in the least with human affairs, and what passed in the world: it was enough for him to know that there was a world, and to pray that it might be improved in goodness. The saint lived on the fruit of his tree till he was forty-three years of age, and from that time till his death, like Elias, he was miraculously fed with bread brought him every day by a raven. His method of life and what he did in this place during ninety years, is unknown to us.

St Antony, after two days and a night spent in the search, discovered the saint's abode by a light that was in it. While they were talking together, a raven flew towards them and dropped a loaf of bread before them.

St Paul said, "Our good God has sent us a dinner. In this manner have I received half a loaf every day these past sixty years; now you have come to see me, Christ has doubled his provision for his servants."

The next morning St Paul told his guest that the time of his death approached, adding, "Go and fetch the cloak given you by St Athanasius, Bishop of Alexandria, in which you must wrap my body." St Antony was surprised to hear him mention the cloak, which he could not have known but by divine revelation.

Having found the cloak, St Antony returned with it in all haste, fearing lest the holy hermit might be dead. Whilst on the road he saw his happy soul carried up to heaven, attended by choirs of angels, prophets and apostles. St Antony could not help lamenting for having lost a treasure so lately discovered. As soon as his sorrow would permit, he arose, continued his journey and came to the cave. Going in he found the body kneeling, and the hands stretched out. Full of joy, and supposing him alive, he knelt down to pray with him, but by his silence soon knew he was dead. Having paid his last respects to the holy corpse, he carried it out of the cave. Whilst he stood perplexed how to dig a grave, two lions came up quietly and tearing up the ground, made a hole large enough to take a human body. St Antony then buried the corpse, singing hymns and psalms.

He always kept as a great treasure, and wore himself on festivals, the garment of St Paul, of palm-tree leaves patched together. St Paul died in 342, in his one hundred and thirteenth year, and is usually called the "first hermit" to distinguish him from others of that name.

The following feasts are also celebrated today:
St Alexander Akimetes, Confessor, 430: **St Bonitus**, Bishop of Auvergn: **St Ceolwulf**, king and confessor: **St Emebert**, Bishop of Cambrai, Confessor: **St Ephysius**: **St Isadore**, priest of Scété and hermit in that desert: **St Ita** or **Ida** or **Mida**, Abbess of a nunnery at Newcastle in Limerick, died 570: **St John Calybites**, about 450: **St Malard**, Bishop of Chartres, Confessor: **St Maurus**, brought up by St Benedict: **St Tarsitia**, virgin.

January 16
SAINT MACARIUS
The Elder of Egypt – AD 390

St Macarius, the Elder, was born in Upper Egypt, c300, and brought up in the country tending cattle. In his childhood, in company with some others, he once stole a few figs and ate one of them, but from his conversion to his death, he never ceased to weep bitterly for this sin. He retired from the world in his youth and dwelling in a little cell in a village, made mats, in continual prayer and great austerities.

To shun the esteem of men, he fled into the vast hideous desert of Scété being then about thirty years of age. In this solitude he lived sixty years. He was compelled by an Egyptian bishop to receive the order of priesthood c340. The austerities of St Macarius were excessive; he usually ate once a week, saying, "For these twenty years I never once ate, drank or slept as much as nature required." His face was very pale, and his body weak and parched. To deny his own will, he did not refuse to drink a little wine when others desired him; but then he would punish himself for this indulgence by abstaining two or three days from all manner of drink. He used to say, "In prayer you need not use many or lofty words."

Our saint, knowing that his end drew near, made a visit to the monks of Nitria, where they all fell weeping at his feet. "Let us weep, brethren," said he, "and let our eyes pour forth floods of tears before we go, lest we fall into that place where tears will only increase the flames in which we shall burn." He went to receive the reward of his labours in 390, aged ninety, having spent sixty years in the desert of Scété.

The following feasts are also celebrated today:

St Ferriolus, Bishop of Grenoble, towards the end of the seventh century: **St Fursey**, born in Ireland and famous for his wonderful visions died on this date in 648: **St Honoratus** founded the famous monastery of Lerins, succeeded St Hilary as Archbishop of Arles in 426: **St James**, Bishop of Tarantaise: **St Marcellus**, pope and martyr: **St Priscilla**, matron: **St Tarantaise**: **St Triverius**, hermit, Monk of Lyons.

January 17
SAINT ANTONY
Abbot, Patriarch of Monks – AD 356

St Antony was born at Coma, a village near Heraclea, or Great Heracleopolis, in Upper Egypt, on the borders of Arcadia, or middle Egypt, in 251. His parents, who were Christians, and rich, to prevent his being tainted by bad example and vicious conversation, kept him always at home. He was remarkable from his childhood for his temperance, a close attendance on church duties and a punctual obedience to his parents.

By their death he found himself possessed of a very considerable estate, and charged with the care of a younger sister, before he was twenty years of age. He heard read in the church those words of Christ to the rich young man: "Go sell what thou hast, and give it to the poor, and thou shalt have treasure in heaven."

He considered these words as addressed to himself; going home, he made over to his neighbours three hundred *aruras*, that is about one hundred and twenty acres of land, that he and his sister might be free for ever from all public taxes and burdens. The rest of his estate he sold, and gave the price to the poor, except what he thought necessary for himself and his sister. He placed his sister in a convent and Antony himself retired to live on his own near his village.

The saint's food was only bread, with a little salt, and he drank nothing but water; he never ate before sunset, and sometimes only once in two or three days: he lay on a rush mat or on the bare floor. In quest of more remote solitude, he withdrew further from Coma, and hid himself in an old sepulchre where a friend brought him from time to time a little bread.

About the year 305, aged fifty-five, he came down from his mountain and founded his first monastery at Phaium. He appeared vigorous and always cheerful: strangers knew him from among his disciples by the joy which always shone from his face. Retirement in his cell was his delight and prayer his perpetual occupation.

His under-garment was sackcloth, over which he wore a white coat of sheepskin with a girdle. He instructed his monks to have eternity always present to their minds and to reflect every morning that perhaps they might not live till night and every evening that perhaps they might never see the morning; and to perform every action as if it were the last of their lives.

St Antony always looked upon himself as the least and the very outcast of mankind; he listened to the advice of everyone. He cultivated and pruned a little garden on his desert mountain, that he might have herbs always at hand to present as refreshment to those who, on coming to see him, were weary by travelling over a vast wilderness and inhospitable mountains.

At the request of the bishops, about the year 355, he took a journey to Alexandria where he converted many and wrought several miracles.

When certain philosophers asked him how he could spend his time in solitude without the pleasure of reading books, he replied that nature was his great book. When others, despising him as an illiterate man, ridiculed his ignorance, he asked them with great simplicity, which was first, reason or learning and which had produced the other? The philosophers answered, "Reason, or good sense." "This, then," said Antony, "suffices." The philosophers went away astonished at the wisdom and dignity with which he prevented their objections.

No one visited St Antony who did not return home full of comfort and joy; many miraculous cures were wrought by him, also several heavenly visions and revelations with which he was favoured.

His death happened in the year 356, probably on the 17th January. He was one hundred and five years old, the founder of monasticism.

Patron saint of basket makers his emblems are a T-shaped staff and bell.

The following feasts are also celebrated today:
St Genulfus or **Genou**, Bishop of Cahors (?) about 250 (?): **St Julian Sabas**, hermit, who lived in a cave, 377: **St Mildgytha**, virgin, grand-daughter of Penda, King of Mercia: **St Richimirus**, Abbot: **St Sabinas**, Bishop of Piacenza: **Saints Speusippus, Eleusippus** and **Meleusippus**, said to have been three (triplet) brothers, martyred with their grandmother, Leonilla, under Marcus Aurelius: **St Sulpicius (St Sulpice)**, second Bishop of Bourges, Confessor.

January 18
The following feasts are celebrated today:
St Deicolus, Abbot. In Irish **Dicuil** and called by the French **Desle**; he left Ireland with St Columban, who once asked him why he was always smiling. "Because no one can take my God from me," said the holy youth; died in the seventh century: **St Prisca**, a Roman virgin believed to have known St Peter and to have been martyred in the first century; others, however, place her in the third century: **St Ulfrid**, and Englishman of great learning, who converted many to Christ, first in Germany and later in Sweden. In 1028 preaching against Thor and hewing his idol down with a hatchet, he was killed by the pagans: **St Volusianus**, Bishop of Tours (496).

January 19
SAINT WULSTAN,
Bishop of Worcester – AD 1095

St Wulstan was a native of Icentum in Warwickshire. He laid the foundation of his education in the Monastery of Evesham, but completed his studies at Peterborough. Under the direction of Brithege, Bishop of Worcester, he advanced to the priesthood.

Not long after, he entered as a novice, the abbey at Worcester, where he was remarkable for the sanctity of his life. The first charge with which he was entrusted in the monastery was the care of instructing the children. He was afterwards made precentor, and then treasurer of the church. In these two last stations he devoted himself totally to prayer, and watched whole nights in the church. He was made Prior of Worcester, and in 1062, bishop.

When the Conqueror had deprived the English, both nobility and clergy, of the posts of honour they possessed in the church and state, in favour of his Normans, Wulstan kept his see.

When any English complained of the oppression of the Normans, he used to tell them, "This is a scourge of God for your sins, which you must bear with patience."

The following feasts are also celebrated today:

St Canutus of Knut, King of Denmark, martyr: **St Germanicus**, martyred in 156. He provoked the wild beasts in the arena to attack him so that he might sooner be delivered from the ungodly companionship in which he found himself: **St Lomer** or **Launomar**, Abbot (about 590). He was a shepherd boy, afterwards becoming a priest. Many gathered around his hermitage because of his spirit of prayer and gift of miracles: **Saints Marius, Martha, Audifax** and **Abachum**, the first named two being husband and wife and the two last their sons. Being converted they came from Persia, leaving their fortune to the poor, to Rome, where they gathered the ashes of Christian martyrs under Aurelian and buried them. For this they were apprehended, the three men being beheaded and St Martha being drowned at a place now called Santa Ninfa, near Rome: **St Nathalan**, Bishop: **St Regimius**, Bishop of Rouen.

January 20
SAINT FABIAN
Pope – AD 250

St Fabian succeeded St Anterus in the pontificate in the year 236. Eusebius relates that in an assembly of the people and clergy, held for the election of a pope, a dove, unexpectedly appearing, settled, to the great surprise of all present, on the head of St Fabian, and that this united the votes of the clergy and people in promoting him, though not thought of before, as being a layman and a stranger. He governed the church sixteen years. St Fabian died a martyr in the persecution of Decius in 250.

and
SAINT SEBASTIAN
Martyr – AD 283

St Sebastian was born at Narbonne, in Gaul, but his parents were of Milan in Italy and he was brought up in that city. He went to Rome and entered the army under the emperor Carinus about the year 283. As a Christian in Rome he encouraged persecuted believers such as Mark and Marcellian who were in prison before their martyrdom, and as his faith was unknown he was appointed captain of the praetorian guard. Sebastian continued to support and encourage the Christians under persecution.

When the Emperor finally discovered Sebastian's faith he ordered him to be shot to death with arrows. The sentence was carried out and Sebastian was left for dead but Irene, the widow of St Castulus, going to bury him, found him still alive, and took him to her lodgings where, by care, he recovered. He refused to leave the city for a place of safety, but went instead to confront the Emperor, who was naturally taken aback at the apparition. Recovering from his surprise, he gave orders for him to be seized and beaten to death with cudgels, and his body thrown into the common sewer. A pious lady called Lucina got the body privately removed and buried it in the catacombs at the entrance of the cemetery of Calixtus. A church was afterwards built over his relics by Pope Damasus, which is one of the seven ancient churches at Rome, the Basilica of St Sebastian.

He became popular as the patron saint of archers, soldiers and police.

The following feasts are also celebrated today:
St Euthymius, Abbot, whose birth was an answer to his parents' prayers (473) and whom the Greeks style "the Great": **St Fechin** or **Vigaenus**, Abbot, 665.

January 21
SAINT AGNES
AD 304 or 305

St Jerome says that the tongues and pens of all nations are employed in the praises of this saint. St Austin observes that her name signifies chaste in Greek, and a lamb in Latin. Rome was the theatre of the triumph of St Agnes. She suffered not long after the beginning of the persecution of Diocletian, in 303. We learn from St Ambrose and St Austin that she was only thirteen years of age at the time of her death. Her riches and beauty excited the young noblemen of the first families in Rome to vie with one another to gain her in marriage.

When she was betrayed to the Roman authorities as a Christian by a rejected suitor, at the age of 12 or 13, she endured martyrdom rather than compromise her faith or her virginity.

To this basic story many traditions add elaborations such as the story of the soldier who looked on her in her imprisonment with impure thoughts and immediately lost his eyesight; it was restored by the prayers of Agnes. During her arrest she is said to have been unmoved by the governor's range of torture implements, until in desperation and enraged by her radiant purity he sent her to a house of prostitution in Rome, where she might be supposed to lose her innocence. But Agnes, by her holiness, was impervious to the corruption around her.

Agnes is variously supposed to have been beheaded, pierced through the throat and burned to death. These conflicting accounts of her martyrdom suggest that the details of her story were lost in myth by time. She was buried in a catacomb on the Via Salaria that was later named after her, and by 349 a basilica had been built over her tomb by Constantina, daughter of the emperor Constantine. From the sixth century at least, Agnes's emblem has been that of a lamb. At St Agnes in Rome, where the nuns weave the pallia for archbishops, the lambs which provide the wool are specially blessed on her feast-day. In art she is usually depicted with long hair and a lamb, sometimes with the sword of her martyrdom at her throat. Patron saint of betrothed couples, gardeners and virgins, invoked for chastity.

The following feasts are also celebrated today:

St Epiphanius, Bishop of Pavia, who by his eloquence tamed savage barbarians, won life and liberty for whole armies of captives and secured the abolition of oppressive taxes; for he was powerful with the weak Roman emperors of his time: **St Fructuosus and Companion**, martyrs. The martyrs were burned to death with arms extended in the form of a cross: **St Meinrad**, hermit and martyr: **St Patroclus**, martyr: **St Vinim** or **Wynnin,** or **Gwynnin**, Bishop and Confessor in Scotland.

January 22
SAINT ANASTASIUS
Martyr – AD 628

St Anastasius was a Persian, son of a Magian, and a young soldier in the Persian troops. Upon hearing of the news of the taking of the cross by his king, he became very inquisitive concerning the Christian religion; and what he learnt made such an impression on his mind that he left the army with his brother and went to live in Hierapolis. In that city he lodged with a devout Persian Christian, a silversmith, with whom he went often to prayer. The holy pictures which he saw moved him exceedingly.

At length, desirous of baptism, he left Hierapolis and went to Jerusalem, where he received that sacrament. He changed his Persian name Magundat into that of Anastasius, meaning that he was risen from death to a new and spiritual life, and entered a monastery.

In 628 after seven years spent in great perfection, he left and visited the places of devotion in Palestine, at Diospolis, Garizim, and our Lady's church at Cæsarea. This city was then subject to the Persians. The Persian magistrates apprehended him as a suspected spy; but he informed them that he once enjoyed the dignity of Magian with them, and had renounced it to become a humble follower of Christ. Upon this confession he was thrown into a dungeon, where he lay three days without eating or drinking till the return of Marzabanes, the governor, to the city. Being interrogated by him, he confessed his conversion to the faith. Marzabanes commanded him to be chained by the foot to another criminal, and his neck and other foot to be linked together by a heavy chain, and condemned him in this condition to carry stones.

The executioners were preparing themselves to bind him fast on the ground; but the saint told them it was unnecessary, for he had courage enough to lie down under the punishment without moving, and he regarded it as his greatest happiness and pleasure to suffer for Christ. He only begged leave to take off his monk's habit, lest it should be treated with contempt, which only his body deserved. He therefore laid it aside in a respectful manner, and then stretched himself on the ground, and without being bound did not stir all the time of the cruel torment, bearing it without changing his posture.

The following day he was strangled, and after his death his head was cut off. This was in 628. His body, among the other dead, was exposed to be devoured by dogs, but it was the only one the dogs left untouched. It was afterwards redeemed by the Christians, who laid it in the monastery of St Sergius, a mile from Barsaloe, called afterwards Sergiopolis. The saint's body was afterwards brought into Palestine. Some years later it was removed to Constantinople, and lastly to Rome.

The following feasts are also celebrated today:

St Blæsilla, widow: **St Brihtwold**, Bishop and Confessor: **St Dominic of Sora**, Abbot: **St Vincent** a young martyr under Dacien, governor of Spain (304). Vincent was taught by St Valerius, Bishop of Saragossa, who ordained him deacon at an early age. Vincent suffered terrible tortures, preserving through all such peace in his words and gestures as astonished his tormentors. Being asked to compromise, for the last time, he walked with joy to the torture – fire upon a kind of gridiron. After this he was thrown into a dungeon where God sent angels to console him. The gaoler, seeing the prison filled with light and the saint praising God, was converted on the spot. The saint was no sooner laid upon a soft bed than he immediately died. His cult spread widely through the Christian world at a very early date.

January 23
SAINT JOHN THE ALMONER
Patriarch of Alexandria

St John received his surname from his profuse almsdeeds. He was nobly descended, very rich, and a widower, at Amathus, in Cyprus, where, having buried all his children, he employed the whole income of his estate in the relief of the poor. The reputation of his sanctity raised him to the patriarchal chair of Alexandria about the year 608, at which time he was fifty years of age. On his arrival in that city he ordered an exact list to be taken of his masters. Being asked who these were, his answer was, "The Poor!"

Their number amounted to 7,500, whom he took under his special protection and furnished with all necessities. He most rigorously forbade all his officers and servants ever to receive the least presents, saying they are no better than bribes. Every Wednesday and Friday he sat the whole day on a bench before the church, that all might have free access to him to lay their grievances before him, and make known their necessities.

One of his first actions at Alexandria was to distribute the 80,000 pieces of gold, which he found in the treasury of his church, among hospitals and monasteries. He consecrated to the service of the poor the great revenues of his see.

When his stewards complained that he impoverished his church, his answer was that God would provide for them. To vindicate his conduct and silence their complaints, he recounted to them a vision he had in his youth of a beautiful woman, brighter than the sun, with an olive garland on her head, whom he undertook to be Charity, who said to him, "I am the eldest daughter of a great king. If you enjoy my favour, I will introduce you to the great monarch of the universe. No one has so great an interest with him as myself, who was the occasion of his coming down from heaven to become man for the redemption of mankind."

When the Persians had plundered the East and sacked Jerusalem, St John sent the poor there, large sums of money, corn, iron, fish, wine, and 1,000 Egyptian workmen to assist in rebuilding the churches. He also sent two bishops and an abbot to ransom captives.

The patriarch lived himself in the greatest austerity and poverty as to diet, apparel, and furniture. A person of distinction in the city being informed that our saint had but one blanket on his bed, and this a very sorry one, sent him one of value, begging his acceptance of it, and that he would make use of it for the sake of the donor. He accepted it, and put it to the intended use, but it was only for one night. The next morning he sold it, and gave the price to the poor. The friend, being informed of it, bought it back, and gave it him a second and a third time, for the saint always disposed of it in the same way, saying, "We shall see who will be tired first." He was very well versed in the scriptures. The functions of his ministry, prayer and pious reading employed his whole time.

Nicetas, the governor, persuaded the saint to accompany him to Constantinople to pay a visit to the emperor. St John was admonished from heaven whilst he was on his way, at Rhodes, that his death drew near, and said to Nicetas, "You invite me to the emperor of the earth, but the king of heaven calls me to himself."

He therefore sailed for Cyprus, and soon after died at Amathus, about 619, in his sixty fourth year. His body was afterwards carried to Constantinople, where it was kept a long time. The Turkish emperor made a present of it to Matthias, King of Hungary, which he deposited in his chapel at Buda.

In 1530 it was translated to Tall, near Presbourg; and in 1632, to the cathedral itself of Presbourg, where it still remains.

The following feasts are also celebrated today:
St Asclas: **St Barnard**, Archbishop of Vienne, Confessor: **Saints Clement of Ancyra** and **Agathangelus**, martyrs: **St Erementiana**, virgin and martyr: **St Eusebius**, Abbot in the fourth century: **St Ildephonsus**, Archbishop of Toledo: **St Lufthild**: **St Maimbod**, martyr: **St Raymund of Pennafort.**

January 24
SAINT TIMOTHY
Martyr, Disciple of Paul – AD 97

St Timothy, the beloved disciple of St Paul, was of Lycaonia, and probably of the city of Lystra. Timothy's father was a Greek and his mother Eunice a converted Jewess, and he himself studied the Jewish scriptures as a child. He was converted by Paul and became his disciple when the apostle preached at Lystra and travelled with him as a close friend and co-worker. St Paul wrote his first epistle to Timothy from Macedon, in 64; and his second in 65 from Rome, while there in chains, to press him to come to Rome, that he might see him again before he died.

St Timothy was slain with stones and clubs by the heathens whilst he was endeavouring to oppose their idolatrous ceremonies on one of their festivals called Catagogia, kept on 22 January, and was buried in Ephesus, from where his relics were supposedly translated in 365 to a shrine in Constantinople. From Paul's admonition that he should 'take a little wine' with his food for the sake of his stomach, Timothy has been traditionally invoked in cases of stomach complaint. He is usually represented in art with his emblem of a club and a stone recalling his death; another common depiction has him receiving his epistle from Paul.

The following feasts are also celebrated today:
St Arthemius, Bishop of Clermont, Confessor: **St Babylas**, the most celebrated of the Bishops of Antioch after St Ignatius, martyred about the year 250: **St Cadocus of Cadoc**, Abbot in Wales, eldest son to a Welsh prince who followed his father's example in renouncing the world and entering the religious life. He built a church and a monastery called Llancarven and a school: **St Felician**, Bishop of Foligno, martyr: **St Macedonius.**

Fellowship – on Earth
To dwell above with saints we love –
Ah yes! that will be glory.
To live below with saints we know,
Well, that's another story.

Anon

January 25
SAINTS JUVENTINUS AND MAXIMINUS
Martyrs – AD 363

These martyrs were two officers of distinction in the foot-guards of Julian the Apostate who wished for death rather than to see the profanation of holy things, Julian informed the emperor of this who sent for them and, finding that they could not be prevailed upon by any means to retract what they had said, he confiscated their estates and had them scourged. Some days later they were beheaded in prison at Antioch, on 25 January 363. The Christians stole away their bodies and after the death of Julian erected for them a magnificent tomb. On their festival St Chrysostom says of these martyrs, "They support the church as pillars, defend it as towers, and repel all assaults as rocks."

The following feasts are also celebrated today:
St Apollo, about 395, who, after passing many years as a hermit, assembled and governed a company of five hundred monks when he was eighty. Miracles are told of him, including multiplication of bread in time of famine: **St Artemas**, martyr: **St Poppo**, Abbot of Stavelot, born in Flanders 987. His mother died a nun at Verdun: **St Præjectus**, Bishop of Clermont, martyred January 25, 676: **St Publius**, Abbot, who died about 380.

January 26
SAINT POLYCARP
Bishop of Smyrna, Martyr – AD 166

St Polycarp was one of the most illustrious of the apostolic fathers, who, being the immediate disciple of the apostles, received instructions from them. He embraced Christianity whilst young, about the year 80. He seems to have been the angel or bishop of Smyrna who was commended above all the bishops of Asia by Christ himself in the Apocalypse and the only one without a reproach.

About the year 158 he undertook a journey to Rome to confer with Pope Anicetus about certain points of discipline, especially about the time of keeping Easter. We find no further particulars concerning our saint recorded before the acts of his martyrdom.

In the sixth year of Marcus Aurelius and Lucius Verus, Statius Quadratus being proconsul of Asia, a violent persecution broke out in that country. When the persecutors sought him he changed his retreat but was betrayed by a boy. They unanimously demanded that he should be burnt alive. The plle being prepared, Polycarp put off his garments, untied his girdle, and began to take off his shoes, a thing he had not been accustomed to, the Christians having always striven to do these things for him, regarding it as a happiness to be admitted to touch him. The wood and other combustibles were heaped all round him. The executioners would have nailed him to the stake; but he said to them: "Suffer me to be as I am. He who gives me grace to undergo this fire will enable me to stand still without that precaution." They therefore tied his hands behind his back and in this posture looking up towards heaven he prayed.

He had scarce said Amen when fire was set to the pile, which increased to a mighty flame. The flames forming themselves into an arch, like the sails of a ship swelled with the wind, gently encircled the body of the martyr, which stood in the middle, resembling not roasted flesh, but purified gold or silver, appearing bright through the flames; and his body sending forth such a fragrancy which seemed to smell of precious spices. The persecutors were exasperated to see his body could not be consumed, and ordered a spearman to pierce him through which he did, and such a quantity of blood issued out of his left side that it quenched the fire.

His tomb is still shown with great veneration at Smyrna in a small chapel.

The following feasts are also celebrated today:
St Conan, Bishop of the Isle of Man: **St Paula**, widow.

January 27
SAINT JOHN CHRYSOSTOM
Archbishop of Constantinople, and Doctor of the Church – AD 407

This incomparable doctor, on account of his eloquence, obtained soon after his death the surname of Chrysostom or Golden Mouth. He was born in Antioch about the year 344. He had one elder sister, and was the only son and heir of Secundus, master of the horse, that is, chief commander of the imperial troops in Syria. His mother Anthusa, left a widow at twenty years of age, continued the remainder of her life, dividing her time between the care of her family and the exercise of devotion.

Eloquence was esteemed the highest accomplishment, especially among the nobility. John studied the art under Libanius, a famous orator of that age; and such was his proficiency that even in his youth he excelled his masters. About 390 John became a priest, his principal care was to study Christ and to learn His spirit. He changed his garb for a penitential habit as a public sign and declaration to the world that he had turned his back on its vanities. His clothing was a coarse grey coat, he fasted every day and spent the greater part of his time in prayer and meditation on the holy scriptures: his bed was no other than the hard floor.

After four years, in 374, he went into the mountains near Antioch to live among certain holy hermits and whose life is described by our saint. They devoted all the morning to prayer, pious reading and meditating on the holy scriptures. Their food was bread with a little salt, some added oil and those who were very weak a few herbs or pulses. No one ever ate before sunset. After eating it was allowed to converse with one another, but only on heavenly things.

These monks had no other bed than a mat spread on the bare ground. Their garments were made of the rough hair of goats or camels, or of old skins and such as the poorest beggars would not wear, though some of them were of the richest families, and had been tenderly brought up. They wore no shoes; no one possessed anything as his own.

They inherited their estates only to distribute them among the poor. The cold words *mine* and *thine* were banished from use. They rose at the first crowing of the cock – that is at midnight, and after the morning hymns and psalms – matins and lauds – all remained in their private cells, where they read the holy scriptures and some copied books.

All met in the church at the canonical hours of tierce, sext, none, and vespers, but returned to their cells none being allowed to speak, to jest or to be one moment idle. Their meal took up very little time, and after a short sleep they resumed conversing not with men but with God, with the prophets and apostles in their writings and pious meditation; and spiritual things were the only subject of their entertainment.

They made baskets, tilled and watered the earth, hewed wood, attended the kitchen, washed the feet of all strangers and waited on them whether they were rich or poor.

In 381 John was ordained deacon by St Meletius and priest by Flavian in 386, our saint then being in his forty-third year.

He was elected Patriarch of Constantinople in 398. Because he courageously branded vice, his enemies caused him to be exiled to Comana in Pontus.

There he died on 14 September 407.

The following feasts are also celebrated today:
St Julian, first Bishop of Le Mans, Confessor: **St Marius**, Abbot, who spent the forty days of Lent as a recluse in the forest, every year, where he experienced prophetic visions: **St Vitalian**, Pope, 657-72, who sought to restore the connection with Constantinople. He was successful in England where disputes had arisen between the Anglo-Saxons and the British clergy respecting ecclesiastical customs.

January 28
The following feasts are celebrated today:
St John, Abbot of Reomay: **St Paulinus**, Patriarch of Aquileia.

January 29th
SAINT FRANCIS OF SALES
Bishop, Confessor and Doctor of the Church – AD 1622

The eldest son of the Seigneur de Nouvelles, Francis was born in the family castle in Savoy on 21 August and christened Francis Bonaventure. He was privately educated in Annecy, then at Clermont, a Jesuit college in Paris.

in 1588 he went on to study rhetoric, philosophy and theology at the University of Padua, where he became a doctor of law in 1591.

Francis, however, had decided to become a priest and despite strong opposition from his family he was ordained in 1593 and become provost of Geneva.

In 1599 he was appointed coadjutor to the Bishop of Geneva and despite his initial reluctance succeeded to the see in 1602. As bishop he was a leading figure in the Counter-Reformation movement, famed for his simple, straightforward preaching, his administrative prowess and his untiring intellect.

It was in a Visitandine convent in Lyons that Francis died 12 years later on 28 December. His body was translated to Annecy the following month, and into a new shrine there in 1912. He was declared a Doctor of the Church in 1577 and was named patron saint of writers in 1923.

Two of his works are still very popular today: his *Treatise on the love of God* and *Introduction to the devout life*, the first guide to piety to be written for laymen.

He is immediately recognisable in art by his bald head and long beard; dressed in Franciscan robes and often holding a book. He is also shown with a heart pierced by a crown of thorns, or occasionally with a picture of the Virgin. Patron saint of writers, editors and journalists.

The following feasts are also celebrated today:

St Gildas, "The Wise", Patron of Vannes; surnamed Badonicus because being the son of a British lord, he was born in the year in which the British gained a victory over the Saxons at Mount Badon, now Bannesdown, near Bath. He crossed to Ireland to learn from those taught by St Patrick, then to a small isle in Brittany: **St Sabinianus**, martyr: **St Sulpicius Severus**, lived about 425. He built and furnished many churches, employing the revenue of his estates in giving alms: **St Sulpicius (Severus)**, Archbishop of Böurges (about 591): **St Valerius**, Bishop of Treves (or Trier) about the year 100.

It was never loving that emptied the heart nor giving that emptied the purse.

January 30
SAINT BATHILD
Queen of France – AD 680

Anglo-Saxon Bathild was captured by pirates in 641 and sold into slavery in the household of Erchinoald, mayor of the imperial palace. King Clovis II of the western Franks soon noticed this beautiful and capable young Englishwoman, who had risen to a position of responsibility and trust within her master's household, and in 649 he wedded her.

In their short marriage of only eight years, Bathild bore Clovis three sons, all future kings: Clotaire III, Childeric II and Thierry III. After Clovis's death in 657 Bathild acted as regent for the five-year-old Clotaire and proved herself worthy of her new role. She ruled intelligently and compassionately, promoting the activities of the church. Among the many monasteries which she endowed were St Denis, Corbie and Chelles.

A revolution led by nobles at the palace in 665 forced Bathild to quit the regency and withdraw to her convent at Chelles, where she spent the rest of her life quietly under obedience to the abbess there, distinguished only by an attitude even more humble than that of her sisters. She died in the convent after a long and painful illness.

In art her emblem is a ladder extending towards heaven. Bathild herself is shown as a crowned nun, often performing menial tasks such as sweeping, or giving money to the poor. Patron saint of children.

The following feasts are also celebrated today:
St Adelelmus, Abbot: **St Aldegund**, virgin and Abbess of the royal house of France: **St Barsimæus (Barsamja)**, third Bishop of Odessa, martyred under Trajan 250: **St Hyacintha Mariscotti**, virgin: **St Martina**, virgin and martyr.

January 31
SAINT PETER NOLASCO
AD 1258

Peter, of the noble family of Nolasco, in Languedoc, was born in the diocese of St Papoul about the year 1189. His parents were very rich.

In his childhood he gave to the poor whatever he received for his own use. He rose at midnight, and assisted at matins in the church. At the age of fifteen he lost his father, who left him heir to a great estate, and he remained at home under the government of his pious mother, who brought him up in the practices of virtue. He gave no part of his time to amusements, but spent all the moments which the instruction of his pupils left free in holy prayer, meditation and pious reading. By his begging, he moved others to contribute large alms towards charity and formed a religious order to carry on his charitable undertakings.

The king declared himself the protector of the order and assigned them a large quarter of his own palace for their use.

St Peter was presented to the Bishop of Barcelona who received his three solemn religious vows to which the saint added a fourth, to devote his whole substance and his very liberty, if necessary, to the ransoming of slaves; the like vow he required of all his followers. They chose a white habit, to put them continually in mind of innocence; they wore a scapular, which is also white but the king asked them for his sake, to bear the royal arms of Arragon, which were interwoven on their habit upon the breast.

Their numbers increasing very fast, the saint petitioned the king for another house who, on this occasion, built for them in 1232, a magnificent convent at Barcelona.

In 1249 he resigned the offices of ransomer and general, which was six or seven years before his death. His relics are honoured by many miracles.

The following feasts are also celebrated today:

St Aidanus, Bishop of Ferns: **Saints Cyrus** and **John**, the former a physician who converted many to the faith, the latter an Arabian. Syrians, Egyptians, Greeks and Latins all venerate these two saints: **St Eusebius**, hermit and martyr: **St Germinianus**, Bishop of Modena 348: **St John Bosco**, Confessor, born in Piedmont in 1815. From early childhood he had a great influence on children. After his ordination he established himself in Turin where, with the help of his saintly mother, Margaret, he founded the Congregation of the Salesian Fathers. Later he also founded that of the Daughters of Our Lady Help of Christians. He is known as one of the greatest educators of youth: **St Marcella**, widow: **St Ulphia**, virgin.

February 1
SAINT IGNATIUS
Bishop of Antioch, Martyr – AD 107

St Ignatius, surnamed Theophorus, a word implying a divine or heavenly person, was a convert disciple of St John the Evangelist; also the apostles SS Peter and Paul, who united their labours in planting the faith at Antioch. During the persecution of Domitian, St Ignatius defended his flock by prayer, fasting, and daily preaching the word of God. He was condemned to death by the Emperor Trajan.

and
SAINT BRIGID (BRIDE)
AD c523

Second only to St Patrick in the love of the Irish and credited with countless miracles and blessings, she was foundress of the first convent in Ireland.

It seems possible that she was born into a peasant family near Dundalk in Ireland, of parents baptised by St Patrick himself. She became a nun at an early age. The central achievement of her life came in c470 when she founded the first convent in Ireland at Kildare.

Brigid died at Kildare and was buried there, but her relics were reburied at Downpatrick, along with those of Patrick, during invasions by the Danes.

In art she is shown as an abbess usually holding a lamp or candle and often with a cow nearby recalling the legend that the cows she kept as a nun once produced milk three times a day for the benefit of her visitors. Patron saint of Ireland (after St Patrick), poets, blacksmiths, healers, cattle, dairymaids, midwives, newborn babies and fugitives.

Her name means "a bright light".

The following feasts are also celebrated today:
St Kinnea of Ireland, baptised by St Patrick: **St Pionius**, martyr, a priest of Smyrna: **St Sigebert**, the French king of Austrasia.

February 2
The following feasts are celebrated today:
St Laurence, who came to England with **St Augustine** c597. He died in 619.

February 3
SAINT BLAISE (Blase, Blasius)
Bishop and martyr – AD 316

Blaise was born of wealthy, noble Christian parents and was consecrated as bishop of Sebastea while still very young. When the persecutions began he withdrew to live in a cave as a hermit, where he healed wild animals. Sought out by a woman, whose son was choking to death on a fishbone, Blaise miraculously healed the boy. But he was eventually discovered by hunters of the emperor out searching for wild beasts for entertainment in the amphitheatre: they were astonished to find Blaise surrounded by animals and yet unharmed by them. They took him before Agricolaus, governor of Cappadocia and Lesser Armenia, found him guilty of being a Christian and had him imprisoned.

Blaise refused to recant and underwent horrific tortures for his faith; he is thought to have been torn with iron wool-combs before his execution by beheading, hence he is regarded as the patron saint of wool-combers and his iconographic emblem is a comb. He is also usually shown with two candles (sometimes only one), recalling the legend that while in prison he was visited by the woman whose son he had healed who brought him food and candles.

The blessing of St Blaise began in the 16th century and is still practised today, in which two candles are placed on the throat of the sufferer. Other representations have him as a hermit tending wild animals or healing the choking boy.

Patron saint of wool-combers, invoked against throat diseases.

The following feasts are also celebrated today:
St Anscharius, Archbishop of Hamburg and Bremen, 865: **St Margaret** of England: **St Wereburghe**, Abbess and patron of Chester who died at Trentham about the end of the seventh century.

February 4
SAINT ANDREW CORSINI
Bishop and Confessor – AD 1373

The saint at his baptism was called Andrew, from the apostle of that name, on whose festival he was born in Florence, in 1302. The family of the Corsini was then one of the most illustrious. Before St Andrew was born, his mother dreamed that she gave birth to a wolf which, while running towards a Carmelite Church suddenly changed into a lamb.

He spent the first part of his youth in vice and extravagance, in the company of such as were as wicked as himself. His devout mother, Peregrina, who never ceased praying for his conversion, one day said to him, "I see you are the wolf I saw in my sleep." She added that she and her husband had in a particular manner devoted him to the service of God, and that, in consequence of his being born not for them, nor for the world, but for God, a very different kind of life from what he led was expected from him.

This made so strong an impression on his heart that he went immediately to the church of the Carmelite friars, and having prayed there for some time he resolved upon the spot to return no more to his father's house, but to embrace the religious state of life professed in that convent. He never departed from the first fervour of his conversion.

In 1328 he was ordained priest. After some time employed in preaching at Florence, he was sent to Paris, where he studied three years.

He stayed some time at Avignon with his uncle, Cardinal Corsini, and, in 1332, returning to Florence, was chosen prior of that convent.

Being consecrated bishop in the beginning of the year 1360, he redoubled his former austerities. His time was taken up in prayer, meditation and reading the scriptures. His tenderness and care of the poor were incredible. He was accustomed every Thursday to wash the feet of the poor; one excused himself, alleging that his feet were full of ulcers. The saint insisted upon washing them notwithstanding and they were immediately healed. He kept a list of the names of all the poor and never dismissed any without alms, for which purpose he once miraculously multiplied bread. He was taken ill whilst he was singing high mass on Christmas night in 1372. He died on 6 January 1373. He was honoured with many miracles, and immediately canonized by the voice of the people.

The Marquis of Corsini, sumptuously adorned the chapel of the Carmelite friars' church in Florence, in which the saint's body is kept.

The following feasts are also celebrated today:
St Gilbert, Abbot, Founder of the Gilbertins: **St Isadore** of Pelusium, priest: **St Joan** or **Jane** of Valois, Queen of France: **St Joseph of Leonissa**: **St Modan**, Abbot in Scotland in the seventh century: **St Phileas** and **St Philoromus**, the former a rich noble who became Bishop of Thmuis, the second a governor in Egypt: **St Rembert**, Archbishop of Bremen.

February 5
SAINT AGATHA
Virgin and Martyr – AD c251

Little is known of the historical figure of Agatha. She was a young noble Sicilian, born in either Palermo or Cantania, who had dedicated herself and her virginity to God as a child. When she was pursued by an amorous consul named Quintian, she rejected his advances out of hand despite his threats to implicate her as a Christian in a climate of imperial persecution.

She was tortured and humiliated but refused to renounce her faith: one of her most famous ordeals was the cutting off of both her breasts, but she was healed and encouraged by a vision of St Peter coming to her aid as she lay in prison, mutilated and in agony. She eventually died after being rolled over red-hot coals.

Her cult became hugely popular in Sicily, Italy and beyond; she is invoked against fire, particularly against the unpredictable eruptions of Mount Etna, and against the associated dangers of earthquakes and lightning. Her iconography is especially interesting. As she is usually shown as a virgin martyr, who carries on a tray before her her two shorn breasts, the resulting image has understandably given rise to much confusion and the breasts have frequently been wrongly identified as bells or loaves of bread. As a result Agatha is venerated as the patroness of bell-founders and many churches celebrate her feast with a tradition of blessing bread.

Other representations show her with pincers or shears, the instruments of her torture, and she sometimes wears the veil that is her most famous relic. Patron saint of Catania, bell-founders and wet-nurses, invoked against eruptions of Etna, diseases of the breast, earthquakes, fire and sterility.

The following feasts are also celebrated today:
St Abraamius, Bishop of Arbela in Assyria: **St Alice** or **Adelaide**, Abbess in Cologne, who died in 1015: **St Avitis**, Archbishop of Vienne.

February 6
The following feasts are celebrated today:
St Amandus, Bishop and Confessor: **St Barsanuphius** who lived as hermit in the Holy Land: **St Vedast**, Bishop of Arles.

February 7
SAINT ROMUALD
Abbot, Founder of the Order of Camaldoli – AD 1027

St Romuald, of the family of the dukes of Ravenna, called Honesti, was born in that capital c956. Being brought up in the maxims of the world, in softness and the love of pleasures, he grew every day more and more enslaved to his passions; yet he often made a resolution of undertaking something remarkable for the honour of God.

Romuald, then twenty years of age entered the neighbouring Benedictine monastery of Classis, within four miles of Ravenna. He passed seven years in this house in great austerity. Romuald retired into the marsh of Classis, and lived in a cell, remote from all mankind.

He built many monasteries, and often foretold things to come and gave directions full of heavenly wisdom to all who came to consult him. He obtained the pope's licence, and set out to preach the gospel in Hungary, but a violent illness which seized him on his entering Hungary, and returned as often as he attempted to do so, forced him to return home.

In his old age instead of relaxing, he increased his austerities and fasts. His disciples also were remarkable for their austere lives, and went always barefoot, and looked excessively pale with continual fasting. No other drink was known among them but water, except in sickness.

The most famous of all his monasteries is that of Camaldoli near Arezzo, in Tuscany. It lies beyond a mountain, which then belonged to a lord called Maldoli, who gave it to the saint, and from him it retained the name Camaldoli.

On entering the monastery, we meet with a chapel of St Antony for travellers to pray in before they advance any further. Next are the cells and lodgings for the porters.

Somewhat further is the church, which is large, well built and richly adorned. Over the door is a clock, which strikes so loud that it may be heard all over the desert. On the left side of the church is the cell in which St Romuald lived when he first established these hermits. Their cells, built of stone, have each a little garden walled round. A constant fire is allowed to be kept in every cell on account of the coldness of the air throughout the year; each cell has also a chapel in which they may say mass.

The whole hermitage is now enclosed with a wall: none are allowed to go out of it; but they may walk in the woods and valleys within the enclosure.

Everything is sent them from the valley: their food is every day brought to each cell; and all are supplied with wood and necessities. They keep strict silence in all public places.

For a severer solitude, St Romuald added a third kind of life; that of a recluse. After a holy life in the hermitage, the superior grants leave to any that ask it to live for ever shut up in their cells, never speaking to any one but to the superior when he visits them and to the brother who brings them necessities. Their prayers and austerities are doubled, and their fasts more severe and more frequent. St Romuald condemned himself to this kind of life for several years.

St Romuald died in his monastery in the valley of Castro in Ancona. As he was born c956 he must have died seventy years and some months old, not a hundred and twenty as the present copies of his life have it. His body was found entire and uncorrupt five years after his death, and again in 1466.

and
SAINT RICHARD
King and Confessor – AD 722

This saint was an English prince, in the kingdom of the West-Saxons. His three children, Winebald, Willibald and Warburga, are all honoured as saints. Taking with him his two sons, he undertook a pilgrimage of penance and devotion, and sailing from Hamble-haven, landed in Neustria on the western coast of France.

He arrived at Lucca in Italy and on the road to Rome died suddenly. He was buried in St Fridian's church there. His relics are venerated to this day in the same place.

The following feasts are also celebrated today:
St Augulus: **St Theodorus** of Heraclea: **St Tresian**, an Irish priest who preached to the French; he is greatly venerated at Avenay in Champaigne.

February 8
SAINT JOHN OF MATHA
Founder of the Order of the Trinitarians – AD 1218

St John was born of very pious and noble parents, at Faucon, on the borders of Provence, on 24 June 1169, and was baptised John in honour of St John the Baptist. His father Euphemius sent him to Aix, where he learned grammar, fencing, riding and other exercises fit for a young nobleman. But his chief attention was to advance in virtue.

He gave the poor a considerable part of the money his parents sent him; he visited the hospital every Friday, assisting the sick, dressing and cleansing their sores and affording them all the comfort in his power. He returned home and begged his father's leave to continue the pious exercises he had begun and went to a little hermitage not far from Faucon.

Finding his solitude interrupted by the frequent visits of his friends, he went to Paris to study divinity. He was soon ordained priest, and having heard of a holy hermit, St Felix Valois, living in a great wood near Gandelu, he went to him.

Felix soon discovered John was no novice, and would not treat him as a disciple, but as a companion. Together they founded a new religious order. The Bishop of Paris drew up their rules, which the pope approved in 1198. He ordered the religious to wear a white habit, with a red and blue cross on the breast, and to take the name of the order of the Holy Trinity.

The two saints founded many other convents in France, and sent several of their religious to accompany the counts of Flanders and Blois, and other lords, to the holy war.

St John died on 21 December, 1213 aged sixty-one. He was buried in his church of St Thomas, where his monument yet remains, though his body has been translated into Spain.

The following feasts are also celebrated today:
St Cuthman, much honoured in England: **St Paul**, Bishop of Verdun, died in 631: **St Stephen** of Grandmont, 1124, son of the Viscount of Thiers.

February 9
SAINT APOLLONIA
AD 249

During a riot in Alexandria in the last year of the reign of Emperor Philip, a mob hunted down and killed Christians in the town, looting their houses, torturing them to make them renounce their faith and murdering them.

One of the victims of the atrocities was an old deaconess, 'that marvellous aged virgin Apollonia', according to Dionysius. She was struck on the jaw so hard and so frequently that her teeth were knocked out and a pyre was built outside the city on which to burn her alive if she refused to renounce her faith. Apollonia begged for a moment's respite then she seized her opportunity and leapt dramatically into the flames.

Her usual emblem is a tooth, sometimes gilded and suspended on a neckchain or held by forceps to indicate its removal, and she is the patron saint of dentists. Invoked against toothache.

The following feasts are also celebrated today:
St Ansbert, Archbishop of Rouen, who left the Court of Clotaire III to enter a monastery: **St Attracta** or **Tarahata**: **St Erhard**, a Scotsman who preached in Germany: **St Nicephorus**: **St Theliau**, Bishop.

February 10
SAINT SCHOLASTICA
Virgin – AD c543

This saint was sister to the great St Benedict. She consecrated herself to God from her earliest youth, as St Gregory testifies. Where her first monastery was situated is not mentioned; but after her brother went to Mount Cassino she chose her retreat at Plombariola, where she founded and governed a nunnery about five miles to the south from St Benedict's monastery.

St Gregory informs us that as St Benedict governed nuns as well as monks, his sister must have been their abbess under his rule and direction. She visited her holy brother once a year, and as she was not allowed to enter his monastery, he went out with some of his monks to meet her at a house some small distance away.

St Gregory relates a remarkable circumstance of the last of these visits. Scholastica having passed the day as usual in singing psalms and prayer, they sat down in the evening to take their meal. After it was over, Scholastica, perhaps knowing it would be their last interview in this world asked her brother to delay his return till the next day. St Benedict, unwilling to transgress his rule, told her he could not pass a night out of his monastery. Scholastica laying her hands joined upon the table, and her head upon them, begged of Almighty God to interpose in her behalf.

Her prayer was scarce ended when there was such a storm of rain, thunder and lightning that neither St Benedict nor any of his companions could set a foot out of doors. He complained to his sister, saying "God forgive you, sister; for what you have done." She answered, "I asked you a favour and you refused it me; I asked it of Almighty God and he has granted it me." St Benedict was therefore obliged to comply with her request. The next morning they parted, and three days later St Scholastic died.

St Benedict was then alone in contemplation on Mount Cassino, and lifting up his eyes to heaven, he saw the soul of his sister ascending in the shape of a dove.

The following feasts are also celebrated today:
St Erluph, a native of Scotland who went to north-western Germany to preach: **St Soteris**, virgin and martyr: **St William of Maleval**, who lived and died (in 1157) a hermit, founder of the Gulielmites, an order of Hermits long since extinct.

February 11
SAINTS SATURNINUS, DATIVUS
And Many Other Martyrs of Africa – AD 304

The emperor Diocletian had commanded all Christians under pain of death to deliver up the holy scriptures to be burnt. This persecution had raged a whole year in Africa. Abitina, a city of the proconsular province of Africa, was the theatre of their triumph.

Saturninus, priest of that city, celebrated the mass on a Sunday, in the house of Octavius Felix. The magistrates having notice of it, came with a troop of soldiers, and seized 49 persons of both sexes. The principal among them were the priest Saturninus, with his four children, young Saturninus and Felix, Mary and Hilarianus; also Dativus, a noble senator, Ampelius, Rogatianus and Victoria. Dativus marched at the head of this holy troop. Saturninus walked by his side, surrounded by his family. The others followed in silence. Being brought before the magistrates, they confessed Jesus Christ so resolutely that their very judges applauded their courage.

They underwent severally the tortures of the rack, iron hooks and cudgels. These martyrs ended their lives under the hardships of their confinement and are honoured in the ancient calendar of Carthage.

The following feasts are also celebrated today:
St Severinus, Abbot of Agaunum: **St Theodora**, Empress. She spent the last years of her life in a monastery.

February 12
SAINT BENEDICT OF ANIAN
Abbot – AD 821

He was the son of Aigulf, count or Governor of Languedoc and served King Pepin and his son Charlemagne enjoying under them great honours and possessions. At 20 years of age he took a resolution of seeking the kingdom of God with his whole heart. He led a most mortified life in the court itself for three years, eating very sparingly and of the coarsest fare, allowing himself very little sleep, and mortifying all his senses. In 774, having narrowly escaped being drowned in the Tesin, near Pavia, in endeavouring to save his brother, he made a vow to quit the world entirely.

Returning to Languedoc he went to the Abbey of St Seine, and having sent back all his attendants, became a monk there. He spent two years in abstinence, treating his body as a furious wild beast, to which he would show no other mercy than barely not to kill it. He took no sustenance on any account but bread and water; and when overcome with weariness, he allowed himself nothing softer than the bare ground whereon to take a short rest. He frequently passed the whole night in prayer, and stood barefoot on the ground in the sharpest cold.

He wrote, whilst a private monk at Seine, the Code of Rules, being a collection of all the monastic regulations, also a book of homilies for the use of monks. This great restorer of the monastic order in the West, worn out with mortification and fatigues, suffered much from continual sickness during the latter years of his life, died at Inde, with extraordinary tranquillity and cheerfulness.

The following feasts are also celebrated today:
St Anthony Cauleas, Patriarch of Constantinople, died on this date 896: **St Eulalia**, virgin and martyr, who suffered on the rack before she was crucified: **St Meletius**, Patriarch of Antioch.

February 13
SAINT CATHARINE DE RICCI
Virgin – AD 1589

The Ricci are an ancient family, still flourishing in Tuscay. Peter de Ricci, the father of our saint, was married to Catharine Bonza. The saint was born at Florence in 1522 and called at her baptism Alexandrina, but she took the name of Catharine at her religious profession. Having lost her mother in her infancy she was brought up by a very pious godmother. When she was between six and seven years old, her father placed her in the Convent of Monticelli near the gates of Florence, where her aunt, Louisa de Ricci, was a nun. This place was to her a paradise: at a distance from the noise and tumult of the world, she served God without distraction. After some years her father took her home. She continued in the world as much as she was able but in 1535 at 14 she received the religious veil in the convent of Dominicanesses at Prat, in Tuscay, to which her uncle, F. Timothy de Ricci, was director.

Saint Catharine was chosen whilst still very young to be first, mistress of the novices, then sub-prioress, and at 25 was appointed perpetual prioress. The reputation of her extraordinary sanctity and prudence drew her many visits from a great number of bishops, princes and cardinals.

She died after a long illness.

The following feasts are also celebrated today:
St Gregory II, Pope, "skilled in the knowledge of the Scriptures": **St Licinius**, Bishop of Angers: **St Martinianus**, hermit at Athens: **St Modomnoc,** or **Dominick**, of Ossory: **St Polyeuctus**, martyr about the year 250: **St Stephen**, Abbot.

February 14
SAINT VALENTINE
Priest and Martyr – AD 269

There are in fact two Valentines, whose feasts are both celebrated on 14 February in the Roman martyrology, and neither of whom has any obvious connection with courting couples.

One was a Roman priest and doctor who is believed to have been martyred under Claudius II on the Flaminian Way where a basilica was erected in his honour in 350. The other was a bishop of Turni (about 60 miles distant from Rome) who was brought to Rome and tortured and executed there c273 at the command of Placidus, the ruling prefect. Some believe that the two Valentines are in fact one person, that the Roman priest became bishop of Turni, was condemned there and brought to Rome for execution of his sentence.

The present popularity of Valentine's day has little to do with the historical saint or saints. It was a commonly held belief, attested from the time of Chaucer, that birds began to choose their mates on Valentine's feast-day, the very beginning of Spring and this is thought by many to be the origin of the tradition of choosing one's object of love as a 'Valentine'.

Some scholars believe that Chaucer was actually referring to the feast-day of the bishop Valentine of Genoa celebrated on 2 May, and that he may have had in mind the betrothal of Richard II to Anne of Bohemia on 3 May 1381. If this is the case, the conflation of the various Valentines on to a single fast-day probably occurred some time after the death of Chaucer.

He is often represented in art with a crippled or epileptic child at his feet whom he is believed to have cured. For this reason, too, he is often invoked against epilepsy. Other depictions show his beheading, or his refusal to worship idols, which led to his martyrdom.

Patron saint of bee-keepers, affianced couples, travellers and the young, invoked against epilepsy, fainting and plague and for a happy marriage.

The following feasts are also celebrated today:
St Abraames, Bishop of Carres: **St Auxentius**, hermit. In his youth one of the equestrian guards of Theodosius the Younger: **St Conran**, Bishop of Orkney: **St Gilbert** of Sempringham, founder of the Gilbertines. He was the friend of St Thomas of Canterbury: **St Maro**, Abbot, who lived on a mountain in Syria.

February 15
SAINTS FAUSTINUS AND JOVITA
Martyrs – AD 121

Faustinus and Jovita were brothers, nobly born, and zealous professors of the Christian religion, which they preached without fear in their city of Brescia, whilst the bishop of that place lay concealed during the persecution. The acts of their martyrdom seeming of doubtful authority, all we can affirm with certainty of them is that their remarkable zeal excited the fury of the heathens against them, and procured them a death for their faith at Brescia in Lombardy, under the emperor Adrian. The city of Brescia honours them as its chief patrons and possesses their relics.

The following feast is also celebrated today:
St Sigefride or **Sigfrid**, Bishop, Apostle of Sweden.

February 16
SAINT ONESIMUS
Disciple of St Paul – AD 95

He was a Phrygian by birth, slave to Philemon, a person of note in the city of Colossæ, converted to the faith by St Paul. Having robbed his master, and being obliged to fly, he providentially met with St Paul, then a prisoner for the faith at Rome, who there converted and baptised him, and sent him with his canonical letter of recommendation to Philemon, by whom he was pardoned, set at liberty and sent back to St Paul whom he afterwards faithfully served. The Greeks say he was crowned with martyrdom under Domitian, in 95.

The following feasts are also celebrated today:
Saints Elias, Jeremy, Isaias, Samuel and **Daniel**, five Egyptians martyred at Cæsaria in Palestine 1309: **St Gregory X**, Pope and Confessor: **St Juliana**, martyred in Nicomedia: **St Tanco** or **Tatta**, Bishop and martyr, a native of Scotland.

February 17
SAINT FLAVIAN
Martyr, Archbishop of Constantinople – AD 449

St Flavian was a priest of distinguished merit, and treasurer of the church of Constantinople.

The following feasts are also celebrated today:
St Finnan, a monk of Iona who succeeded St Aidan as Bishop of Northumbria, died 661, honoured in Scotland: **St Fintan**, Abbot of Chuainednech. He is said to have raised one of his disciples from the dead by his prayers: **St Loman** or **Luman**, a disciple if not a sister's son of St Patrick's, first Bishop of Trim in Meath: **St Silvin** of Auchy, Bishop and Confessor: **St Theodulas** and **St Julian**, martyred at Cæsarea in Palestine.

February 18
SAINT SIMEON
Bishop of Jerusalem, Martyr – AD 116

St Simeon was the son of Cleophas, otherwise called Alpheus, brother to St Joseph, and of Mary, sister of the Blessed Virgin. He was therefore, nephew both to St Joseph and to the Blessed Virgin and cousin to Christ.

Simeon and Simon are the same name, and this saint is, according to the best interpreters of the holy scripture, the Simon mentioned who was brother to St James the Lesser, and St Jude, apostles and to Joseph or José. He was eight or nine years older than Christ. St Simeon travelled into Asia and from there to Rome.

Vespasian and Domitian had commanded all to be put to death who were of the race of David. St Simeon had escaped their searches; but Trajan having given the same order accused him of being both of the race of David and a Christian and so the holy bishop was condemned to be crucified. He died in 107.

God gives us a pencil for the Book of Life, but He alone holds the eraser.

and
SAINT BERNADETTE
The visionary of Lourdes – AD 1879

Marie Bernarde Sourbrious was born on 7 January, the first child of a poverty-stricken miller named François Soubrious and his young wife Louise. Given the diminutive pet name Bernadette as a child, she suffered from asthma, poverty and a lack of education. Her delicate health was not improved by a bout of cholera, contracted during the epidemic of 1854, or by the insanitary conditions of the dark, damp basement in which she lived. But at the age of 14 on 11 February 1858, Bernadette experienced a vision of the Virgin Mary while collecting firewood on the bank of the river Gave near Lourdes. Over the next six months she saw a series of 18 visions, in which 'the Lady', who identified herself as 'the Immaculate Conception', indicated a nearby spring from which she told Bernadette to drink: opinion is divided as to whether this was a forgotten spring or one created miraculously. She also directed Bernadette to erect a chapel on the site; beyond this the content of the visions was mostly concerned with the importance of prayer and penance.

Bernadette's claims were subjected to enormous scepticism. She was questioned exhaustively by church and state authorities but, in spite of her youth and her intellectual simplicity, her story was unshakeable. Unlike many visionaries Bernadette was a stable character not given to emotional outbursts, and those investigating the claims were forced to acknowledge her disinterestedness and veracity. The incessant attention and questioning was a mental and physical ordeal for the sensitive girl, whose asthma was worsened by the fatigue of cross-examination.

Finally, however, the visions were ecclesiastically approved, and work began to make the site of the visions one of the largest pilgrimage sites the Christian world has ever known. The spring has regularly produced 27,000 gallons of water each week since its discovery, and countless miracles of healing have been reported in its waters and at the shrine there.

Bernadette herself retired to the convent of the Sisters of Charity at Nevers in 1866, wishing only to escape the unwanted publicity and the equal measures of suspicion, curiosity and enthusiasm with which she was regarded. She was not involved with the development of Lourdes, and did not even attend the consecration of the basilica there in 1876, but spent the rest of her life patiently suffering ill health, proving a quiet and self-effacing nun renowned for her simple piety until she died aged only 35. She was beatified in 1925, and when she was canonized by Pope Pius XI in 1933 it was not so much for her visions as for the integrity and humility of her life. She is listed in the official records of the Church as Marie Bernarde, but to the faithful who honour and invoke her she is always known by her pet name, Bernadette.

The following feasts are also celebrated today:
St Colman, bishop and Confessor, honoured in Ireland: **St Leo** and **St Paregorius**.

February 19
SAINT BARBATUS OR BARBAS
Confessor, Bishop of Benevento – AD 682

St Barbatus was born in the territory of Benevento, in Italy, toward the end of the pontificate of St Gregory the Great, in the beginning of the seventh century. His parents gave him a Christian education. He became a priest as soon as the church would allow it. He was immediately employed by his bishop in preaching for which he had an extraordinary talent; and, after some time, made curate of St. Basil's in Morconia, a town near Benevento.

His parishioners desired only to slumber on in their sins, they could not bear this new pastor, who endeavoured to awake them to a sense of their faults. They treated him as a disturber of their peace and persecuted him with the utmost violence. Such was their success that he was obliged to withdraw. But Barbatus returned to Benevento, where this time he was received with great joy by those who had previously persecuted him.

Totila, the Goth, laid the city of Benevento in ruins in 545. When St Barbatus entered that city, the Christians themselves retained many idolatrous superstitions. They expressed a religious veneration to a golden viper, and prostrated themselves before it: they paid also a superstitious honour to a tree, on which they hung the skin of a wild beast. St Barbatus preached zealously against these abuses, and laboured long to no purpose. At length he roused their attention by foretelling the distress of their city and the calamities which it was to suffer from the army of the emperor Constans who, landing soon after in Italy, laid siege to Benevento.

In their extreme distress, and still more grievous alarms and fears, they listened to the holy preacher and renounced their errors and idolatrous practices. Upon their repentance, the saint cut down the tree which was the object of their superstition, and afterward melted down the golden viper which they adored and made a chalice for the use of the altar. St Barbatus was consecrated bishop of Benevento on 10 March 663.

Barbatus destroyed every trace of the least remains of superstition in the whole state. He died in 682 being about seventy years old.

The following feasts are also celebrated today:
St Mansuetus, Bishop of Milan: **St Gabinus**, priest and martyr: **St Georges**, Bishop of Lodavia.

February 20
SAINT TYRANNIO
Bishop of Tyre
SAINT ZENOBIUS AND OTHERS
Martyrs in Phœnicia – AD 304-310

Eusebius, an eye-witness, relates the following account of them – "Several Christians of Egypt had settled in Palestine, others at Tyre, and gave astonishing proofs of their faith. After innumerable blows, which they cheerfully underwent, they were exposed to wild beasts, such as leopards, wild bears, boars and bulls. I myself was present when these savage creatures, accustomed to human blood, being let out upon them, instead of devouring them or tearing them to pieces, as it was natural to expect, stood off, refusing even to touch or approach them. At the same time they fell foul on their keepers and others that came in their way.

The persecutors tossed about their arms, which was thought a ready way to provoke the beasts and stir them up against the martyrs. Sometimes, indeed, the beasts were perceived to rush towards them then suddenly withdraw, and this many times, to the great admiration of all present.

A second and third time the animals were let out upon them, but in vain; the martyrs standing all the while unshaken, though many of them very young."

After repeated trials of this kind with other wild beasts, with as little success as the former, the saints were slain by the sword, and their bodies cast into the sea. This happened in 304, under Veturius, a Roman general in the reign of Diocletian.

The following feasts are also celebrated today:
St Eleutherius, Bishop of Tournay, born of a Christian family, converted to St Paul 150 years earlier: **St Eucherius**, Bishop of Orleans: **St Mildred**, Abbess, a grand-daughter of King Penda, she, with two sisters and a brother, served God in the cloister and are honoured as saints: **St Sadoth**, Bishop of Seleucia, with Ctesiphon and 128 companion-martyrs. Threatened with death, they cried with one voice: "We shall not die but shall live for ever, with God and His Son, Jesus Christ.": **St Ulrick**, a recluse in Dorset, died 1154.

February 21
The following feasts are celebrated today:
St Daniel, a priest and **St Verda** (in Chaldiac "a Rose", a virgin consecrated to God; they were first tortured and then martyred in Persia, 344: **St German**, Abbot of Granfel and **St Radaut**, martyred about 666: **St Margaret** of Cortona: **St Severianus**.

February 22
SAINT MARGARET OF CORTONA
AD 1297

Margaret of Cortona was born into a Tuscan peasant family; her mother died when she was only seven, and when her father remarried two years later his wife was unsympathetic towards her young stepdaughter.

At the age of 18, Margaret, now renowned for her beauty, ran away from home to become the mistress of a young nobleman from Montepulciano. She lived with her lover for nine years in ostentation and luxury, and bore him a son, before his death at the hands of an unknown murderer in 1273.

According to legend his hound returned alone to lead Margaret to his master's body, hence she is frequently represented with a dog pulling at her robe and a skull beneath her feet.

The death of her lover shocked Margaret into penitence; she made a public confession of her sins in a church near Cortona in Tuscany and appealed to her father but he refused to allow her back into his house. She and her son were finally taken in by two ladies of the church, Mariana and Raneria.

From now on Margaret's life was as self-denying as it had previously been self-indulgent. She enrolled as a Franciscan tertiary and underwent a reclusive probation of three years, during which time her spiritual advisors were Friars John da Castiglione and Giunta Bevegnati.

She devoted herself to works of charity and to prayer and counsel which converted many, but she faced slanderous gossip concerning her relationship with the friars. The rumours, later proved to be unfounded, were so serious that in c1289 Friar Giunta was transferred to Siena.

Margaret is renowned for her supernatural experiences, including visions of Christ as a peacemaker.

In 1286 Margaret set up a community of women to care for the poor and sick, to extend the charity she had hitherto practised from her own home, which she named *Le Poverelle*. She established a hospital for the work of the order in Cortona, and she also founded the Confraternity of Our Lady of Mercy, whose members were pledged to support it.

Margaret died at the age of 50, and her allegedly incorrupt body lies in the church at Cortona with a statue by Giovanni Pisano showing her with the dog that led her to her lover's body.

Patron saint of female penitents.

The following feasts are also celebrated today:
St Baradat, of Cyr: **St Thelassius** and **St Limneus**.

February 23
SAINT PETER DAMIAN
Cardinal, Bishop of Ostia – AD 1072

Peter, surnamed Damian, was born about 988 in Ravenna, of a good family. He was the youngest of many children, and losing his father and mother very young, was left in the hands of a brother who was married, in whose house he was treated more like a slave, or rather like a beast, than one so nearly related; and when grown up he was sent to keep swine.

Peter went to school, first at Faenza, afterwards at Parma, where he had Ivo for his master. By the means of close application, it was not long before he found himself in a capacity to teach others.

He began to wear a rough hair shirt under his clothes and to fast and pray. He not only gave much away in alms, but was seldom without some poor person at his table. He resolved entirely to leave the world and embrace a monastic life.

He joined the order of St Benedict, going to a hermitage founded by Blessed Ludolf, about twenty years earlier. The hermits here remained in separate cells, occupied chiefly in prayer and reading. They lived on bread and water for four days in the week: on Tuesdays and Thursdays they ate pulse and herbs. They never used any wine (the common drink of the country) except for mass, or in sickness: they went barefoot.

Peter gave a considerable time to sacred studies and became well versed in the scriptures and other sacred learning.

Being recalled home some time after, and commanded by his abbot, he founded five other hermitages. Pope Stephen IX in 1057 made him Cardinal-bishop of Ostia.

Old age did not make him lay aside his accustomed mortifications. On his return towards Rome, he was stopped by a fever in the monastery of Our Lady outside the gates of Faenza, and died there on the eighth day of his sickness. He is honoured as patron at Faenza and Font-Avellano.

The following feasts are also celebrated today:
St Boisel, prior of Melross: **St Milburge**, virgin, sister to St Mildred (7th century): **St Serenus**, a gardener, beheaded on this date in 327.

Art thou lonely, O my brother?
Share thy little with another!
Stretch a hand to one unfriended,
And thy loneliness is ended.

JOHN OXENHAM – Lonely Brother

February 24
SAINT MATTHAIS
Apostle

St Clement of Alexandria assures us, from tradition, that this saint was one of the seventy-two disciples who were in constant attendance on our Lord from the time of his baptism by St John to his ascension.

St Peter having declared from holy scripture the necessity of choosing a twelfth apostle, chose Matthias. He was accordingly associated with the eleven, and ranked among the apostles.

Never put off till tomorrow the smile you can give today.

and
SAINT ETHELBERT
First Christian King among the English

Ethelbert was King of Kent. He succeeded his father, Ermenric in 560. His queen, Bertha, was a very zealous and pious Christian princess, and by the articles of her marriage had free liberty to exercise her religion. The merit of the queen in the great work of her husband's conversion is acknowledged by our historians.

From the time St Augustine landed in Kent, Ethelbert appeared quite changed. For the remaining twenty years of his life his only ambition and endeavour was to establish the perfect reign of Christ, both in his own soul and in the hearts of all his subjects.

His royal palace at Canterbury he gave for the use of the archbishop St Austin; he founded in that city the cathedral called Christchurch.

King Ethelbert, after having reigned fifty-six years, died in 616 and was buried in the Church of SS Peter and Paul.

St Ethelbert is sometimes known as St Albert, under which name he is titular saint of several churches in England – particularly of one in Norwich, which was built before the cathedral.

The following feasts are also celebrated today:
Saints Montanus, Lucius, Flavian, Julian, Victoricus, Primolus, Rhenus and **Donatian**, martyred at Carthage, 259: **St Lethard**, Bishop of Senlis, who came to England as chaplain to Bertha, daughter of the King of the French, when she married Ethelbert: **St Pretextatus** or **Prix**, Archbishop of Rouen, martyr.

February 25
SAINT TARASIUS
Confessor, Patriarch of Constantinople – AD 806

Tarasius was born about the middle of the eighth century. His father, George, was a judge, well-known for his justice, and his mother, Eucratia, no less celebrated for her piety. She brought him up in the practice of the most eminent virtues.

The young man, by his talents and virtue, gained the esteem of all, and was raised to the greatest honours of the empire, being made consul, and afterwards secretary of state to the Emperor Constantine and the Empress Irene, his mother. In the midst of the court, and in its highest honours, surrounded by all that could flatter pride or gratify sensuality, he led a life of a religious man.

Paul, Patriarch of Constantinople, being asked whom he thought would provide the church of Constantinople with a worthy pastor immediately named Tarasius who was accordingly chosen patriarch by the unanimous consent of the court, clergy, and people. The life of this holy patriarch was a model of perfection to his clergy and people. He allowed himself very little time for sleep. Reading and prayer filled all his leisure hours.

His charity and love for the poor seemed to surpass his other virtues. He often took the dishes of meat from his table to distribute among them and he assigned them a large fixed revenue; and that none might be overlooked, he visited all the houses and hospitals in Constantinople.

The saint, under his successor, Icphorus, persevered peaceably in his practices of penance, and in the functions of his pastoral charge. In his last sickness he still continued to offer daily mass so long as he was able to move. In great serenity this holy man died in 806.

The following feasts are also celebrated today:
St Cæsarius, a physician, brother to St Gregory Nazianzen: **Saints Victorinus and Six Companions**, martyrs; they were seven citizens of Corinth: **St Walberge**, Abbess, daughter to King Richard, she was educated in the monastery of Wimborne in Dorset.

February 26
The following feasts are celebrated today:
St Alexander: **St Porphyrius**, Bishop of Gaza: **St Victor** or **Vittre** of Arcis, hermit.

He will always be a slave who does not know how to live upon a little.

February 27

The following feasts are celebrated today:

St Alnoth, hermit, murdered by robbers: **St Galmier**, a locksmith of Lyons. He gave all, even his tools, to the poor: **Saints Julian, Chronion** and **Besas**, martyrs, three soldiers: **St Leander**: **St Nestor**: **St Thalilæus**, a Cilician recluse in Syria.

Let me live in my house by the side of the road,
Where the race of men go by;
They are good, they are bad; they are weak, they are strong,
Wise, foolish, – so am I;
Why should I sit in the scorner's seat,
Or hurl the cynic's ban?
Let me live in my house by the side of the road,
And be a friend to man.

  SAM WALTER FOSS – House by the Side of the Road

February 28
SAINTS ROMANUS AND LUPICINUS
Abbots

Romanus at 35 years of age left his relations and spent some time in the monastery of Ainay at Lyons.

He then went into the forests of Mount Jura, between France and Switzerland and stayed at a place called Condate, where he found a spot of ground fit for culture, and some trees which furnished him with wild fruit. Here he spent his time in praying, reading and labouring for his subsistence. Lupicinus, his brother, came to him some time after, in company with others, who were followed by several more, drawn by the fame of the virtue and miracles of these two saints.

They built the monastery of Condate, and, their members increasing, that of Leuconne, two miles away to the north, and, on a rock, a nunnery called La Beaume (now St Romain de la Roche), which no men were allowed ever to enter. The brothers governed the monks jointly and in great harmony, though Lupicinus was more inclined to severity of the two. He usually resided at Leuconne with one hundred and fifty monks.

St Romanus died c460. St Lupicinus survived him almost twenty years.

The following feast is also celebrated today:
St Proterius, Patriarch of Alexandria, martyr, ordained by St Cyril.

February 29
SAINT OSWALD
Bishop of Worcester and Archbishop of York – AD 992

St Oswald was nephew to St Odo, Archbishop of Canterbury, and to Oskitell, Bishop first of Dorchester, afterwards of York. He was educated by St Odo, and made Dean of Winchester, but going to France, took the monastic habit at Fleury. Being recalled to serve the church, he succeeded St Dunstan in the see of Worcester about the year 959.

He was employed by Duke Aylwin in superintending his foundation of the great monastery of Ramsey in an island formed by marshes and the river Ouse in Huntingdonshire, in 973. St Oswald was made Archbishop of York in 974 and was almost always occupied in visiting his diocese, preaching and reforming abuses. He was a great encourager of learning and learned men.

After 33 years as Bishop, he fell sick at St Mary's in Worcester and died amidst his monks on 29th February 992.

> **St Oswald is the only Saint whose feast is celebrated on this date, which only recurs every fourth year.**

March 1
SAINT DAVID
Archbishop, Patron of Wales – AD c544

St David, in Welsh Dewid, was son of Xantus, prince of Ceretica, now Cardiganshire. He was brought up in the service of God, and, being ordained priest, retired to the Isle of Wight and embraced an ascetic life, under the direction of Paulinus, a learned and holy man, who had been a disciple of St Germanus of Auxerre. He is said by the sign of the cross to have restored sight to his master, which he had lost by old age.

He studied a long time to prepare himself for the functions of the holy ministry. At length, coming out of his solitude, like the Baptist out of the desert, he preached the word of eternal life to the Britons. He built a chapel at Glastonbury, a place which had been consecrated to divine worship by the first apostles of this island. He founded twelve monasteries, the principal of which was in the vale of Ross, near Menevia, where he formed many great pastors and eminent servants of God.

By his rule he obliged all his monks to assiduous manual labour in the spirit of penance. They were never to speak but on occasions of absolute necessity, and they never ceased to pray, at least mentally, during their labour. They returned late in the day to the monastery, to read, write and pray; then took a little rest, rose at cock-crowing, and continued in prayer till they went out to work. Their habit was of the skins of beasts.

The Pelagian heresy springing forth a second time in Britain, the bishops, in order to suppress it, held a synod at Brevy, in Cardiganshire in 512. St David, being invited to it went, and in that venerable assembly confuted and silenced them by his eloquence, learning and miracles. On the spot where this council was held a church was afterwards built called Llan-Devi Brevi, or the church of St David near the river Brevi. At the close of the synod, St Dubritius, the Archbishop of Caerleon resigned his see to St David. As for St David, Giraldus adds that he spoke with great force and energy, but his example was more powerful than his eloquence; and he has in all succeeding ages been the glory of the British church. He continued in his last see many years; and having founded several monasteries, and been the spiritual father of many saints, both British and Irish, died about the year 544, at a very advanced age.

The following feasts are also celebrated today:
St Albinus, Bishop of Angers: **St Monan** of Fife in 874: **St Swidbert** or **Swibert** "The Ancient", Bishop, an English monk who preached in Holland and Germany.

March 2
SAINT CEADA, OR CHAD
Bishop and Confessor – AD 673

He was brother to St Cedd, Bishop of London, and the two holy priests Celin and Cymbel, and had his education in the monastery of Lindisfarne, under St Aidan. For his greater improvement in sacred letters and divine contemplation he went into Ireland, and spent a considerable time in the company of St Egbert till he was called back by his brother, St Cedd, to assist him in settling the monastery of Lestingay, which he had founded in the mountains of the Deiri, that is, the Wolds of Yorkshire.

St Chad was ordained Bishop of Winchester in 666. He zealously devoted himself to all the laborious functions of his charge, visiting his diocese on foot, preaching the gospel, and seeking out the poorest and most abandoned persons to instruct and comfort in the meanest cottages and in the fields. St Chad, leaving the see of York, retired to his monastery of Lestingay, but was not allowed to bury himself long in that solitude.

He became the fifth bishop of the Mercians at Lichfield, the name signifying the field of carcasses. This city bears for its arms a landscape, covered with the bodies of martyrs. St Theodorus, considering St Chad's old age, and the great extent of his diocese, absolutely forbade him to make his visitations on foot, as he used to do at York.

By the bounty of King Wulfere, he founded a monastery at the place called Barrow. When allowed to retire, he enjoyed God in solitude with seven or eight monks, whom he had settled in a place near his cathedral. St Chad died in the great pestilence on 2 March 673.

The following feasts are also celebrated today:
St Charles, Earl of Flanders, martyr: **St Joavin** or **Joevin**, Bishop, a disciple of St Paul of Leon in Great Britain: **St Marman**, Bishop, who instructed the Northumbrian princes, Oswald and Oswi, in religion: **St Simplicius**, who succeeded Hilarius as pope in 497.

March 3
SAINT CUNEGUNDES
Empress – AD 1040

St Cunegundes was the daughter of Sigefride, the first Count of Luxemburg, and Hadeswige, his pious wife. They instilled into her from her cradle the most tender sentiments of piety, and married her to St Henry, Duke of Bavaria, who, upon the death of the Emperor Otho III, was chosen King of the Romans, and crowned on 6 June 1002.

In the year 1014 she went with her husband to Rome, and received the imperial crown with him from the hands of Pope Benedict VIII. She had, by St Henry's consent before her marriage, made a vow of virginity. They lived from that time conspiring to promote in everything God's honour and the advancement of piety.

Going once to make a retreat in Hesse, she fell dangerously ill and made a vow to found a monastery, if she recovered, in a place then called Capungen, now Kaffungen, near Cassel, which she had built and gave it to nuns of the order of St Benedict. Before it was finished St Henry died in 1024. She had already exhausted her treasures and her patrimony in founding bishoprics and monasteries, and in relieving the poor. Whatever was rich or magnificent she thought better suited churches than her palace. She had therefore, little now left to give.

On the anniversary day of her husband's death, in 1025, she joined her convent at Kaffungen. After she was consecrated to God in religion, she seemed entirely to forget that she had been empress. Thus she passed the fifteen last years of her life. Her mortifications at length reduced her to a very weak condition and brought on her last sickness.

She died on 3 March 1040. Her body was carried to Hamberg, and buried near that of her husband. The greatest part of her relics still remain in the same church.

The following feasts are also celebrated on 3 March:
St Ælred, Abbot, an Englishman: **St Emeterius** and **St Chelidonius**, soldiers of the Roman army in Spain: **St Marinus** and **St Asterius**, martyrs about the year 272: **St Lamalisse**, after whom a small Scottish island is still called: **St Winwaloe (or Winwaloc?)** of the family of the princes of Wales.

March 4
SAINT CASIMIR
Prince of Poland – AD 1433

St Casimir was the third among the thirteen children of Casimir III, King of Poland and of Elizabeth of Austria, daughter to the Emperor Albert II, a most virtuous woman, who died in 1505. He was born in 1458 on 3 October. From his childhood he was remarkably pious and devout. His tutor was John Dugloss, called Longinus, canon of Cracow, a man of extraordinary learning and piety. Casimir and the other princes were so affectionately attached to the holy man, who was their tutor, that they could not bear to be separated from him. But Casimir profited most by his pious maxims and example.

In 1471 the Palatines and other nobles of Hungary, dissatisfied with Mathias Corvin, their king, begged the King of Poland to allow them to place his son Casimir on the throne. The saint, not then quite fifteen years of age, was very unwilling to consent; but in compliance with his father's will he went.

At Vila, the capital of Lithuania on 4 March 1484, being twenty-three years old he died and was buried in the Church of St Stanislas. So many were the miracles wrought by his intercession that Swiecicki, a canon of Vilna, wrote a whole volume of them from memoirs in 1604.

His body was found quite entire and exhaling a sweet smell one hundred and twenty years after his death, notwithstanding the excessive moisture of the vault. It is honoured in a large rich chapel of marble. St Casimir is the patron of Poland.

The following feasts are also celebrated today:
St Adrian, Bishop of St Andrews: **St Lucius**, Pope and martyr, 253, whose body is now venerated in the church of St Cecily, in Rome.

There is a land of pure delight,
Where saints immortal reign;
Infinite day excludes the night,
And pleasures banish pain.
  ISAAC WATTS – Hymns and Spiritual Songs

March 5
The following feasts are celebrated today:
St Adrian and **St Eubulus**: **St John Joseph of the Cross**, Franciscan, 1654-1739: **St Kiaran** or **Kenerin**, styled by the Irish the first-born of their saints. He was somewhat older than St Patrick: **St Philip** of Jesus, Patron of Mexico City: **St Roger**, a disciple of St Francis of Assisi. His gift of prophecy and of miracles made him illustrious in life and after death.

March 6
SAINT CHRODEGANG
Bishop of Metz, Confessor – AD 766

This saint, nobly born in Brabant, then called Hasbain, was educated in the Abbey of St Tron, and for his great learning and virtue was made referendary, chancellor of France, and prime-minister by Charles Martel, Mayor of the French Palace, in 737. He was always meanly clad from his youth; he macerated his body by fasting and hair-cloths. His charity to all in distress seemed to know no bounds; he supported an incredible number of poor, and was the protector and father of orphans and widows. Soon after the death of Charles Martel, he was chosen Bishop of Metz, in 742. He died on 6 March 766 and was buried at Gorze.

The following feasts are also celebrated today:
St Baldrede, immediate successor of St Mungo as Bishop of Glasgow: **St Cadroe**, A Scotchman, who reformed the monastery of St Clement at Metz in 960: **St Colette**, Abbess, a carpenter's daughter whose parents gave her this name, a diminutive of Nicholas, having a great devotion for that saint: **St Fridolin**, Abbot: **St Kineburge, St Kineswide** and **St Tibba**, the first two daughters of Penda, king of Mercia, and the last named their kinswoman.

March 7
SAINT THOMAS OF AQUINO
Doctor of the Church and Confessor – AD 1274

The counts of Aquino, who have flourished in the kingdom of Naples these last ten centuries, derive their pedigree from a certain Lombard prince. Our saint's grandfather having married the sister of the Emperor Frederick I, was himself grand-nephew to that prince, and second cousin to the Emperor Henry VI, and in the third degree to Frederick II. His father, Landulph, was Count of Aquino, and Lord of Loretto and Belcastro: his mother Theodora was daughter to the Count of Theate. The saint was born towards the end of the year 1225.

The Count of Aquino took Thomas to the Abbey of Mount Cassino, when he was five years old, to be instructed by the monks; his tutors soon saw the rapidity of his progress, his great talents and his happy dispositions to virtue. He was ten years old when the abbot told his father that it was time to send him to a university. The count took him to see his mother at her seat at Loretto, the place which about the end of that century grew famous for devotion to Our Lady. Thomas was the admiration of the whole family. Amidst so much company, and so many servants, he appeared always as much recollected, and occupied on God, as he had been in the monastery; he spoke little and employed all his time in prayer, or serious and profitable exercises. His great delight seemed to be to distribute his parent's plentiful alms among the poor at the gate.

His father then sent him to Naples where the Emperor Frederick II had lately founded a university. Thomas soon missed the sanctuary of Mount Cassino. He learned with such wonderful progress that he repeated the lessons more clearly than the master had explained them. At that time the order of St Dominic abounded with men full of the Spirit of God. The saint received their habit in the convent of Naples in 1243 being then seventeen years old.

His humility made him conceal his progress insomuch that his school-fellows thought he learned nothing, and on account of his silence called him the Dumb Ox and the Great Sicilian Ox. But the brightness of his genius and his quick learning were at last discovered in spite of all his endeavours to conceal them: for his master, Albertus, having asked him several questions on the most knotty and obscure points was astonished at his answers and in admiration, said, "We call him the Dumb Ox, but he will give such a bellow in learning as will be heard all over the world."

In 1248, being twenty-two years of age, he was appointed by the general chapter to teach at Cologne, together with his old master Albertus, whose high reputation he equalled. He then also began to publish his first works. St Thomas, after teaching four years at Cologne, was sent in 1252 to Paris, and admitted doctor, on 23 October 1257.

In 1261 Urban IV called St Thomas to Rome, and appointed him to teach there. He taught and preached in all the towns where that pope resided, as in Rome, Viterbo, Orvieto, Fondi, and Perugia. He also taught at Bologna and Naples.

The fruits of his preaching were no less wonderful than those of his pen. Whilst he was preaching on Good Friday on the love of God for man, and our ingratitude to him, his whole congregation melted into tears to such a degree that he was obliged to stop several times that they might recover themselves.

Though seriously ill he set out from Naples till, his fever increasing, he was forced to stop at Fossa-Nuova, a famous abbey of the Cistercians, where formerly stood the city called Forum Appii.

The good monks treated him with veneration and esteem, as if he had been an angel from heaven. He died on 7 March 1274 a little after midnight.

The following feasts are also celebrated today:
St Paul, hermit, surnamed "The Simple", who served God in a poor and toilsome life: **Saints Perpetua** and **Felicitas**, martyred with their companions in Africa in 203.

March 8
SAINT JOHN OF GOD
Confessor, Founder of the Order of Charity – AD 1550

St John, surnamed of God, was born in Portugal in 1495. His parents were of the lowest rank in the country, but devout and charitable. John spent a considerable part of his youth in service to the Count of Oropeusa in Castile, in great innocence and virtue. He served in the wars between the French and Spaniards; as he did afterwards in Hungary against the Turks whilst the Emperor Charles V was king of Spain. The troop which he belonged to being disbanded, he went into Andalusia in 1536, where he entered the service of a rich lady near Seville as a shepherd. Being now about forty years of age, he began to have very serious thoughts of a change of life.

Making his way to Gibraltar he met a Portuguese gentleman whose estate had been confiscated by King John III. He was with his wife and children, and on his way to Ceuta in Barbary. John, out of charity and compassion, served him without any wages. At Ceuta, the gentleman falling sick was soon reduced to the small remains of his shattered fortune for the family's support. John went out to earn all he could for their subsistence.

The great preacher, John D'Avila, preached that year at Granada. John, having heard his sermon, was so affected with it that he filled the whole church with his cries and lamentations. Not content with this, he ran about the streets like a distracted person, tearing his hair and behaving in such a manner that he was followed everywhere by a rabble with sticks and stones, and came home all besmeared with dirt and blood. He then gave away all he had in the world, and having thus reduced himself to absolute poverty, he began again to counterfeit the madman, running about the streets as before, till some had the charity to take him to the venerable John D'Avila, covered with dirt and blood.

The holy man advised him to employ himself for the time to come in something more conducive to his own and the public good. He then thought of doing something for the relief of the poor. Soon after he hired a house to harbour sick persons whom he served. This was the foundation of the Order of Charity in 1540 which has since spread all over Christendom. John was occupied all day in serving his patients.

Worn out at last by ten years' hard service in his hospital, he fell sick. His illness increasing, the news of it spread. The Lady Anne Ossorio was no sooner informed of his condition but she came in her coach to the hospital to see him. The servant of God lay in his habit in his little cell, covered with a piece of an old coat instead of a blanket, and having under his head, not indeed a stone, as was his custom, but a basket, in which he used to beg alms in the city for his hospital. The poor and sick stood weeping round him. The lady, moved with compassion, had him carried into her coach, in which she conveyed him to her own house. The whole city was in tears. The saint died on 8 March 1550, being exactly fifty-five years old. He was buried by the archbishop accompanied by all the court, and city, with the utmost pomp.

The following feasts are also celebrated today:

St Apollonius, St Philemon and their companions, martyred in Egypt. The first was a holy hermit and the second a famous physician: **St Duthak**: **St Felix,** a holy bishop in Dunwich, Suffolk. Founder of many schools. Some have called him the founder of the University of Cambridge. Pressed into the army by the people of the East Angles to defend them against King Penda, he carried nothing but a staff in his hand: **St John of Avilila**, the spiritual father of many eminent saints in Spain in the sixteenth century: **St Julian**, Abbot of Toledo, who died in 690: **St Psalmod**, hermit: **St Rose of Viterbo**. she lived and died in her father's house: **St Senan**, an Irish abbot and bishop, who loved St David and died on the same day as his friend.

March 9
SAINT FRANCES
Widow, Foundress of the Collatines – AD 1440

St Frances was born at Rome in 1384. Her parents, Paul de Buxo and Jacobella Rofredeschi, were both of illustrious families. She had always an aversion to the amusements of children, and loved solitude and prayer. At eleven years of age she desired to enter a monastery, but in obedience to her parents was married to a rich young Roman nobleman, named Laurence Ponzani, in 1396. All her delight was in prayer, meditation, and visiting churches. She treated her domestics not as servants, but as brothers and sisters. She abstained from wine and fish, with a total abstinence from flesh, unless in her greatest sicknesses. Her ordinary diet was bread. She drank nothing but water, making use of a human skull for her cup and ate once a day. Her garments were of coarse serge, and she never wore linen, not even in sickness. Her example was such that many Roman ladies, having renounced a life of idleness, pomp, and softness, joined her in pious exercises and put themselves under the direction of the Benedictine monks of the congregation of Monte-Oliveto.

She founded a monastery of nuns, called Oblates. The house being too small for the numbers that fled to this sanctuary, she enlarged it in 1433.

Going out to see her son John Baptist, who was dangerously sick, she felt so ill herself that she could not return to her monastery at night. She died on 9 March. Her shrine in Rome is most magnificent and rich, and her festival is kept as a holy-day in the city, with great solemnity.

Her biographers attributed many mystical experiences and revelations to her. The most famous of all of these was her vision of her guardian angel, said to have guided her for 23 years invisible to everybody else. Patron saint of motorists.

The following feasts are also celebrated today:
St Catherine of Bologna, Abbess of the Poor Clares in that city, born 1413: **St Gregory** of Nyssa, a younger brother of St Basil the Great: **St Pacian**, Bishop of Barcelona, in the fourth century.

March 10
THE FORTY MARTYRS OF SEBASTE
AD 320

These holy martyrs suffered at Sebaste in Armenia, under the Emperor Licinius in 320. They were of different countries, but enrolled in the same troop. St Gregory of Nyssa says they were of the Thundering Legion, famous under Marcus Aurelius for the miraculous rain and victory obtained by their prayers. This was the twelfth legion, and then quartered in Armenia. Lysias was duke or general of the forces and Agricola the governor of the province.

The cold in Armenia is very sharp, especially in March, and towards the end of winter, when the wind is north. Under the walls of the town stood a pond, which was frozen so hard that it would bear walking upon with safety. The judge ordered the saints to be exposed quite naked on the ice and in order to tempt them to renounce their faith, a warm bath was prepared at a small distance from the frozen pond. The martyrs, on hearing their sentence, without waiting to be stripped, undressed themselves. The guards in the meantime tried to persuade them to take the warm bath. Of the whole number only one losing courage went off from the pond and no sooner entered the warm water but he died.

In the morning, the judge ordered both those that were dead with the cold and those that were still alive, to be cast into a fire. Their bodies were burned, and their ashes thrown into the river; but the Christians secretly carried off or purchased part of them. Some of these precious relics were kept in Cæsarea.

The following feasts are also celebrated today:
St Droctovæus, first abbot of St Germain-des-Prez, where he died in 590: **St Mackessoge of Kessoge**, Bishop in the provinces of Lerin and Boin, in Scotland.

March 11
SAINT EULOGIUS OF CORDOVA
Priest, martyr – AD 859

St Eulogius was of a senatorian family of Cordova, at that time the capital of the Moros of Saracens, in Spain. Our saint was educated among the clergy of the church of St Zoilus, a martyr, who suffered at Cordova, with nineteen others, under Diocletian. Here he distinguished himself by his virtue and learning; and being made priest, was placed at the head of the chief ecclesiastical school in Spain.

The Archbishop of Toledo dying in 858, St Eulogius was elected to succeed him. A woman named Leocritia, of a noble family among the Moors, had been instructed from her infancy in the Christian religion by one of her relations, and privately baptised. St Eulogius and his sister Anulona secretly concealed her for some time, but the matter was at length discovered and they were all brought before the judge. He received the stroke of death out of the city gates on 11 March 859. St Leocritia was beheaded four days after him and her body thrown into the river Boetis, or Guadalquiver, but taken out by the Christians. The church honours both of them on the days of their martyrdom.

The following feasts are also celebrated today:
St Ængus, Bishop, surnamed "Kele-De" or "Worshipper of God", of Ulster: **St Constantine**, martyr, said to have been a British king, who preached the Gospel among the Picts with St Columba; died in 576: **St Sophronius**, Patriarch of Jerusalem, called "The Sophist" because of his progress in wisdom.

March 12
SAINT GREGORY THE GREAT
Pope, Confessor – AD 604

St Gregory, from his illustrious actions and extraordinary virtues surnamed the Great, was born at Rome about the year 540. Gordianus, his father, enjoyed the dignity of a senator, and was very wealthy. His mother Sylvia, consecrated herself to God in a little oratory near St Paul's. Our saint was called Gregory, which in Greek implies a watchman. In his youth he applied himself with diligence to the studies of grammar, rhetoric and philosophy; and after these to the civil law and the canons of the church, in which he was perfectly skilled. He was only thirty-four years old when, in 574, he was made by the Emperor Justin the Younger, prætor, or governor and chief magistrate, of Rome.

After the death of his father, he built and endowed six monasteries in Sicily out of the estates which he had in that island, and founded a seventh in his own house in Rome, which was the famous monastery of St Andrew, on the hill Scaurus, now possessed by the Order of Camaldoli.

Not long after, the pope, Pelagius II, made him one of the seven deacons of the church at Rome. Pope Pelagius II, dying in the beginning of the great pestilence,

in January 590, the clergy, senate and Roman people unanimously agreed to choose St Gregory for their bishop. It is incredible how much he wrote and, during the thirteen years that he governed the church, what great things he achieved for the glory of God, the good of the church, the reformation of manners, the edification of the faithful, the relief of the poor, the comfort of the afflicted, the establishment of ecclesiastical discipline and the advancement of piety and religion.

But our surprise redoubles when we remember his continual bad state of health and frequent sicknesses, and his assiduity in prayer and holy contemplation. This holy pope laboured many years under great weakness and was afflicted with fevers which once confined him to his bed for two years. He died aged sixty-four. His holy remains rest in the Vatican church.

Bede claims that on seeing some fair-haired young slaves in the forum and being told their nationality he answered with the immortal words, "Not Angles, but angels" and immediately resolved to convert their country. Yet Gregory's attitude to his position is revealed in the title which he chose and which has been retained by Popes ever since: "Servant of the Servants of God".

Patron saint of masons, singers, musicians, students and teachers.

The following feasts are also celebrated today:
St Maximilian, son of a Christian solder in Numidia: **St Paul**, Bishop of Laon, a native of Cornwall, a cousin of St Samson.

March 13
The following feasts are celebrated today:
St Euphrasia: **St Gerald**, Bishop, an Englishman in the Abbey of Mayo: **St Kennocha**, virgin, joined a nunnery in Fife, died in 1007: **St Mocheomoc**, in Latin **Pulcherius**, Abbot: **St Nicephorus**, Patriarch of Constantinople: **St Theophans**, Abbot, who was left at three years old heir to a great estate, forced to marry by his friends, but he and his young wife suffered much and was banished after being imprisoned and scourged.

The Moving Finger writes; and having writ,
Moves on; nor all thy Piety nor Wit
Shall lure it back to cancel half a Line,
Nor all thy Tears wash out a Word of it.

OMAR KHAYYAM – RUBAIYAT

March 14
SAINT MAUD OR MATHILDIS
Queen of Germany – AD 869

This princess was daughter of Theodoric, a powerful Saxon count. Her parents placed her whilst still very young in the monastery of Erford of which her grandmother, Maud, was then abbess.

She remained in that house an accomplished model of all virtues till her parents married her to Henry, son of Otho, Duke of Saxony, in 913. Her husband, surnamed the Fowler, from his fondness of hawking, then much in vogue, became Duke of Saxony by the death of his father in 916, and in 919, upon the death of Conrad, was chosen King of Germany. He was a pious and victorious prince and very tender to his subjects. Whilst he, by his arms, checked the Hungarians and Danes and enlarged his dominions by adding to them Bavaria, Maud gained domestic victories over her spiritual enemies.

It was her delight to visit and comfort the sick, to serve and instruct the poor and give to prisoners their liberty. After twenty-three years of marriage, the king died in 936. Maud had three sons: Otho, afterwards emperor; Henry, duke of Bavaria; and St Bruno, Archbishop of Cologne. Otho was crowned King of Germany in 937 and Emperor of Rome in 962, after his victories over the Bohemians and Lombards. Maud, in the contest between her two elder sons for the crown, favoured Henry, who was the younger. These two sons conspired to strip her of her dowry on the unjust pretence that she had squandered away the revenues of the state on the poor. She then became more liberal in her alms than ever, and founded many churches, with five monasteries, of which the principals were that of Polden, in the duchy of Brunswick, in which she maintained three thousand monks, and that of Quedlinbourg, in the duchy of Saxony. She buried her husband in this place and when she had finished the buildings, made it her usual retreat. Lying on a sackcloth with ashes on her head, she died on 14 March 968. Her body remains at Quedlinbourg.

The following feasts are also celebrated today:
Saints Acepsimas, bishop, **Joseph**, priest and **Aithilahas**, deacon, martyr: **St Boniface**, Bishop of Ross, brought from Italy to north Britain, where he preached in the Provinces of Ross, Elgin and Murray.

To see a World in a Grain of Sand,
And Heaven in a Wild Flower,
Hold Infinity in the palm of your hand,
And Eternity in an hour.

WILLIAM BLAKE (1757-1827)

March 15
SAINT ABRAHAM
hermit
SAINT MARY
St Abraham's niece – c360

St Abraham was born in Cidana, in Mesopotamia, of wealthy and noble parents, who, after giving him a most virtuous education wanted him to marry. His wife, who was a pious and noble virgin, earnestly desired to live and die in the state of virginity, So as soon as the marriage ceremony and feast were over he secretly withdrew to a cell two miles from the city of Edessa, where his friends found him at prayer after a search of seventeen days. After their departure he walled up the door of his cell, leaving only a little window through which he received what was necessary for his subsistence.

He had no other earthly goods but a cloak and a piece of sackcloth which he wore and a little vessel out of which he both ate and drank. For fifty years he was never wearied with his austere penance and holy exercises and seemed to draw from them every day fresh vigour. Of his parents, he inherited their great estates, but commissioned a virtuous friend to distribute the revenues in alms-deeds.

The bishop ordained him priest and sent him to preach through Edessa. This he did for four years before going back to his cell.

His brother, dying soon after his return, left an only daughter, called Mary, whom the saint undertook to train in a religious life. St Abraham died five years before her. After he died everyone strove to procure for themselves some part of his clothes and many sick were cured by the touch of these relics.

The following feasts are also celebrated today:
St Clement Hofbauer, Confessor, 1751-1820, one of the German dramatist's "three men of tremendous energy", the other two being Napoleon and Goethe: **St Zachary**, Pope, who succeeded Gregory III in 741.

March 16
SAINT JULIAN OF CILICIA
Martyr

This saint was a Cilician, of a family in Anazarbus, and a minister of the gospel. In the persecution of Diocletian, he fell into the hands of a judge who, by his brutal behaviour, resembled more a wild beast than a man. For a whole year he forced him to be dragged through the towns of Cilicia. He suffered every kind of torture. The bloody executioners had torn his flesh, furrowed his sides, laid his bones bare and exposed his bowels to view.

Scourges, fire, and the sword were employed in various ways to torment him with the utmost cruelty. The judge was forced at length to condemn him to death.

The martyr was sewn up in a sack with scorpions, serpents and vipers and so thrown into the sea. The body was taken out of the sea and conveyed to Alexandria of Cilicia and afterwards to Antioch.

The following feast is also celebrated today:
St Finian, surnamed "The Leper", who suffered the disease.

March 17
SAINT PATRICK
Bishop, Confessor, Apostle of Ireland – AD 464

St Patrick was born in the fourth century in a village called Bonaven Taberniæ, which seems to be the town of Kilpatrick, on the mouth of the river Cluyd, in Scotland, between Dunbriton and Glasgow. He calls himself both a Briton and a Roman and says his father was of a good family, named Calphurnius. Some writers call his mother Conchessa, and say that she was niece to St Martin of Tours.

At fifteen years of age he committed a fault, which appears not to have been a great crime, yet was to him a subject of tears during the remainder of his life. He says that when he was sixteen he lived still ignorant of God. In his sixteenth year he was carried into captivity by certain barbarians. They took him into Ireland, where he kept cattle on the mountains and in the forests, in hunger and nakedness, amidst snows, rain and ice. St Patrick, after six months spent in slavery under the same master escaped to the sea-coast and found a ship, but could not obtain his passage probably for want of money. The saint was about to return when the sailors called him back and took him on board. After three days' sail they landed, probably in the north of Scotland; but wandered twenty-seven days, finding nothing to eat. At last they found a place that was cultivated and inhabited. Some years afterwards he was again led captive, but recovered his liberty.

The authors of his life say that after his second captivity he travelled into Gaul and Italy, but it seems he was ordained deacon, priest and bishop in his own country. He forsook his family, sold, as he says, his birthright and dignity, to serve strangers and consecrated his soul to God to carry His name to the end of the earth.

He founded a monastery at Armagh; another called Domnach-Padraig, or Patrick's Church; also a third, named Sabhal-Padraig, and filled the country with churches and schools. He died and was buried at Down, in Ulster. His body was found there in a church of his name in 1185. Later legends had Patrick expelling snakes from Ireland, and explaining the doctrine of the Trinity by reference to a shamrock, and these have become his emblems.

The following feasts are also celebrated today:

St Gertrude, Abbess of Nivelle, born 626: **St Joseph** of Arimathea, a faithful disciple of Jesus, who embalmed and buried His Sacred Body after His crucifixion. Joseph is said to have visited Glastonbury.

March 18
SAINT EDWARD
King and Martyr – AD 979

He was monarch of all England, and succeeded his father, King Edgar, in 975, being thirteen years old. His stepmother, Elfrida, had attempted to set him aside that the crown might fall on her own son, Ethelred, then seven years old.

The young king had reigned three years when one day, weary with hunting in a forest near Wareham in Dorset, he paid a visit to his stepmother at Corfesgeate, now Corfe Castle in the Isle of Purbeck. Here he was treacherously stabbed by a servant of the queen.

Though seriously wounded he managed to mount his horse, but fell off and died on 18 March 979. His body was hidden deep in a marsh, but was discovered by a pillar of light and honoured by many miraculous cures. It was taken up and buried in the church of our Lady at Wareham; but found entire three years after and translated to the monastery of Shaftesbury.

The following feasts are also celebrated today:

St Alexander: **St Anselm**, Bishop of Lucca, a native of and patron of Mantua, where he died 1086, a distinguished scholar: **St Cyril**, Archbishop of Jerusalem, died 386: **St Fridian**, an earlier bishop of Lucca, of Northern Irish extraction: **St Gabriel**, "one of the seven Spirits that stand before the throne of God". His feast is kept on this date in England, but he is also honoured on March 24.

March 19
SAINT JOSEPH
The foster-father of Christ – 1st century AD

Although descended from King David, Joseph was a poor man who earned his living as a carpenter: "an upright man" as he is called in the Gospels.

When he learned that his fiancé was pregnant Joseph was understandably concerned, knowing that the child was not his, but he resolved to spare Mary public humiliation and even death by breaking off the engagement quietly.

He was reassured of her virtue by an angel in a dream, and the marriage went ahead. He witnessed the visit of the Magi in Bethlehem.

According to Matthew, it was to Joseph that the angel appeared with first a warning to flee to Egypt and then the command to return when the massacre of the Innocents took place. Matthew's gospel largely presents the nativity story from the point of view of Joseph, while Luke concentrates more on the experiences of the Virgin Mary.

Suspicious of Herod's successor in Israel, Joseph took his wife and the Christ-child back to Nazareth where he presumably recommenced his trade. He and Mary took Jesus to be circumcised and presented to God in the temple at Jerusalem and he was present and concerned, as Mary was, when the 12-year-old Jesus was left behind in the temple at Jerusalem after Passover.

This is the last mention of him in the Gospels. It seems likely that he died before Jesus's ministry began; Mark records that Jesus was told that his mother and brothers wished to see him and at the crucifixion Jesus entrusted his mother to the care of John the Evangelist.

As a human father-figure and tradesman, he is widely loved and respected, with many churches and hospitals being dedicated to him.

In art he nearly always appears in groups of the Holy Family, usually as an old man carrying a flowering rod and sometimes surrounded by his carpentry tools. Patron saint of carpenters, fathers, workers, social justice and travellers, invoked in doubt and when house-hunting.

The following feast is also celebrated today:
St Alcmund, martyr, son and brother of Northumbrian kings.

March 20
SAINT CUTHBERT
Confessor, Bishop of Lindisfarne – AD 687

St Cuthbert was born not very far from Mailros. In his youth he kept his father's sheep. One night, whilst watching his flock, he saw the soul of St Aidan carried up to heaven by angels, that very instant the young man went to Mailros where he joined the monastery whilst Eata was abbot and St Boisil prior. Eata being called to govern the new monastery of Rippon, founded by King Alcfrid, he took with him St Cuthbert.

When St Wilfred was made Abbot of Rippon, St Cuthbert returned with Eata to Mailros; and St Boisil dying in 664, he was chosen provost or prior in his place. After St Cuthbert had lived many years at Mailros, St Eata, abbot, also of Lindisfarne, appointed him prior of that larger monastery.

The saint had governed the monastery of Lindisfarne for several years, when he retired into the little isle of Farne, nine miles from Lindisfarne to lead an austere life. The place was then uninhabited and he had neither water, tree, nor corn.

Cuthbert built himself a hut with a wall and trench around it and sowed first wheat, which failed, then barley, which though sowed out of season, yielded a plentiful crop. He built a house at the entry of the island from Lindisfarne to lodge the brethren that came to see him. Afterwards he confined himself within his own wall and trench, and gave spiritual advice only through a window, without ever stirring out of his cell.

He was consecrated bishop at York from the hands of St Theodorus, assisted by six other bishops. St Cuthbert, foreseeing his death approach, resigned his bishopric, which he had held two years, and retired to his solitude in Farne Island. Two months after he fell sick and he died in the island of Farne, but his body was buried in the monastery of Saint Peter in Lindisfarne, on the right side of the high altar.

In the Danish invasions, the monks carried it away from Lindisfarne, and, after several removals on the continent, settled by the river Were. There they built a church of stone and in 995 placed in it the body of St Cuthbert with great solemnity. The present cathedral was built in 1080. When the shrine of the saint was plundered and demolished by the order of King Henry VIII, the body of St Cuthbert was found still entire.

The following feast is also celebrated today:
St Wulfran, Archbishop of Sens, famed for many miracles. His mother was St Bathildes and in his youth he spent some years at the court of Clotaire III. He resigned as archbishop in 684 (or 685?) and entered Friseland as a poor priest.

March 21
SAINT BENEDICT
Abbot, Patriarch of the Western Monks - AD 543

Saint Benedict, or Bennet, was a native of Norcia, and born about the year 480. When he was fit for higher studies, he was sent by his parents to Rome. He left the city privately and made his way towards the desert mountains of Sublacum, nearly forty miles from Rome; a barren, hideous chain of rocks, with a river and lake in the valley. Near here he met a monk of a neighbouring monastery, called Romanus, who gave him the monastic habit, and showed him a deep narrow cave in the midst of these mountains, almost inaccessible to men.

In this cavern, now called the Holy Grotto, the young hermit chose to live and Romanus, who kept his secret, brought him from time to time, bread and slender provisions and let them down to the recluse with a line. Bennet seems to have been about fourteen or fifteen years old when he came to Sublacum.

In 497 a certain priest in that country whilst he was preparing a dinner for himself on Easter Sunday, heard a voice which said, "You are preparing for yourself a banquet, whilst my servant Bennet, at Sublacum, is distressed with hunger." The priest immediately set out to look for the hermit and with much difficulty found him. At length the priest invited the saint to eat, saying it was Easter Day. St Bennet answered him saying he knew not what day it was. Certain shepherds discovered the saint near his cave, but at first took him for a wild beast; for he was clad with the animal skins, and they imagined no human creature could live among those rocks. From that time he began to be known, and many visited him and brought him food. The monks of Vicovara, asked him to be their abbot. He built twelve monasteries, placing in each twelve monks with a superior.

St Benedict's reputation drew the most illustrious from Rome, and other remote parts to see him. To escape, Bennet left Sublacum and went to Mount Cassino. He governed also a monastery of nuns, situated near Mount Cassino and founded an abbey of men at Terracina, and sent St Placidus into Sicily to establish another in that island.

The death of this great saint seems to have happened soon after that of his sister, St Scholastica. he died on Saturday 21 March, probably in 543 having spent fourteen years at Mount Cassino.

The following feasts are also celebrated today:
St Enna or **Endeus**, Abbot, a naive of Ulster and lord of Ergall, a brother of St Fanchea: Three **Saints Serapion**, all belonging to Egypt – **St Serapion**, Abbot of Arsinoe in Upper Egypt, who governed ten thousand monks dispersed in the desert and monasteries around that place: **St Serapion**, Bishop of Thmuis, called "The Scholastic" because of his great learning: **St Serapion**, called "The Sindonite" from the single garment of coarse linen he always wore.

"If we sit down at set of sun,
And count the things that we have done,
And counting find
One self-denying act, one word
That eased the heart of him who heard,
One glance most kind,
That fell like sunshine where it went,
Then we may count the day well spent."

Anon

March 22
The following feasts are celebrated today:
St Basil of Ancyra: **St Catherine** of Sweden: **St Deogratias**, bishop of Carthage, who sold even the gold and silver vessels of the church to redeem the captives of Genseric when he plundered Rome: **St Lea**, widow, a rich Roman: **St Paul**, Bishop of Narbonne, sent from Rome to Gaul.

March 23
SAINT ALPHONSUS TURIBIUS
Confessor, Archbishop of Lima – AD 1606

St Toribio, or Turibius Alphonsus Mogrobejo, was second son to the lord of Mogrobejo, and born in the kingdom of Leon on 16 November 1538.

He began his higher studies at Valladolid, but completed them at Salamanca. He was introduced early to King Philip II, who made him president or chief judge at Granada. The pressing necessities of the infant church of Peru required a prelate who inherited, in a distinguished manner, the spirit of the apostles; and the archbishopric of Lima falling vacant, Turibius was unanimously judged the person best qualified to be bishop. He set out for Peru, and landed at Lima in 1581. On his arrival he visited every part of his vast diocese and would sometimes stay two or three days in places where he had neither bed nor any kind of food.

The flourishing state of the church of Peru, the great numbers of saints and eminent pastors with which it abounded and the establishment of hospitals for the poor, were the fruit of his zeal. By his last will he ordered whatever he possessed to be given to the poor.

In art he is shown in his bishop's robes kneeling at an altar, surrounded by angels. Patron saint of Peru and the bishops of Latin America.

The following feasts are also celebrated today:
St Edelward, priest: **St Joseph Oriol**, 1650-1702, known as "The Thaumaturge of Barcelona".

March 24
The following feasts are celebrated today:
St Gabriel ("Power of God"), Archangel: **St Irenæus**, Bishop of Sirmium: **St Simon**, an infant and **St William**, martyrs.

March 25
The following feast is celebrated today:
St Cammin, Abbot, who retired to Lough Derg, where he built a monastery.

For well you know that not life nor health nor riches nor honour nor dignity nor lordship is your own. Were they yours, you could possess them in your own way. But in such an hour a man wishes to be well, he is ill; or living, and he is dead; or rich, and he is poor; or a lord, and he is made a servant and vassal. All this is because these things are not his own, and he can only hold them in so far as may please Him who has lent them to him. (St Catherine of Siena)

March 26
SAINT LUDGER
Bishop of Munster, Apostle of Saxony – AD 809

St Ludger was born in Friseland about 743. His father, who was a nobleman in that country, and at the child's own request, committed him to the care of St Gregory. Gregory educated him in his monastery. Ludger then went to England and spent four years at school in York.

In 773 he returned home, and St Gregory dying in 776 his successor, Alberic, compelled our saint to become a priest and employed him for several years in preaching in Friseland. He travelled to Rome to consult Pope Adrian II, then retired for three years to Mount Cassino. He founded the monastery of Werden in the county of La Mark, twenty-nine miles from Cologne. In 802, Hildebald, Archbishop of Cologne, ordained him Bishop of Mimigardeford (or ford of the river Mimigard), a city which afterwards changed this name for that of Munster.

He was very learned in the holy scriptures.

St Ludger was favoured with the gift of miracles and prophecy. He foretold the invasions of the Normans from Denmark and Norway and what ravages they would make in the French empire. His last sickness though violent, did not stop him from continuing his work to the very last day of his life. His relics are still kept at Werden.

> **The following feasts are also celebrated today:**
> **St Bernadine** of Fossa, 1420-1503: **St Braulio**, Bishop of Saragossa: **The Good Thief**, known as **St Mismas**.

March 27
SAINT JOHN OF EGYPT
Hermit – AD 394

St John was born about the year 305, brought up to the trade of a carpenter. At twenty-five years of age he put himself under the guidance and direction of a hermit.

He seems to have lived about twelve years with this old man, till his death, and about four more in different neighbouring monasteries.

Being about forty years of age, he retired alone to the top of a rock near Lycopolis. His cell he walled up, leaving only a little window through which he received all necessities and spoke to those who visited him.

He never ate till after sunset and never anything that had been cooked by fire such as bread. In this manner he lived to his ninetieth year. He was illustrious for miracles, and a wonderful spirit of prophecy. Such was the fame of his predictions that they drew the admiration of the world upon him.

This saint restored sight to a senator's wife; being his custom never to allow any woman to speak to him this was a remarkable incident.

Another story has it, a general in the emperor's service, visiting the saint asked him to permit his wife to speak to him for she had come to Lycopolis through many dangers and difficulties. The holy man answered that during his strict enclosure of the last forty years he had not seen nor conversed with a woman.

The officer returned to his wife who was not satisfied. The husband went back to the old man and told him that she would die if he refused her request. The saint said to him, "Go to your wife, and tell her that she shall see me tonight." This answer he took to his wife and both were very keen to know in what manner the saint would perform his promise.

When she was asleep in the night the man of God appeared to her in her dream, and said: "Your great faith, woman, made me come to visit you." The woman, awaking, described to her husband the person she had seen in her dream, in such a manner as to leave no room to doubt that it was John that had appeared to her.

In 394, St Petronius, with six other monks, made a long journey to pay St John a visit. The blessed John entertained Petronius and his company for three days. Some days after their leaving him to return home, they were informed he had died.

The following feasts are also celebrated today:
St John Damascene, Doctor of the Church: **St Rupert (or Robert?)** Bishop of Saltzbourg, a Frenchman of royal blood.

March 28
The following feasts are celebrated today:
St Gontran, king, a grandson of Clovis: **St John Capistran**: **St Priscus, St Malchus** and **St Alexander**: **St Sixtus III**, Pope.

March 29
SAINTS JONAS, BARACHISIUS AND THEIR COMPANIONS
Martyrs – AD 327

Jonas and Barachisius, two brothers of the city Beth-Asa, hearing that several Christians lay under sentence of death at Hubaham, went to encourage and serve them. After their execution, Jonas and Barachisius were apprehended for having helped them to die. The president mildly entreated the two brothers to obey the king of kings, meaning the King of Persia, and to worship the sun, moon, fire, and water. Their answer was that it was more reasonable to obey the immortal King of heaven and earth. Barachisius was cast into a very narrow close dungeon. Jonas they detained with them to be beaten with clubs and with rods. The judge ordered him next to be set in a frozen pond, with a cord tied to his foot.

The following feasts are also celebrated today:
St Armogastes, **St Archinimus** and **St Saturas**, martyrs: **St Eustasius**, Abbot of Luxeu, succeeded his master St Columban: **St Gundleus**, greatly honoured in Wales, son of a king and father of two saints: **St Mark**, Bishop of Arethusa in Syria.

March 30
SAINT JOHN CLIMACUS
Abbot – AD 605

St John was born about 525, probably in Palestine. By his extraordinary progress in the arts and sciences he obtained the surname of the Scholastic. But at sixteen years of age he dedicated himself to God in a religious state. He retired to Mount Sinai, which, from the time of the disciples of St Anthony and St Hilarion, had been always peopled by holy men. John chose not to live in the great monastery on the summit but in a hermitage on the descent of the mountain, under the discipline of Martyrius.

In 560, Martyrius died. He then lived as a hermit in a plain called Thole, near the foot of Mount Sinai. His diet was very sparing. Prayer was his principal employment. As if this cell had not been sufficiently remote, St John frequently retired into a neighbouring cavern which he had made in the rock, where no one could come to disturb him.

St John was now seventy-five years old and had spent forty of them in his hermitage, when, in 600, he was unanimously chosen Abbot of Mount Sinai and superior-general of all the monks and hermits in that country.

He died in his hermitage being eighty years old.

The following feasts are also celebrated today:
St Regulus or **Rieul**, first Bishop of Senlis: **St Zosimus**, Bishop of Syracuse.

March 31
The following feasts are celebrated today:
St Acasius or **Achates**, Bishop of Antioch, in Asia Minor, surnamed "good angel": **St Benjamin**: **St Guy**, was forty years Abbot of Pomposa.

April 1
SAINT HUGH
Confessor, Bishop of Grenoble – AD 1132

Saint Hugh was born at Château-neuf, in the territory of Valence, in Dauphiné in 1053. His father, Odilo, served his country in an honourable post in the army. He went through his studies with great applause, and his progress in piety always kept pace with his advancement in learning.

Having chosen to serve God in an ecclesiastical state, he accepted a position in the cathedral of Valence. He was tall and very comely, but exceedingly shy. The bishop of Die was so charmed at first sight with the saint when he came to Valence that he took the good man into his household. In 1080 the Legate Hugh held a synod at Avignon, in which it was decided St Hugh was the person best qualified to reform and restore the Grenoble church. The legate took St Hugh, the newly appointed bishop, with him to Rome.

St Hugh, after his ordination, hastened to Grenoble. He found the people in general immersed in ignorance of religion and spiritual disorders. Many lands belonging to the church were taken over by laymen; and the revenues of the bishopric were non-existent, so that the saint, upon his arrival, found nothing either to enable him to assist the poor, or to supply his own necessities. He set himself in earnest to reform the abuses.

Through his endeavours his diocese in a short time was exceedingly changed. After two years he privately resigned his bishopric and entered the austere abbey of Chaise-Dieu, or Casa-Dei, in Auvergne. There he lived a year till Pope Gregory VII commanded him to resume his pastoral charge. He later asked Pope Innocent II for leave to resign his bishopric, that he might die in solitude; but was never able to obtain his request.

Some time before his death he lost his memory for everything but his prayers. He died saying, "This life is given us for weeping and penance."

The following feasts are also celebrated today:
St Gilbert, Bishop of Caithness: **St Melito**, Bishop of Sardes, in Lydia.

April 2
SAINT FRANCIS OF PAULA
Confessor, Founder of The Order of Minims – AD 1508

This saint was born about the year 1416, at Paula, a small city near the Tyrrhenian Sea, in Calabria, midway from Naples to Reggio. His parents were very poor but industrious, and happy in their condition. Francis, whilst yet a child, made prayer his delight. When he was thirteen years of age, his father, whose name was James Mertotille, placed him in the convent of

Franciscan friars at St Mark's. Having spent one year here, he went with his parents on a pilgrimage to Rome.

When he returned to Paula he chose to live in the corner of a rock upon the sea-coast, where he made himself a cave. He was fifteen years old when he shut himself up in this hermitage, in 1432. He had no other bed than the rock itself, nor other food than the herbs which he gathered in the neighbouring wood, or what was sometimes brought him by his friends. Before he was twenty years old, two other persons joined him, imitating his holy exercises. The neighbours built them three cells and a chapel. This is reputed the first foundation of his religious Order, in 1436. Nearly seventeen years after, their number much increased, a large church and monastery was built for them in the same place towards the year 1454.

The Archbishop of Cosenza approved the rule and Order of this holy man in 1471. Pope Sixtus IV confirmed it and established Francis superior-general. About the year 1476, the saint founded another convent at Paterno, on the gulf of Tarentum; and a third at Spezza, in the diocese of Cosenza. In the year 1479, being invited into Sicily, he built several monasteries. Returning to Calabria, in 1480, he built another at Corigliano, in the diocese of Rossano.

King Charles VIII honoured the saint even more than his father Lewis had done. He built for him a beautiful convent in the park of Plessis, in a place called Montils; and another at Amboise, the very spot where he met him when he was dauphin; and on Mount Pincio, a stately monastery for his Order under the name of the Blessed Trinity, in which none but Frenchmen can be admitted.

St Francis spent the three last months of his life within his cell, to prepare himself for a happy death. He fell sick of a fever on Palm Sunday, and died on the 2 April 1508 being ninety-one years old. His body remained uncorrupted in the church of Plessis-les-Tours till the year 1562, when the Huguenots broke open the shrine and found it entire, fifty-five years after his death. They dragged it about the streets, and burned it in a fire which they had made with the wood of a great crucifix.

Many of the miracles attributed to Francis were connected with the sea, most famously the story that he once used his cloak as a boat. Needing to cross the Straits of Messina, Francis was unable to find a boat. Nothing daunted, he laid his cloak on the sea, tied one end to his staff to serve as a sail, and took his companions safely to Sicily. He was therefore named patron of seafarers in 1943.

In art he is shown with the word "charitas", sometimes levitated above the crowd or holding a skull and discipline, or scourge. He is also depicted sailing on his cloak. Patron saint of sailors.

> *Fear less, hope more; Eat less, chew more;*
> *Whine less, breathe more; Talk less, say more:*
> *Hate less, love more; and all good things will be yours.*
> *(Swedish proverb)*

The following feasts are also celebrated today:

St Apian, born in Lycea of illustrious parents; he studied philosophy and the Roman laws; only nineteen years of age be became a Christian, was tortured and finally martyred: **St Bronacha**, titular saint of the parish of Kill-Broncha, Dromore: **St Ebba and her Companions**, nuns of the monastery of Coldingham, Berwick: **St Nicetius**, Archbishop of Lyons: **St Theodosia**, virgin and martyr.

April 3
SAINT AGAPE, SAINT CHIONIA AND ST IRENE
Sisters and their companions, Martyrs – AD 304

These three sisters lived at Thessalonica, when they suffered martyrdom. In the year 303, the Emperor Diocletian published an edict forbidding, under pain of death, any person to keep the holy scriptures. These saints concealed many volumes of those sacred books, but were not discovered or apprehended till the year following when they were condemned to be burnt alive with their companions.

The following feasts are also celebrated today:

St Nicetas, Abbot, brought up under austere monastic rules by his father, who had become a monk after the death of his wife; he lived a life of mortification and was famed for many miracles: **St Richard**, Bishop of Chichester and Confessor, Chancellor of the University of Oxford: **St Ulpian** of Tyre.

April 4
SAINT ISIDORE
Bishop of Seville – AD 636

Isidore's noble Cartagenian family was blessed with an extraordinary number of saints; his siblings Leander, Fulgetius and Florentian are all venerated. It was under his elder brother Leander that the young Isidore mainly acquired his education, developing a monastic and learned turn of thought that would serve him well in later, clerical life.

In c600 Isidore succeeded Leander as Bishop of Seville, and he ruled the see for the next 36 years. Among his priorities was the completion of his brother's work of converting the Arian Visigoths, and also the more effective organization of the Spanish church by means of synods and councils. Isidore also encouraged the development of monasticism in Spain, and was renowned for his austerity and his charity to the poor. He died at Seville on 4 April.

His works were considered essential reading for any medieval cleric or monk, and Dante mentions both him and Bede in his *Paradiso*. Surprisingly, Isidore was not officially canonized until 1598, and he was declared a Doctor of the Church by Pope Benedict XIV in 1722.

In art he is generally shown as an aged bishop with a prince at his feet, often holding a pen and a book, or with his sainted brothers and sister. Patron saint of farmers.

The following feast is also celebrated today:
St Plato, Abbot of the monastery on top of Mount Olympus.

April 5
SAINT VINCENT FERRER
Confessor – AD 1419

St Vincent Ferrer was born at Valentia, in Spain, on 23 January 1357. His parents were persons distinguished for their virtue and alms-deeds. They made it their rule to distribute in alms whatever they could save out of the necessary expenses of their family at the end of every year. Two of their sons became eminent in the church: Boniface, who died general of the Carthusians, and St Vincent, who brought with him into the world a happy disposition for learning and piety.

He began his course of philosophy at twelve years of age, and his theology at the end of his fourteenth year. Vincent said it was his earnest desire to enter the Order of St Dominic. His parents took him to a convent of that Order in Valentia in 1374 in the beginning of his eighteenth year. Soon after he read lectures of philosophy, and at the end of his course published a treatise on Dialectic Suppositions, being not quite twenty-four years old. He was then sent to Barcelona, where he continued his scholastic exercises. From there he was sent to Lerida, the most famous university of Catalonia. St Vincent had lived thus six years at Valentia, when Cardinal Peter de Luna, legate of Clement VII in Spain asked the saint to accompany him into France.

In the beginning of the year 1394 the legate returned to Avignon, and St Vincent, refusing his invitations to the court of Clement VII, went to Valentia. Clement VII dying at Avignon in 1394, during the great schism, Peter de Luna was chosen pope by the French and Spaniards and took the name of Benedict XIII. He commanded Vincent to go to Avignon and made him master of the Sacred Palace.

Before the end of the year 1398, St Vincent being forty-two years old, set out from Avignon towards Valentia. He preached in every town with wonderful efficacy; and the people having heard him in one place followed him in crowds to others. He converted a prodigious number, and visited every province of Spain except Galicia.

He returned to France, and stayed in Languedoc, Provence, and Dauphiné. He went preaching on the coasts of Genoa, in Lombardy, Piedmont, and Savoy; as he did in part of Germany, about the Upper Rhine, and through Flanders. Such was the fame of his missions that Henry IV, King of England, sent one of his own ships to fetch him from the coast of France. The saint then preached in the chief towns of England, Scotland, and Ireland. Returning into France, he did the same from Gascony to Picardy.

His gift of miracles, and the sanctity of his penitential life, gave to his words the greatest weight. He laboured so for twenty years, till 1417, in Spain, Majorca, Italy and France. During this time, preaching in Catalonia, among other miracles he restored the use of his limbs to John Soler, a crippled boy, judged by the physicians incurable, who afterwards became a very eminent man and Bishop of Barcelona.

In the year 1400 he was at Aix, in Provence; in 1401 in Piedmont and neighbouring parts of Italy. Returning into Savoy and Dauphiné, he found a valley called Vaupute, or Valley of Corruption, in which the inhabitants were abandoned to cruelty. He converted them and changed the name of the valley into Valpure, or Valley of Purity, which name it has retained.

Normandy and Brittany were where St Vincent laboured the two last years of his life. He was then sixty years old, and so worn out and weak that he was scarce able to walk a step without help; yet no sooner was he in the pulpit but he spoke with as much strength as in his youth.

At last his companions persuaded him to return to his own country. Accordingly he set out with that view, riding on an ass, as was his manner of travelling on long journeys. But they found themselves again near the city of Vannes, where the saint's illness increased. On the tenth day he died. Joan of France, daughter of King Charles VI, Duchess of Brittany, washed his corpse with her own hands. The duke and bishop appointed the cathedral for the place of his burial. His relics were taken up in 1456 where they are still exposed to veneration.

The following feasts are also celebrated today:
St Becan, Abbot in Ireland; known as one of the twelve apostles of Ireland: **St Gerald**, Abbot of Suauve or Sylva-major, near Bordeaux: **St Tigernach**, Bishop and Confessor in Ireland; his mother was daughter to an Irish king and St Bridget was his godmother. Carried to Britain by pirates he returned to Ireland, where he founded Clones Abbey. He became blind in his old age and spent his time in a cell in continual prayer.

April 6
The following feasts are celebrated today:
St Celestine, Pope, chosen to succeed Pope Boniface: **St Celsus**, in Irish **Ceallach**, Bishop in Ireland: **St Prudentius**, Bishop of Troyes, a Spaniard by birth: **St Sixtus**, Pope: **St William**, Abbot of Eskille.

April 7
The following feasts are celebrated today:
St Aibert, recluse, who had applied himself to prayer from his infancy:
St Aphraates: **St Finian** of Ireland a disciple of St Brendan:
St Hegesippas, a Jew by birth.

April 8
The following feasts are celebrated today:
St Ædecius, brother to St Apian: **St Perpetuus**, the eighth Bishop of
Tours: **St Walter**, Abbot of St Martin's near Pontoise.

April 9
SAINT MARY OF EGYPT

In the reign of Theodosius the Younger there lived in Palestine a holy monk
and priest named Zosimus, famed for the reputation of his sanctity. He had
served God for fifty three years, and was tempted to think that he had
attained a state of perfection, and could be taught nothing more in regard
to a monastic life. The members of his community had no communication
with the rest of mankind. The whole employment of their lives was manual
labour, accompanied with prayer, the singing of psalms, and their chief
subsistence was on bread and water.

It was their yearly custom on the first Sunday in Lent, to cross the river
and disperse themselves over the vast deserts which lie towards Arabia,
to stay in solitude until Palm Sunday. About the year 430, Zosimus
passed over the Jordan with the rest at the usual time. He stopped at
noon to rest and saw the figure of somebody that appeared naked,
extremely sunburnt and with short white hair, who walked very quick,
and fled from him. Zosimus thinking it to be some holy hermit, ran to
overtake him. Drawing nearer, he cried out to the person to stop, who
answered, "Abbot Zosimus, I am a woman; throw me your mantle to
cover me, that you may come near me." He was surprised to hear her
call him by his name.

Having covered herself with his garment, she approached him and told him
how long and in what manner she had lived in that desert, she said, "My
country is Egypt. When my father and mother were still living, at twelve
years of age, I went without their consent to Alexandria."

She then described how she lived as a prostitute for seventeen years. She
added: "At twenty-nine I went to Jerusalem to celebrate the feast of the
Exaltation of the glorious Cross of our Saviour. On the day of the festival, I

---

mixed with the crowd to get into the church where the holy cross was shown, but found myself withheld from entering by some secret but invisible force. This happened to me three or four times. I sat in a corner and began to consider my criminal life and I melted into tears. I saw above me the picture of the Mother of God. Fixing my eyes upon it, I addressed that holy virgin. I asked her that I might be allowed to enter the church doors promising from that moment to consecrate myself to God by a life of penance."

"After this prayer, I attempted again to enter the church, I went up with ease into the very middle of it. I cast myself on the ground and after having kissed the pavement, I arose and went to the picture of the Mother of God. I addressed my prayers to her. After my prayer I seemed to hear this voice: 'If thou goest beyond the Jordan, thou shalt there find rest and comfort.' After these words I went out in haste, bought three loaves, and asking the baker which was the gate of the city which led to the Jordan, I walked all of the day, and at night arrived at the church of St John Baptist on the banks of the river. Having ate half of one of the loaves, I slept on the ground. Next morning I passed the Jordan and have since carefully shunned any human creature."

She told Zosimus she had lived in the desert for forty-seven years and subsisted upon the loaves she took with her and no other food but what the wild and uncultivated land afforded her. Her clothes being worn out, she suffered severely from the heat and the cold, with which she was often so afflicted that she was not able to stand.

Zosimus taking notice that in her speech she from time to time made use of scripture phrases, asked her if she had ever applied herself to the study of the sacred books. Her answer was that she could not even read, neither had she conversed nor seen any human creature since she came into the desert till that day, that could teach her to read the holy scripture or read it to her: "but it is God," said she, "that teacheth man knowledge."

She concluded by asking him next Maunday Thursday to wait for her on the banks of the river on the side which is inhabited. The year following, on Maunday Thursday, taking a small chalice and also a little basket of figs, dates and lentils, he went to the banks of the Jordan. At night she appeared on the other side, walking upon the surface of the water as if it had been dry land till she reached the opposite shore.

She begged Zosimus to pardon the trouble she had given him and asked him to return the following Lent to the place where he first saw her. He begged her to accept the sustenance he had brought her. But she took only a few of the lentils and left him and then went over the river as she came.

Zosimus returned home until the time fixed for their next meeting. He set out with the intention of a further conversation with her and to learn her name. But on his arrival at the place where he had first seen her he found her corpse stretched out on the ground with an inscription declaring her name Mary and the time of her death. Zosimus being miraculously assisted by a lion, dug a grave and buried her. And returned to his monastery where he recounted all that he had seen.

The following feasts are also celebrated today:
St Dotto, founded and governed a great monastery in the sixth century on one of the isles of Orkney. He lived to be one hundred years old: **St Gaucher**, Abbot in Limousin: **St Waltrude**, widow.

April 10
SAINT BADEMUS
Abbot, Martyr – AD 376

Bademus was a rich and noble citizen of Bethlapeta in Persia, who founded a monastery near that city. In this amiable retreat he enjoyed a calmness and happiness which the great men of the world would view with envy. He was apprehended by King Sapor and lay four months in a dungeon loaded with chains.

At the same time a Christian lord of the Persian court named Nersan, prince of Aria, was cast into prison because he refused to adore the sun. The king ordered Bademus to be introduced to Nersan. Nersan, after a disagreement, with a sword advanced to plunge it into the breast of the abbot, but he stopped short and remained some time without being able to lift up his arm.

The king determined to rid himself of both Bademus and Nersan ordered a servant to slay them both. Nersan died immediately but so great was the number of Bademus's wounds that those who watched stood in admiration at his invincible patience. The body of St Bademus was cast out of the city but was secretly carried away by the Christians.

April 11
SAINT LEO THE GREAT
Pope – AD 461

St Leo, surnamed the Great, was descended of a noble Tuscan family, but born at Rome. The maturity of his judgment helped in the rapid progress which he made in his studies. Being made archdeacon of the church, he was invited to Rome and was consecrated bishop on Sunday 29 September in 440.

This great saint for his humility, mildness and charity, was reverenced and beloved by emperors, princes and all ranks of people. He was pope for twenty-one years, dying on the 10 November 461. His body was interred in the church of St Peter. His relics were translated with great solemnity and devotion, enclosed in a case of lead and placed in the altar in the Vatican church in the year 1715.

The writings of this great pastor are the monuments of his extra-ordinary genius and piety. His thoughts were true, bright and strong.

The following feasts are also celebrated today:
St Aid, Abbot in Ireland and titular saint of a parish church, an old abbey and a number of chapels there: **St Antipas**, martyr. His tomb at Pergamus is famous for many miracles: **St Guthlake**, hermit, Paton of the Abbey of Croyland. A nobleman who, in his youth, served in the armies of Ethelred, King of Mercia. He sought admission into a monastery in his twenty-fourth year: **St Maccai**, Abbot, a disciple of St Patrick; he flourished in the Isle of Bute.

April 12
The following feasts are celebrated today:
St Julius, chosen Pope, 337: **St Sabas the Goth**, martyr, 372: **St Victor of Braga**: **St Zeno**, Bishop of Verona.

April 13
SAINT HERMENEGILD
Martyr – AD 586

Levigild, or Leovigild, the Goth, King of Spain, had two sons by his first wife Theodosia, namely, Hermenegild and Recared. Hermenegild, the eldest married Ingondes, daughter of Sigebert, King of Austrasia, in France. Levigild, to secure his posterity allotted to each a portion of his dominions Seville fell to the eldest. Levigild, who was already exasperated with his son and of his open profession of the faith, in a rage divested him of the title of king, and resolved to deprive him of his possessions, his princess, and even his life, unless he returned to his former beliefs.

Levigild held his son besieged in Seville for more than a year, till Hermenegild, no longer able to defend himself in his capital, fled secretly to join the Roman camp.

He shut himself up in this fortress with three hundred chosen men; but the place was taken and burnt by Levigild. The prince sought a refuge in a church. The king not wanting to violate that sacred place, permitted his second son, Recared, to go to him and to promise him pardon. Hermenegild believed his father was sincere, and going out, threw himself at his feet. Levigild embraced him and renewed his promises, till he had got him into his own camp. He then ordered him to be stripped of his royal robes, loaded with chains, and conducted prisoner to the tower of Seville in 586.

There he again employed all manner of threats and promises to draw him back to his former ways and beliefs. The martyr repeated, "I value the crown as nothing; I am ready to lose sceptre and life rather than abandon the divine truth." He clothed himself in sackcloth and added other voluntary austerities to the hardships of his confinement.

The furious father sent soldiers to kill him. They entered the prison and found the saint fearless and ready to receive the stroke of death. They instantly cut his head with an axe, leaving his brains scattered on the floor. The merits of this martyr gained the conversion of his brother, King Recared, and that of the whole kingdom of the Visigoths in Spain. His body remains at Seville.

The following feasts are also celebrated today:

St Caradoc, a Welsh nobleman. He became priest and then a hermit. Many miracles attested his sanctity. He died in 1124: **St Guinoch**, for many years the support of Church and State among the Scots in the ninth century, in the reign of Kenneth II.

April 14
SAINT TIBURTIUS, VALERIAN AND MAXIMUS
Martyrs – AD 229

Valerian was espoused to St Cecily and converted by her to the faith; and with her he became the instrument of the conversion of his brother Tiburtius. Maximus, the officer appointed to attend their execution, was brought to the faith by the example of their piety and received with them martyrdom in the year 229. It is likely this happened in Rome, though some say they suffered in Sicily.

The following feasts are also celebrated today:

St Benezet, Patron of Avignon, called Little Bennet, a shepherd boy inspired by God to build a bridge across the Rhone at Avignon. He died when this was accomplished, the work having taken seven years: **St Carpus**, Bishop of Thyatira in Asia Minor, **Papylas**, his deacon and **Agathodorus**, his servant, martyrs: **Saints Anthony**, **John** and **Euatachius**, martyrs. They were three noblemen of Lithuania, Anthony and John being brothers: **St Justin,** martyr, a converted philosopher and notable writer in the second century.

Present and Future
The tissues of the life to be
We weave with colours all our own,
And on the fields of destiny
We reap what we have sown.
Still shall the soul around it call
The shadows gathered here,
And painted on the eternal wall,
The past shall reappear.

(1 Tim. 4. 8)

April 15
SAINT PETER GONZALES
Confessor, commonly called St Telm or Elm, Patron of Mariners – AD 1246

Historians place the birth of St Peter Gonzales, in the year 1190 at Astorga, in the kingdom of Leon, in Spain, where he was descended of an illustrious family. His wonderful progress in his studies showed him endowed with an extraordinary quickness. His uncle, the Bishop of Astorga, made him dean of his chapter. He entered the Order of St Dominic. The world pursued him into his retreat, men left no stone unturned to find him.

King Ferdinand III though always taken up in his wars with the Saracens, wanted to see him so much that he would have him always near both in the court and in the field. The holy man reformed the corrupt manners both of the troops and court. His example gave the greatest weight to his words; for he lived in the court as he would have done in a cloister.

The saint accompanied Ferdinand, King of Leon and Castille, in all his expeditions against the Moors, particularly in the siege and taking of Cordova in 1236. The great mosque of Cordova, the most famous of all Spain, became the cathedral church. Neither mountains nor places of the most difficult access in Asturia and other parts, nor the ignorance and brutality of the people, could daunt his courage.

At Bayona, in Galicia, he preached in a great plain, and a violent storm arose with wind, thunder and lightning, his whole audience became very uneasy. The holy preacher told them to pray. All places round about them were deluged but not a drop fell upon the plain.

He foretold his death on Palm Sunday and wanting to die in the arms of his brethren at Compostella, set out from Tuy but growing worse on the road returned to the former place on foot. Luke, the famous Bishop of Tuy, his great friend, attended to him and buried him in his cathedral; and in his last will gave directions for his own body to be laid near the remains of Peter's. They are now exposed to public veneration in the same church in a magnificent silver shrine. St Peter Gonzales is the patron of mariners.

The following feasts are also celebrated today:
Saints Basilissa and **Anastasia**, two noble women, disciples of Saints Peter and Paul at Rome, beheaded at the order of Nero: **St Munde**, Abbot: **St Paternus**, Bishop of Avranches: **St Ruadhan**, Abbot in Ireland, called one of the twelve apostles of Ireland. He died in 584.

Give the Devil his due, but be very careful there isn't much due to him.

April 16
EIGHTEEN MARTYRS OF SARAGOSSA, AND ST ENCRATIS, OR ENGRATIA
Virgin, Martyr – AD 304

St Optatus, and seventeen other holy men were martyred on the same day at Saragossa in the persecution of Diocletian in 304. Two others, Caius and Crementius died of their torments after a second conflict.

St Encratis, or Engratia was a native of Portugal. Her father had promised her in marriage to a man in Tousillon, but she fled privately to Saragossa, where the persecution was hottest, under the eyes of Dacian. She reproached him for his barbarities, upon which he ordered her to be long tormented in the most inhuman manner: her sides were torn with iron hooks and one of her breasts was cut off so that the inner parts of her chest were exposed to view and part of her liver pulled out. In this condition she was sent back to prison, and died by her wounds in 304.

The relics of all these martyrs were found in Saragossa in 1389.

The following feasts are also celebrated today:
St Benedict Joseph Labre, Confessor: **St Druon**, or **Drugo**, patron of shepherds: **St Fructuosis**, Archbishop of Braga: **St Joachim of Siena**, of the Order of Servites: **St Mans**, or **Magnus**, who gave his life to save the lives of those committed to his care: **St Turibius**, Bishop of Astorga.

April 17
SAINT STEPHEN
Confessor, Abbot of Citeaux – AD 1134

St Stephen Harding was an Englishman and heir to a rich estate. He had his education in the monastery of Sherborne in Dorset. Out of a desire of learning he, with one devout companion, travelled into Scotland and afterwards to Paris and to Rome. Stephen, heard at Lyons of the Benedictine monastery of Molesme, lately founded by St Robert in 1075.

Such was the extreme poverty of this place that the monks for want of bread, were often obliged to live on the wild herbs. The neighbourhood at length supplied their wants in profusion, but with plenty and riches, a spirit of relaxation crept in and drew many aside from their duty. St Robert, Alberic his prior, and Stephen left the house; but were called back again. Stephen was then made superior.

Seeing no hopes of sufficient reformation, St Robert, St Stephen and other monks went to Citeaux, a marshy wilderness not far from Dijon. The viscount of Beaune gave them the ground, the Duke of Burgundy, built them a little church. The monks cut down trees and built themselves a monastery of wood, and this was the foundation of the Cistercian Order.

In the two years 1111 and 1112, sickness swept away the greater part of this small community. St Stephen then founded other monasteries. He lived to found thirteen abbeys. In order to maintain strict discipline he made frequent visits to every monastery and abbey. Twenty abbots of his Order assembled at Citeaux to attend at his death.

The following feasts are also celebrated today:
St Anicetus, Pope: **St Simeon**, Bishop of Ctesiphon and his companions, martyrs for the Church in Persia.

April 18
SAINT APOLLONIUS THE APOLOGIST
Martyr – AD 186

Apollonius was a Roman senator. He was a person very well versed both in philosophy and the holy scripture. He was publicly accused of Christianity by one of his own slaves. Perennis, prefect of the Prætorium sent an order to St Apollonius to renounce his religion. The saint rejected the order and Perennis then referred him to the Roman senate who condemned him to be beheaded.

The following feasts are also celebrated today:
St Galdin, Archbishop of Milan: **St Laserian**, Bishop of Leighlin, in Ireland (by some called **Molaisre**).

April 19
SAINT LEO IX
Pope, Confessor – AD 1054

This great pope received in baptism the name of Bruno. He was born in Alsace in 1002. He was of the family of Dapsborough, had his education under Berthold, the virtuous and learned Bishop of Toul; and after his first studies was made a canon in that cathedral. His time was principally divided between prayer, pious reading and his studies; and the hours of recreation he employed in visiting the hospitals and instructing the poor.

When he was deacon he was called to the court of the Emperor Conrad. The young clergyman displayed an extraordinary talent for business. In 1026 he was chosen Bishop of Toul. Bruno began with the reformation of the clergy and monks. By his care the monastic discipline and spirit were revived in the great monasteries of Senones, Jointures, Estival, Bodonminster, Middle-Moutier, and St Mansu or Mansuet. He reformed the manner of performing church music in which he took great delight.

His life was an uninterrupted severe course of penance. After the death of Pope Damasus II in 1048, Bruno who had been Bishop of Toul twenty-two years was considered the most worthy person to be pope. After this declaration he returned to Toul, and soon after Easter set out for Rome in the clothes of a pilgrim; and alighting from his horse, some miles before he arrived at the city, walked to it and entered it barefoot. He was received with universal acclamations. He became pope on 12 February 1049 under the name of Leo IX, being about forty-seven years old. He held it only five years, but they were filled with good works. He died in April 1054.

The following feasts are also celebrated today:
St Elphege, Archbishop of Canterbury: **St Ursmar**, Bishop.

April 20
SAINT AGNES OF MONTE PULCIANO
Virgin and Abbess – AD 1317

Agnes was a native of Monte Pulciano in Tuscany. At nine years of age she was placed by her parents in a convent of Sackins, so called from their clothes being made of sackcloth. At fifteen years of age she went to Proceno, in the county of Orvieto and was appointed abbess by Pope Nicholas IV. She slept on the ground, with a stone under her head instead of a pillow; and for fifteen years she fasted on bread and water. The gifts of miracles and prophecy made her famous. She died at Monte Pulciano. Her body was removed to the Dominicans' church of Orvieto in 1435 where it remains.

The following feasts are also celebrated today:
St James of Scavonia: **St Seref**, the first bishop and apostle of the isles of Orkney in the fifth century.

Life

Life is too brief
Between the budding and the falling leaf,
Between the seedtime and the golden sheaf,
For hate and spite.
We have no time for malice and for greed;
Therefore, with love make beautiful the deed;
Fast speeds the night.

Margaret E. Sangster

April 21
SAINT ANSELM
Confessor, Archbishop of Canterbury – AD 1109

St Anselm was born of noble parents at Aoust, in Piedmont, about the year 1033. At the age of fifteen, wanting to serve God in the monastic state, he asked an abbot to admit him into his house, but was refused. He lost this inclination and after his mother's death he left his own country and for three years lived in Burgundy.

On his father's death Anselm was determined to enter the monastic state at Bec, and became a member of that house at the age of twenty-seven in 1060 under the Abbot Herluin. Three years after Anselm was made Prior of Bec.

Whilst he was prior at Bec, he wrote his Monologium explaining the metaphysical proofs of the existence and nature of God. Anselm's reputation drew to Bec great numbers from all the neighbouring kingdoms. Herluin dying in 1078, he was chosen Abbot of Bec. The abbey of Bec at that time had some land in England.

In the year 1092, Hugh, Earl of Chester asked Anselm to come to England, to assist him and to give advice about the foundation of a monastery which had been undertaken at St Wereburge's church at Chester. He moreover nominated Anselm to be Bishop of Canterbury.

Anselm had not been long at Canterbury when finding William Rufus the king always seeking occasions to oppress his church unless he fed him with its treasures, Anselm wanted to leave England. The king refused him twice; and on his applying to him a third time, he assured the saint that if he left that kingdom, he would seize upon the whole revenue of Canterbury.

But the saint could no longer be witness of the oppression of the church and set out from Canterbury in October 1097 in the clothes of a pilgrim; took a ship from Dover and landed at Witsan. He stayed at Cluni with St Hugh the abbot and at Lyons. Anselm falling sick soon after stayed longer at Lyons than he had designed.

King William Rufus havIng died, St Anselm, who was then in the abbey of Chaize-Dieu in Auvergne, made haste back to England. He landed at Dover on 23 September 1100 and was received with great joy. The last years of his life, his health was entirely broken. He died at Canterbury and was buried in his cathedral.

The following feasts are also celebrated today:
St Beuno, Abbot of Clynnog in Carnarvonshire: **St Eingan**, a King of the Scots: **St Malrubius**, martyr, who led an austere life in the County of Ross, Ireland.

April 22
SAINT SOTER
Pope and Martyr

St Soter became pope after the death of St Anicetus in 173. He liberally extended his charities to remote churches, particularly to that of Corinth. St Soter governed the church to the year 177.

and
SAINT CAIUS
Pope and Martyr

St Caius was of Dalmatia and related to the Emperor Diocletian. He became pope after St Eutychian in 283.

The following feasts are celebrated today:
Saints Azades, **Tharba**, martyrs in Persia, 341. **Saints Epipodius** and **Alexander**, the latter a Greek, martyred at Lyons: **St Leonides**, a Christian philosopher: **St Opportuna**, virgin, Abbess of Montreuil, three miles from Seez in Normandy, where her brother St Chrodegang was bishop: **St Rufus**, at Glendaloch in Ireland and buried there: **St Theodorus** of Siceon, Bishop.

April 23
SAINT GEORGE
Martyr – AD c303

St George is honoured as one of the most illustrious martyrs.

The Greeks have long distinguished him by the title of The Great Martyr. There stood formerly in Constantinople five or six churches dedicated in his honour, the oldest of which was always said to have been built by Constantine the Great. One of the churches of St George in Constantinople called Manganes, with a monastery adjoining, gave to the Hellespont the name of the Arm of St George.

From frequent pilgrimages to his church and tomb in Palestine, his veneration was propagated over the West. St Clotildis, wife of Clovis, the first Christian king of France, erected altars under his name; and the church of Chelles, built by her, was originally dedicated in his honour.

The help of this saint was implored especially in battles and by warriors, as appears by several instances in the Byzantine history and he is said to have been himself a great soldier. The great national council, held at Oxford in 1222, commanded his feast to be kept a holiday throughout all England.

Under his name and ensign, the most noble Order of knighthood in Europe, consisting of twenty-five knights besides the sovereign was instituted by Edward III, in 1330. Its establishment is dated fifty years before the knights of St Michael were instituted in France by Louis XI; eighty years before the Order of the Golden Fleece, established by Philip the Good, Duke of Burgundy; and one hundred and ninety years before the Order of St Andrew was set up in Scotland by James V. The emperor Fredric IV instituted, in 1470, an Order of knights in honour of St George; and an honourable military Order in Venice bears his name.

The extraordinary devotion of all Christendom to this saint is an authentic proof how glorious his triumph and name have always been in the church. All his acts relate that he suffered under Diocletian at Nicomedia. According to the account given us by Metaphrastes, he was born in Cappadocia, of noble Christian parents.

After the death of his father he went with his mother into Palestine, she being a native of that country, and having there a considerable estate, which fell to her son George. He was strong and robust in body, and having become a soldier, was made a tribune, or colonel, in the army. By his courage and conduct he was soon promoted to higher stations by the Emperor Diocletian.

When that prince waged war against the Christian religion, St George laid aside the marks of his dignity, threw up his commission and posts, and complained to the emperor. He was cast into prison, and tried, afterwards tortured with great cruelty. The next day he was led through the city and beheaded.

The reason why St George has been regarded as the patron of military men is partly because of his profession, and partly because after his death he appeared to the Christian army in the holy war, before the battle of Antioch.

The success of this battle proving fortunate to the Christians, under Godfrey of Bouillon, made the name of St George more famous in Europe. This devotion was confirmed by an apparition of St George to King Richard I, in his expedition against the Saracens.

St George is usually painted on horseback and tilting at a dragon under his feet; but this representation is no more than an emblematical figure, purporting that by his faith and Christian fortitude he conquered the devil, called the dragon in the Apocalypse.

The following feasts are also celebrated today:
St Adalbert, Bishop of Prague, consecrated to God in infancy by his parents, who feared to lose him by sickness: **St Gerard**, Bishop of Toul: **St Ibar** or **Ivor**, bishop in Ireland.

April 24
SAINT MELLITUS,
Archbishop of Canterbury, Confessor – AD 624

St Mellitus was a Roman abbot whom St Gregory sent over in 601 at the head of a second colony of missioners, to assist St Augustine. He was the first Bishop of London and in 604 laid the foundation of the cathedral church of St Paul's and in 609 of the monastery of St Peter, at Thorney, which was rebuilt by King Edgar, and again by St Edward the Confessor and is now called Westminster. St Mellitus went to France but soon returned and upon the death of St Laurence in 619 and was made Bishop of Canterbury. He died in 624.

The following feasts are also celebrated today:
Saints Bona and **Doda**, Abbesses, the latter a niece of St Bona and a faithful imitator of her spirit and her virtues: **St Fidelis of Sigmarengen**: **The Good Thief** who confessed Christ as he was dying.

April 25
SAINT MARK
Evangelist, Patron Saint of Venice – AD 68

St Mark was by birth a Jew of the race of Aaron. He was converted by the apostles after Christ's resurrection and was the disciple and interpreter of St Peter. He is the same Mark whom St Peter calls his son. He wrote his gospel at the request of the Romans who desired to have that committed to writing which St Peter had taught them by word of mouth. St Peter having revised the work, approved of it, and authorized it to be read in the religious assemblies of the faithful. Many by comparing the two gospels argue that St Mark abridged that of St Matthew; for he relates the same things and often uses the same words.

St Peter sent his disciples from Rome to found other churches. Some say St Mark founded that of Aquileia. It is certain, at least that he was sent by St Peter into Egypt, and was by him appointed bishop of Alexandria (which, after Rome, was accounted the second city of the world). The apostle left the city, having ordained St Anianus bishop, in the eighth year of Nero, and returned to Pentapolis and then visited his church of Alexandria.

On account of his miracles, many feared him and called for his death. Having seized him, they tied his feet with cords and dragged him about the streets. The saint was dragged the whole day, staining the stones with his blood and leaving the ground strewed with pieces of his flesh. At night he was thrown into prison. The next day he was again dragged through the streets until he died. The Christians gathered up the remains of his mangled body and buried them at Bucoles. His body was kept there, in a church built on the spot in 310. It is said to have been conveyed by stealth to Venice in 815. The Venetians had carried it to their isles and deposited in the Doge's stately rich chapel of St Mark in a secret place, that it may not be stolen, under one of the great pillars. This saint is honoured by that republic with extraordinary devotion as a principal patron.

Mark's emblem in art is a winged lion, and he is usually shown holding his Gospel as a book or scroll, and occasionally as a bishop on a throne decorated with carved lions. Patron saint of Venice, glaziers and notaries, invoked by captives.

The following feasts are also celebrated today:

St Anianus, second Bishop of Alexandria, a shoemaker of that city whose hand, wounded by an awl, was healed by St Mark. He governed the Church four years with St Mark and eighteen years after his death, and is named on the same day as the Evangelist: **St Ivea**, a Persian bishop who preached the faith in England – St Ives in Cornwall, where he died, is named after him: **St Kebius**, Bishop, who preached penance in Cornwall in the fourth century: **St Macull** of Ireland: **St Phæbadius**, Bishop of Agen in Gaul.

April 26
SAINT CLETUS
Pope and Martyr

St Cletus was the third bishop of Rome and succeeded St Linus. He was buried near St Linus on the Vatican, and his relics still remain in that church.

---

and
SAINT MARCELLINUS
Pope and Martyr

He succeeded St Caius as Bishop of Rome in 296, about the time that Diocletian set himself up for a deity. In those stormy times of persecution Marcellinus acquired great glory. He was pope for eight years, dying in 304 after the persecution broke out.

He has been styled a martyr, though he did not die in the cause of religion.

If you confer a benefit never remember it;
if you receive one never forget it.

The following feasts are also celebrated today:
St Cletus was the third Bishop of Rome: **St Marcellinus**:
St Pasharius Radbert, Abbot: **St Peter Canisius**, S.J., a Doctor of
the Church: **St Richarius**, Abbot, born of poor parents from whom he
inherited virtue. He lived as a hermit in the Forest of Cressy and
founded the monastery of Centula, which holds his relics.

April 27
SAINT ZITA
Virgin – AD 1272

She was born in the beginning of the thirteenth century as Montsegradi, a
village near Lucca in Italy. She was brought up with the greatest care by her
poor, virtuous mother.

At twelve years of age she was put in service in the family of a citizen of
Lucca, called Fatinelli, whose house adjoined the church of St Frigidian.
Being made housekeeper, and, though head servant, she never allowed
herself the least privilege or exemption in her work on that account.

She would fast the whole year on bread and water, and took her rest on the
bare floor or on a board. Whenever business allowed her a little leisure, she
spent it in prayer and contemplation in a little room in the garret. She
respected her fellow-servants as her superiors.

She never kept anything for herself but the poor garments that she wore,
everything else she gave to the poor. Her master, seeing his goods multiply
in her hands, gave her ample leave to bestow liberal alms on the poor,
which she made use of with discretion, but was scrupulous to do nothing
without his express authority.

She died in 1272, being sixty years old. Her body was found entire in 1580
and is kept in St Frigidian's church, richly enshrined, her face and hands
are exposed naked to view through a crystal glass.

The following feasts are also celebrated today:
St Anatasius, Pope, called by St Jerome a man of a most rich
poverty: **St Anthimus**, Bishop, and many other martyrs at Nicomedia:
St Egbert, who died on Easter Day in 729.

The great painter boasted that he mixed all his colours with brains,
and the great saint may be said
to mix all his thoughts with thanks.

G. K. Chesterton

April 28
SAINT VITALIS
Martyr – AD c62

St Vitalis is honoured as the principal patron of the city of Ravenna. He was a citizen of Milan. He went to Ravenna, where he saw a Christian named Ursicinus, who was condemned to lose his head for his faith. Vitalis was extremely moved at this spectacle. He boldly and successfully encouraged Ursicinus to triumph over death, and after his martyrdom carried off his body and respectfully interred it. The judge, whose name was Paulinus, being informed of what he had done, had him apprehended, stretched on the rack, and after other torments to be buried alive in a place called the Palm-tree, in Ravenna.

The relics of St Vitalis are deposited in the great church which bears his name in Ravenna, and was magnificently built by the Emperor Justinian in 547.

and
SAINT POLLIO
Lector, and his companions in Pannonia, Martyrs – AD 304

Probus, Governor of Pannonia under Diocletian in 304, having put to death St Montanus, priest of Singidon, St Irenæus, Bishop of Sirmium, and others, arrived at Cibalis, a town between the rivers Save and Drave, afterwards the birthplace of Emperor Valentinian. The very same day on which he arrived, Pollio was apprehended. He was presented to the governor and accused of Christianity. Probus asked if he were a Christian, "I am," said Pollio.

Probus: "Then you must resolve to die."

Pollio: "My resolution is fixed, do what you are commanded."

Probus condemned him to be burnt alive, and the sentence was immediately executed a mile from the town.

The following feasts are also celebrated today:
St Cronan, Abbot of Roscrea, in Ireland, where his relics are treasured: **Saints Didymus** and **Theodora**, martyrs: **St Patricius**, Bishop of Prusa, in Bithynia, martyr: **St Paul of the Cross**, founder of the Passionist Congregation, 1694-1775.

Blessed is the man who is too busy to worry in the daytime and too sleepy to worry at night.

Anon

April 29
SAINT PETER
Martyr – AD 1252

St Peter the martyr was born at Verona in 1205. His father sent him, while very young, to a schoolmaster who prepared him for entry to the University of Bologna.

At fifteen years of age he joined the order of St Dominic. Every hour of the day had its employment allotted to it, he was either studying, reading, praying, serving the sick or occupying himself in sweeping the house.

After he was promoted to the priesthood, he entirely devoted himself to preaching, for which his superiors found him excellently qualified. He converted an incredible number among the Romagna, the marquisate of Ancona, Tuscany, the Bolognese and the Milanese.

He was accused by some of his own of admitting strangers, and even women, into his cell, and as punishment he was banished to the remote little Dominican convent of Jesi, in Ancona, and removed from the office of preaching.

But after some months his innocence was cleared, and he was commanded to return and resume his former functions with honour. He appeared everywhere in the pulpits with greater zeal and success than ever. He was made superior of several houses of his Order.

His enemies conspired his death, and hired two assassins to murder him on his return from Como to Milan. They lay in ambush for him on the road, and one of them, Carinus, gave him two cuts on the head with an axe, and then stabbed his companion, Dominic. Seeing Peter rise on his knees and hearing him pray, they struck him again with the axe.

His body was buried in the Dominicans' church dedicated to St Eustorgius, in Milan, where it still rests; his head is kept apart in a case of crystal and gold.

The history of miracles, performed by his relics and intercessions, fills twenty-two pages in folio in the Acta Sanctorum.

The following feasts are also celebrated today:

St Fiachna, a monk of Lismore and a disciple of St Carthagh: **St Hugh**, Abbot of Cluny, who succeeded to the government of that great monastery when only twenty-five and held it for sixty-two years: **St Peter**, martyr, 1252: **St Robert**, Abbot of Molesme, founder of the Cistercians, died 1109.

There is more to life than increasing its speeds.

April 30
SAINT CATHERINE OF SIENA
Virgin – AD 1380
One of the greatest Christian mystics

Giacomo Benincasa, a dyer of Siena, had 25 children of whom Catherine was the youngest, a high-spirited and good-looking girl much given to penitential prayer who steadfastly refused her parents' entreaties to marry.

At the age of 16 she became a Dominican tertiary, living at home but spending much time in prayer and solitude. It was now that she first experienced visions, divine ones on Christ and his saints, and diabolical ones in periods of spiritual aridity.

After this preparative time she began work in a hospital, nursing patients with advanced cancer or leprosy.

She gradually attracted a group of disciples, but the attention given to her supernatural gifts was not all positive; she was at one stage brought before the General chapter of the Dominicans at Florence and accused of being a fraud.

The charge was dismissed. Catherine and her disciples travelled widely, calling their listeners to respond to the love of God with repentance, reform and commitment, and they are credited with several dramatic conversions.

In an attempt to further communicate her ideals Catherine dictated her mystical *Dialogue* and several other devotional works and letters addressed to people of every social rank (she herself was illiterate).

On 21 April she suffered a paralytic stroke; eight days later she died, and it is said that the marks of the stigmata became clearly visible.

Her body lies in Sta Maria sopra Minerva in Rome, near to that of Fra Angelico, but her head is claimed by Siena.

She was named patron saint of Italy in 1939 and declared a Doctor of the Church by Pope Paul in 1970.

In art she is represented with the stigmata holding a lily and a book, occasionally wearing a crown of thorns.

The following feasts are also celebrated today:
St Ajutre of Adjuntr, recluse at Vernon, in Normandy: **St Erconwald**, Bishop of London. He founded the monastery at Barking, in Essex. **Saints James**, **Marian and their companions**, martyrs in Numidia, 259: **St Maximus**, martyr, a merchant in Asia, who, firmly declaring himself a Christian, under Decius, was stoned to death: **St Sophia**, virgin, martyr, in Italy.

May 1
SAINT PHILIP
Apostle

St Philip was of Bethsaida in Galilee, and called by our Saviour to follow him. He was at that time a married man and had several daughters. Philip had no sooner discovered the Messiah than he wanted to make his friend Nathanael share in his happiness, saying to him, "We have found him of whom Moses in the law and the prophets did write, Jesus, the son of Joseph, of Nazareth." Nathanael was not so ready to believe his friend. Philip then said "Come and see!" Nathanael went along and Jesus, seeing him approach, said within his hearing, "Behold, an Israelite indeed, in whom there is no guile." Nathanael asked him how he came to know him. Jesus replied, "Before Philip called thee, when thou wast under the fig-tree, I saw thee."

The year following, when our Lord formed the college of apostles, Philip was appointed one of that number, and, from the several passages of the gospel, he appears to have been particularly dear to his divine Master. After our Lord's ascension the gospel was to be preached to the whole world by a few persons who had been eye-witness of his miracles. St Philip accordingly preached the gospel in the two Phrygias. St Philip must have lived to a very advanced age. It appears that he was buried at Hierapolis, in Phrygia, which city was indebted to his relics for its preservation by continual miracles. An arm of St Philip was brought from Constantinople to Florence in 1204. His body is said to be in the church of SS. Philip and James, in Rome.

> **The following feasts are also celebrated today:**
> **St Acius** and **St Acheolus**, martyrs of Amiens: **St Andeolus**, martyr, a disciple of St Polycarp: **St Asaph**, Bishop, a disciple of St Kentigern: **St Brieuc**, Bishop: **St James the Less**, the best known of all the apostles, son of Zebedee and a kinsman of our Lord. His Feast is always kept with that of St Philip, Apostle: **St Marcou** or **Marculfus**, 1558, Abbot, famous for miracles: **St Sigismund**, king and martyr.

May 2
SAINT ATHANASIUS
Patriarch of Alexandria, Doctor of the Church – AD 373

St Athanasius was a native of Alexandria, and seems to have been born about the year 296. His parents, who were Christians and remarkable for their virtue, gave him the best education. After he had learned grammar and the first elements of the sciences, St Alexander took upon himself the direction of his studies, and employed him as his secretary.

Athanasius copied the virtues of his master. By writing under so great a master he acquired the most elegant, easy and methodical manner of composition. However, it was the sacred studies of religion and virtue that employed his whole life. From his easy and ready manner of quoting the holy scriptures one would imagine he knew them by heart. In 313, St Alexander became Patriarch of Alexandria and St Athanasius went into the desert to the great St Anthony. When he returned to the city, he was ordained deacon about the year 319.

In 325 St Alexander took the holy deacon with him to the Council of Nice. Five months after this great council, St Alexander, lying on his death-bed, by heavenly inspiration recommended to his clergy and people the choice of Athanasius for his successor, repeating his name, and when he was found to be absent, he cried out, "Athanasius, you think to escape, but you are mistaken." The bishops of all Egypt assembled at Alexandria, and finding the people and clergy unanimous in their choice of Athanasius for patriarch, they confirmed the election about the middle of the year 326. He was then about thirty years of age.

Those perilous times raised many holy pastors; among these St Athanasius was the most illustrious. By his undaunted courage under the most violent persecutions, he merited a crown equal to that of the most glorious martyrs; by his writings he holds an eminent place among the principal doctors of the church. He stemmed the torrent of scandal and iniquity which threatened to bear down all before it. Called the "Hammer of the Arians", he died in 373 after having been exiled five times because of his defence of the cause of the Church.

May 3
The following feasts are celebrated today:
St Alexander, who succeeded St Evaristus as pope in 109 and was martyred about 119: **St Eventius** and **St Theodulus** suffered together with St Alexander: **St Juvenal** was Bishop of Narni.

May 4
SAINT MONICA
Widow – AD 387

She was born in 332, in a pious family. She married Patricius, a citizen of Tagaste, and had by him two sons, Austin and Navigius, and one daughter.

One of the happy fruits Monica reaped from her patience was her husband's conversion. He died the year after he had been baptized.

Her exercises of piety did not hinder her attention in watching over the education of her children, particularly Austin. He was born in November 354. Patricius died about the year 371. Austin, who was then seventeen years of age, still continued his studies at Carthage, almost nine years before his conversion. Upon his arrival at Rome he fell dangerously sick, and he attributes his recovery to the prayers of his mother.

From Rome he went to teach at Milan in 384. Monica followed him, and in a great storm at sea comforted the sailors, assuring them, from a vision, that they would certainly reach the port. St Austin was baptized at Easter in 387, with some of his friends, with whom he continued to live some time.

St Monica took as much care of them all as if they had been her children. They all set out together for Africa, but lost Monica on the road, who fell sick and died at Ostia. Her body was translated from Ostia to Rome in 1430, and remains there in the church of St Austin.

The following feasts are also celebrated today:
St Godard, Bishop, who reformed many monasteries: **St John Fisher** and **St Thomas More**. They refused to acknowledge Henry VIII as head of the Church.

May 5
SAINT PIUS V
Pope, Confessor – AD 1572

Michael Ghisleri, known afterwards by the name of Pius V, was born at Bosco, a little town in the diocese of Tortona, on 27 January 1504. He was descended of a noble Bolognese family, but considerably reduced in its splendour and fortunes. He studied under the care of the Dominican friars at Voghera and took the habit of that Order when he was only fifteen years of age.

He was ordained priest at Genoa in 1528 and taught philosophy and divinity and was employed in instructing the novices and in governing different houses of his Order.

Pope Paul IV, in 1556, made him Bishop of Nepi and Sutri. In 1557 he was created cardinal by the same pope. He was most scrupulously cautious in the choice of his few necessary domestics, admitting none but persons of most exemplary piety, and he treated them as his children rather than as his servants. Pope Paul IV dying in 1559, was succeeded by Pius IV, of the family of Medicis. The Emperor Maximilian II wrote to Pope Pius IV to desire that priests might be allowed to marry, but none spoke more vigorously against this than our saint, who became pope on the death of Pius IV on the 9th December, 1595, and took the name of Pius.

He accordingly directed the large sums of money usually expended on such occasions to be distributed among the poor in the hospitals and elsewhere.

He in like manner sent to the poorer convents in the city the thousand crowns usually employed in an entertainment for the cardinals, ambassadors and lords who assisted at the ceremony.

In the time of a great famine in Rome he imported corn at his own expense from Sicily and France, a considerable part of which he distributed among the poor and sold the rest to the public much under cost. Frugal in all things himself, he was enabled by his good economy to make many useful foundations and to relieve the distressed.

Through his zeal and ardent prayers he obtained the victory at the Battle of Lapanto, thereby saving Christendom from the Turks. He was preparing to pursue the advantage gained by this great victory when he died on the 1 May, 1572, being sixty-eight years. His remains lie in the church of St Mary Major.

The following feasts are also celebrated today:

St Angelus, Carmelite friar, he became a hermit of austere life on the banks of the Jordan, martyred in Sicily by the connivance of a rich man whose scandalous life he had reproved: **St Avertin**, a holy deacon who attended St Thomas of Canterbury in his exile and throughout all his troubles: **St Hilary**, Archbishop of Arles: **St Mauront**, Abbot, born in 634 and baptized by St Riquier.

Deal with the faults of others
as gently as with your own.

By other's faults wise men correct their own.

May 6
SAINT JOHN BEFORE THE LATIN GATE
AD 95

Today we celebrate the martyrdom of St John the Evangelist. St John was apprehended at Ephesus and sent to Rome. There, outside the Roman gate called *Latina*, he was cast into a caldron of boiling oil.

The visible protection of God allowed him to remain unhurt: to the confusion of Emperor Domitian, who then exiled him to the Island of Patmos.

The following feasts are also celebrated today:

St Eadbert, Bishop of Lindisfarne, who, as St Bede tells us, excelled in the knowledge of Holy Scripture; he tells also of the miracles worked at his tomb and that of St Cuthbert, in whose grave he was laid: **St John Damascen**.

May 7
SAINT STANISLAS
Martyr, Bishop of Cracow – AD 1079

Stanislas Sezepanowski was born on 26 July 1030 at Sezepanow, in the diocese of Cracow. His parents both of Poland having been married for thirty years, had lost all hope of children. Young Stanislas from his very infancy showed an unusual affection for prayer, seriousness and mortification. Stanislas was sent to school and his progress in learning surpassed the expectation of all.

He had no relish for superfluous amusements; and the money which was given him for his pocket was always secretly employed in relieving the poor. When grown up, he was sent to study at Gnesna and then to Paris. After seven years spent in the schools of canon law and divinity at Paris, refusing the degree of doctor which was offered him, he returned home. He received the order of priesthood from Lampert Zula, Bishop of Cracow, and was made by him canon of his cathedral and soon after his preacher and vicar-general.

Upon the death of Lampert in 1072, he found himself Bishop of Cracow.

Boleslas II was then King of Poland and by his acts of tyranny and injustice he was known as the "Cruel" Stanislas, however laid before him in private the scandal and enormity of his conduct. He was the only person that had the courage to discharge this duty. After this the king seemed reconciled with the saint; but the succeeding acts of cruelty which he exercised upon his subjects became more inhuman.

Seeing no remedy applied to the evils he deplored, Stanislas made the king a third visit, but he threatened the saint with certain death if he continued to disturb him. Stanislas left nothing untried, but finding all measures ineffectual, he, after a fourth visit, excommunicated the King. He left the city and went to St Michael's a small chapel at a little distance from Cracow.

The king followed him with his guards, whom he ordered to massacre him on the spot; but going into the chapel with this intent they were struck with such a respect and dread at the presence of the venerable bishop that they dare not attempt it, telling the king that a great light from heaven had frightened them and prevented their executing his orders.

The like happened to a second and a third troop; upon which the king went in himself, rushed forward and killed him with his own hand. Then his guards cut the martyr's body into pieces, which they scattered about the fields to be devoured by beasts and birds of prey. But eagles are said to have defended them till the canons of his cathedral three days after, gathered them together and privately buried them before the door of the chapel in which he was martyred. The body was translated into the cathedral in Cracow, in 1088, and honoured with innumerable miracles.

The king fled out of Poland into Hungary and there perished miserably, some say by becoming his own executioner.

The following feasts are also celebrated today:
St Benedict II, Pope: St John of Beverley, Bishop.

May 8
SAINT PETER
Archbishop of Tarentaise, now called Monstiers in Savoy

He was a native of Dauphiné. At twenty years of age he took the Cistercian habit at Bonnevaux. There he employed a great part of the day in hewing wood and tilling the ground in the forest, in perpetual silence and interior prayer.

The monks ate but once a day and their fare was herbs or roots, mostly turnips of a coarse sort. Four hours in the twenty-four was the usual allowance for sleep; so that, rising at midnight, they continued in the church till it was morning and returned no more to rest.

St Peter, by the help of Amedeus III, Count of Savoy, founded a hospital to receive all the poor sick persons at Tamies. In 1142 St Peter was made Bishop of Tarentaise. He altered nothing, his clothes were plain and his food coarse, but he soon made the church a pattern of good order and devotion.

In 1155, after he had been bishop for thirteen years, he disappeared and made his way to a monastery of Cistercians in Germany, where he was not known. A young man, who had been brought up under his care, came to the monastery in which he lay concealed, and upon observing the monks as they were going out of the church to their work, recognised his bishop and made him known to the whole community. He founded hospitals on the Alps for poor travellers.

The saint preached in Alsace, Burgundy, Lorraine, and in many parts of Italy; and confounded the obstinate by numberless miraculous cures of the sick, performed by the imposition of his hands and prayer.

He was ordered by the pope to go into France and Normandy, to endeavour a reconciliation between the kings of England and France, who had made peace in 1169 but quarrelled again the next year. Though then very old, he preached wherever he went. He fell sick and died at Bellevaux, a monastery of his Order in the diocese of Besançon in 1174, being seventy-three years old.

The following feasts are also celebrated today:
St Gybrian or Gobrian of Ireland, priest, who died at a great age in the eighth century: St Odrian, Bishop and titular saint of Waterford: St Victor, an illustrious martyr, beheaded at Milan in 303: St Wiro an Irish bishop.

May 9
SAINT GREGORY NAZIANZEN
Doctor of the Church – AD 389

Son of two sainted parents, Bishop Gregory of Nazianzus and St Nanna, Gregory was born in Cappadocia and began his education there in Cæsarea, Palestine, and then to study law at the University of Athens in the company of Basil and Julian, later the apostate emperor. His studies completed Gregory became a monk, joining Basil at his retreat on the river Iris in Pontus. In c361 he returned to Nazianzus to help his father with the administration of his see. Despite his objections, he was ordained as a priest by the old bishop and in panic fled back to Basil. He quickly recognized the folly of his flight, and returned to face his new duties, writing an *apologia* which has become a classic statement on the responsibility of the clergy.

In 372 Basil appointed Gregory bishop of Sasima, a hostile and troubled see in Arian territory. The post had been created by Basil to strengthen his position against a neighbouring Arian bishop, and Gregory felt that he was being used for a political purpose. He refused even to visit Sasima, and stayed in Nazianzus, administering the see after his father's death in 374 until the post was filled again. The disagreement was to mar the friendship which had once been so close. The following year Gregory suffered a breakdown and retired to Seleucia for the next five years to live in tranquillity as a hermit.

In 380 he was called to the bishopric of Constantinople after the death of Emperor Valens. Persecution had left the church vulnerable to Arian heresy, but Gregory's articulate preaching in the church established in his own house soon restored sound doctrine. He brought upon himself slander and vitriol from the Arians, but was vindicated in 381 when Emperor Theodosius I at the Council of Constantinople confirmed the doctrine preached by Gregory, that of the Council of Nicaea, as the only authentic Christian doctrine. The Arians were called upon to concur or quit; most of them quitted. Gregory was made archbishop of Constantinople, but the hostility towards him resurfaced after his appointment and to preserve the peace Gregory resigned his post. Back in Nazianzus, the see was vacant and Gregory administered while a successor was chosen.

He spent his final years in great austerity, writing his famous poems and an autobiography. He died there on 25 January and his relics were later translated to Constantinople and then to St Peter's in Rome. His impressive theological writings, promoting Nicene orthodoxy especially in teaching on the Trinity, won him the name "the Theologian" during his life and a place among the four great Eastern Doctors after his death.

The following feasts are also celebrated today:
St Brynoth, Bishop of Scara in Sweden: **St Hermas**: **St Nicholas**, Bishop of Lincöpen in Sweden.

May 10
SAINT ISIDORE OF MADRID
Labourer, Patron of Madrid

He was born at Madrid of poor but very devout parents, and was christened Isidore from the name of their patron, St Isidore of Seville. They had not the means to give him learning or education. Whilst his hand held the plough, his heart conversed with God. For forty years he was servant to a gentleman named John de Vargas, of Madrid, to till his land and do his husbandry work. He died on the 15th of May, 1170, being near sixty years of age. After forty years his body was removed out of the churchyard into the church of St Andrew. It has been since placed in the bishop's chapel, and during these five hundred years remains entire and fresh, being honoured by a succession of frequent miracles down to this time.

The following feasts are also celebrated today:
St Anntoninus ("**Little Anthony**"), a famous Dominican of the fifteenth century, Archbishop of Florence; he lodged and rebuilt the houses of the distressed during frequent earthquakes: **St Catuldus**, a learned Irish monk, who became Bishop of Tarentum in Italy: **St Comgall**, Abbot in Ireland: **St Gordian**, a magistrate sentenced to death under Julian the Apostate, and **St Epimachus**, near whose relics his own were laid.

May 11
SAINT MAMMERTUS
Confessor, Archbishop of Vienne – AD 477

Was a prelate renowned in the Church for his sanctity, learning, and miracles. A terrible fire happened in the city of Vienne, which baffled the efforts of men, but by the prayers of the good bishop the fire all of a sudden went out.

The following feast is also celebrated today:
St Maieul, in Latin **Majolus**, Abbot of Cluni.

May 12
The following feasts are celebrated today:
St Epiphanius, Archbishop of Salamis: **St Flavia Domitilla** and **St Nereus** and **St Achilleus**, martyrs: **St Pancras**, a noble boy of fourteen years, suffered in the fourth century under Diocletian: **St Rictrudes**, Abbess, the mother of four saints.

May 13
The following feasts are celebrated today:
St John the Silent, Bishop, Confessor, 550: **St Peter Regalati**, who, having lost his father in his thirteenth year, became a Franciscan friar. He died in 1456: **St Servatius,** who resisted the Arians, entertained St Athanasius during his banishment and foretold the invasion of Gaul by the Huns: **St Walburga,** sister to Saints Willebald and Winebald, devoted, like them, to the conversion of Germany.

May 14
SAINT BONIFACE
Martyr – AD c307

There lived at Rome, about the beginning of the fourth century, a certain lady called Aglaë, young, beautiful, well born and rich. Her chief steward was Boniface. This man, though addicted to wine and all kinds of debauchery, was, however, remarkable for three good qualities: hospitality, liberality, and compassion. Whensoever he saw a stranger or traveller he would assist him very cordially; and he used to go about the streets and into the public places in the night time and care for the poor. Aglaë called Boniface to her, "I have heard say in the East the servants of Jesus Christ every day suffer torments and lay down their lives for his sake. Go then, and bring me the relics of some of those conquerors, that we may honour their memories."

Boniface having raised a considerable sum of money to purchase the bodies of the martyrs from their executioners said to Aglaë on his departure, "I won't fail to bring back with me the relics of martyrs, if I find any; but what if my own body should be brought to you for that of a martyr?" She reproved him for jesting in a matter so serious. The steward set out but was now entirely a new man.

The church at that time enjoyed peace in the West, but in the East persecution was carried on with great cruelty by Galerius Maximianus and Maximinus Daie. It raged most fiercely in Cilicia, under an inhuman governor named Simplicius. Boniface therefore directed his journey to the capital of that country. He went straight to the court of the governor, whom he found seated on his tribunal, and many holy martyrs suffering under their tortures.

Boniface went up to these champions of Christ and saluted them. The governor thought himself insulted by so bold an action and asked him in great anger who he was. Boniface answered that he was a Christian. Simplicius, in a rage, ordered some reeds to be sharpened and thrust under his nails; and then he commanded boiling lead to be poured into his mouth.

The people disgusted at the cruelty, began to raise a tumult. Simplicius was alarmed and withdrew. But the next day, secretly, he had Boniface executed.

His companions in the meantime, not finding him at the inn, searched for him. Being at last informed by the jailer's brother that a stranger had been beheaded the day before and being shown the dead body and the head, they paid five hundred pieces of gold; and having embalmed it, carried it home with them. Aglaë, taking some priests with her, met the corpse with tapers and perfumes half a mile out of Rome, and in that very place raised a monument in which she laid him and some years after built a chapel. She from that time led a penitential retired life and, dying fifteen years after, was buried near his relics.

The following feasts are also celebrated today:
St Garthagh (or **Carthage**) **the Younger**, commonly called **Mochudu**; a poor boy, working as a swineheard, he met the holy Bishop, Carthagh the Elder, became his disciple and, being ordained, took his name. He was made Bishop of Kier-raigh, founded the Monastery of Rathin and governed it for forty years: **St Pachomius**, said to have received instruction regarding the monastic life from an angel: **St Pontius**, an illustrious martyr of primitive times, said to have suffered under Valerian about the year 258.

May 15
SAINT DYMPNA
9th century

When the bodies of an unknown couple were discovered at Gheel (to the east of Antwerp in northern Belgium), together with an inscription of the name Dympna, and miraculous cures were reported at the site, the popular folk-tale that grew up around them soon became regarded as a saint's Life.

According to this tale, Dympna was the daughter of a pagan Celtic chief and a Christian mother. After her mother's death, Dympna was forced to flee with her confessor, St Gerebernus, first to Antwerp and then on to nearby Gheel, to avoid the incestuous attentions of her father.

There they lived peacefully as hermits, but Dympna's father succeeded in tracking them down by tracing the coins they had spent, and demanded that she return home with him. When Dympna refused, he murdered the girl and her confessor on the spot. The bodies were buried there, and at their translation in the 13th century several miracles of healing of insanity and epilepsy were reported.

A cathedral was built in Dympna's honour in the town, and as the saint's reputation for healing spread, it became a centre of pilgrimage for the mentally ill. The pilgrims were housed originally in a sick-room built for the purpose next to the church, but as their number increased this limited accommodation proved inadequate.

By the 14th century the townsfolk of Gheel were accustomed to opening their homes to give hospitality to those who had travelled for healing. In 1850 the government formalized this arrangement under medical supervision, and the hospital system which thus evolved has proved one of the most famous and effective institutions of its kind in the world. Its special concern is the integration of the mentally ill with society, for example by boarding out patients in private homes in the area.

In art Dympna is usually shown as a princess with a sword holding a devil on a leash, and often with St Gerebernus. Patron saint of the insane, invoked against mental illness and epilepsy.

The following feasts are also celebrated today:
St Genebrard or **Genebern**, martyr, a priest who had baptized St Dympna; he followed her in her flight and was beheaded by her murderers: **St John Baptist de la Salle**, the most famous Christian educationist of the seventeenth century; he founded the Institute of the Brothers of the Christian Schools: **St Peter**, **St Andrew and their Companions**.

May 16
SAINT BRENDAN THE NAVIGATOR
AD 577

The son of Findlugh of Tralee, Brendan was fostered as a child by the famous nun Ita and educated at St Jarlath's abbey school in Tuam by the Bishop of Kerry, St Erc. Given this religious background, it is hardly surprising that he went on to become a monk himself.

He was ordained by Erc in 512 and set about founding monasteries throughout Ireland, including Clonfert (in 559) which became an important missionary centre of about 3000 monks and survived until the 16th century,. Annaghdown, Inishadroum and Ardfert.

He also travelled extensively in Scotland, befriending Columba in Argyll according to Adomnan, and very probably in Wales and beyond, but it is impossible to detail the events of his life with any real certainty. He probably died whilst on a visit to his sister Brig in Annaghdown.

Brendan's great influence in southern Ireland is attested by the significant number of place names which are named after him, most famously Mount Brandon on the Dingle Peninsula. From the ninth century onwards there is evidence of a strong cult of St Brendan in Ireland, and he was popular too in Wales, Scotland and Brittany.

The stories of Brendan's wide travelling gave rise to the *Navigation of Brendan*, a 10th or 11th century visionary romance written in Latin which describes Brendan's seven-year voyage to a "Land of Promise" in the west, identified by some as the Hebrides and Northern Isles, by others as Iceland, and by some as the Canary Islands or even North America.

Matthew Arnold's poem *'St Brandan'* retells the story, and the saint is a popular figure in art, standing aboard ship offering mass whilst the fish crowd round to listen. Patron saint of sailors and travellers.

The following feasts are also celebrated today:
St Abdas, martyr, Bishop of Cascar in Chaldea: **St Abdjesus**, or **Habedjesus**, martyr also Bishop of Cascar: **St Honoratus**, in French **Honoré**, Bishop of Amiens about 660: **St John Nepomucen**: **St Simon Stock**, a native of Kent: **St Ubaldus**, Bishop of Gubio or Gubbio.

May 17
SAINT PASCHAL BAYLON
Confessor – AD 1592

Saint Paschal Baylon was born in 1540, at Torre-Hermosa, a small country town in the kingdom of Arragon. His parents were day-labourers and very virtuous.

Their circumstances were too narrow to afford his being sent to school, but the pious child carried a book with him into the fields where he watched the sheep and asked those that he met to teach him the letters and so in a short space of time, being yet very young, he learned to read. Books of amusement he would never look into, but the lives of the saints and the life of Christ were his chief delight.

When he was old enough he was engaged by a master to keep his flocks as under shepherd. At twenty years of age, he left his master, his friends and his country and went into Valentia to an austere convent of barefoot reformed Franciscans called Soccolans, which stood in a desert near the town of Montfort, and was admitted in 1564.

He was a most fervent religious man; the meanest employments always gave him the highest satisfaction. He had never more than one set of clothes and that always threadbare. He walked without sandals in the snows and in the roughest roads.

In all places and seasons he was always content and cheerful. He died at Villa Reale, near Valentia on 17 May 1592. His corpse was exposed three days, during which time great multitudes from all parts visited the church.

The following feasts are also celebrated today:
St Cathan, Bishop; the Isle of Bute, which holds his relics is often called Kilcathan: **St Maden**, or **Madern**, honoured in Brittany, also in Cornwall where he lived and died in a hermitage near Land's End; a chapel there was long famed for his miracles: **St Maw** (in Cornish, "a boy"); the saint an Irishman who came to Cornwall, is associated with a well which bears his name: **St Possidius**, Bishop, educated under the great St Augustine, whose life he wrote and whose works he catalogued: **St Silave** or **Silan**, Bishop in Ireland, an Irish monk who passed the latter part of his life in Italy, where he was called "the father of the poor".

May 18
SAINT ERIC
Martyr, King of Sweden – AD 1151

Eric was descended of an illustrious Swedish family; in his youth he laid a solid foundation of virtue and learning and took as his wife Christina, daughter of Ingo IV, King of Sweden. Upon the death of King Smercher in 1141, he was placed on the throne by the election of the states, according to the ancient laws of that kingdom. He was truly the father and the servant of all his people and often visited in person the poor that were sick and relieved them with bountiful alms.

He built churches and by wholesome laws restrained the brutish and savage vices of his subjects. The holy king was hearing mass on the day after the feast of the Ascension when the news was brought him that the rebels were in arms and on the march against him. After mass he rode out alone. The conspirators rushed upon him, beat him down from his horse and struck off his head. His death happened on 18 May 1151. St Eric was honoured as chief patron of the kingdom of Sweden.

The following feasts are also celebrated today:
St Potamon, bishop of Heraclea in Egypt: **St Theodotus**: **St Venantius**, a very young martyr.

Again let us dream where the land lies sunny
And live, like the bees, on our heart's old honey,
Away from the world that slaves for money –
Come journey the way with me.

MADISON CAWEIN – Song of the Road

May 19
SAINT DUNSTAN
Confessor, Archbishop of Canterbury

He was a native of Glastonbury of noble birth, and received his education under Irish monks who were excellent masters of the sciences and at that time resided at Glastonbury. Dunstan outstripped his companions in every branch of literature, and through the recommendations of Athelmus, Archbishop of Canterbury, his uncle, with whom he had lived some time, was called to the court of King Athelstan. After he left the court he took the monastic habit, being advised by Elphegus the Bald, Bishop of Winchester, also his uncle, who not long after ordained him priest and sent him back to Glastonbury with the view of serving that church.

Here he built for himself a small cell five feet long and two and a half broad, with an oratory adjoining to the wall of the great church. In this hermitage he spent his time in praying and fasting. King Athelstan dying after a reign of sixteen years, the throne was filled by his brother Edmund, who succeeded to the crown in 900. His palace at Cheddar was nine miles from Glastonbury and having been long acquainted with St Dunstan he installed him abbot of that house. King Edmund had reigned only six years when he was treacherously murdered, and buried at Glastonbury. His sons Edwi and Edgar being too young to govern, his brother Edred was called to the crown, who did nothing but by the advice of St Dunstan.

He was succeeded by his nephew Edwi, a most debauched youth who, on the very day he was anointed king, left his nobles at the royal banquet to go to see his mistress. St Dunstan followed him and endeavoured to put him in mind of the duty which he owed to God and men. Edwi banished him, persecuted all the monks in his kingdom and ruined the abbeys.

St Dunstan spent one year in exile in Flanders and at St Peter's at Ghent, where his vestment is still shown. The Mercians and northern provinces shaking off the yoke of the tyrant Edwi, placed the crown on Edgar, who immediately recalled St Dunstan, made him his principal counsellor and in 957 made him the Bishop of Worcester. In 961 St Dunstan became Bishop of Canterbury, and assisted by his two disciples, St Ethelwold, Bishop of Winchester and St Oswald, bishop of Worcester and Archbishop of York, restored most of the great monasteries in England.

He frequently visited the churches over the whole kingdom, everywhere preaching and instructing the faithful. Glastonbury was his dearest solitude and at Canterbury it was always his custom to visit in the night, even in the coldest weather, the Church of St Austin.

Finding himself taken ill in that city he went again to the church and appointed a place for his burial; then he took to his bed. His death happened on 19 May 988. He was buried in his own cathedral in the place he had appointed.

The following feasts are also celebrated today:
St Peter Celestine: **St Pudentiana**, a sister of St Praxedes.

May 20
SAINT BERNARDIN OF SIENA
Confessor – AD 1444

St Bernardin was born at Massa in 1380, of the noble family of Albizeschi, in the republic of Siena. He lost his mother when he was three years old, and his father, who was chief magistrate of Massa, before he was seven. The care of his education was taken by an aunt called Diana, who loved him as a son. One day it happened that his aunt sent away a poor person from the door because there was but one loaf in the house for the dinner of the family. Bernardin was troubled to see the beggar go empty handed and said to his aunt, "For God's sake, let us give something to this poor man; otherwise I will neither dine nor sup this day."

At eleven years of age he was called to Siena by his uncles and put to school under the ablest masters, and at seventeen he enrolled himself in the hospital of Scala to serve the sick. He had served this hospital four years when in 1400 a dreadful plague broke out in several parts of Italy. Bernardin persuaded 12 young men to accompany him in the service of the hospital. The saint was intrusted with the whole care of the hospital which, in the space of four months, he put into excellent order. He escaped the plague but many of his companions died. He then returned home, but sick of a fever. He was scarcely well when with incredible patience he attended his dying aunt for 14 months, as she was blind and bed-ridden. After her death, Bernardin retired to a house some distance from the city, making the walls of his garden the bounds of his enclosure. Later he joined the Order of St Francis a few miles from Siena.

When the saint first preached at Milan, Duke Philip Mary Visconti took offence at certain things which he had said in his sermons, and threatened him with death if he should presume to speak any more on such subjects; but the saint declared that no greater happiness could befall him than to die for the truth. The duke to test him sent him a present of one hundred ducats of gold in a golden bowl. The saint excused himself from receiving the money to two different messengers; but being compelled by a third to accept it, he took the messenger with him to the prisons and laid it all out in his presence in releasing debtors.

St Bernardin preached throughout Italy. Besides several predictions and miraculous cures, the saint is recorded to have raised four dead to life. He was appointed vicar-general of his Order in Italy in 1438. In his old age he continued preaching through Romania, Ferrar, and Lombardy. He returned to Siena in 1444, preached a farewell sermon at Massa and was taken ill on the road. His body is kept in a crystal shrine, enclosed in one of silver, in the church of his Order at Aquila.

The following feast is also celebrated today:
St Ethelbert, King of the East Angles, whom he ruled for forty-four years according to the maxims of a saint; he was treacherously murdered by an officer of King Offa.

May 21
SAINT GODRICK
Hermit – AD 1170

St Godrick was born of very poor parents at Walpole, in Norfolk, and in his youth carried about little peddling wares which he sold in villages. Having improved his stock, he went to cities and fairs and made several voyages by sea to Scotland. In one of these he called at Holy Island or Lindisfarne, where he met the monks and was attracted to their wonderful life. He visited every corner of that island and of the neighbouring isle of Farne. He entered upon a new course of life by a pilgrimage to Jerusalem, and visited Compostella on his way home. After his return into Norfolk he accepted the position of house steward in the family of a very rich man.

St Godrick made a second pilgrimage to Jerusalem. Upon his return he spent some time in Streneshalch, now Whitby, then went to Durham to the shrine of St Cuthbert. For several years before his death he was confined to his bed by sickness and old age. William of Newbridge, who visited him during that time, tells us that though his body appeared dead, his face held a wonderful dignity. His body was buried in the chapel of St John Baptist.

The following feasts are also celebrated today:
St Felix of Cantalicio, of poor parentage, he was from his infancy, called "the saint": St Hospitius, commonly called Sospis, a recluse in Provence. He lived on bread and dates only, in an old tower, girded with a iron chain, and was gifted with prophecy and miracles.

May 22
SAINT YVO
Confessor – AD 1303

St Yvo Helori, or son of Helor, descended from a noble and virtuous family near Treguier in Brittany, was born in 1253. He studied at home and at fourteen years of age was sent to Paris. His mother would frequently say to him that he ought to become a saint to which his answer always was that he hoped to be one. During his ten years' stay at Paris, where he studied theology and canon law, he was the admiration of the university. He made a private vow of perpetual chastity; but this not being known, many honourable matches were proposed to him.

Maurice the Archdeacon of Rennes, appointed him official or ecclesiastical judge for that diocese. St Yvo protected the orphans and widows, defended the poor, and administered justice to all. He was known as the advocate and lawyer of the poor and never took a fee, but pleaded all causes without any gratuity. He preached often in distant churches, sometimes five times on the same day. He built a house near his own for a hospital of the poor and sick.

He distributed his corn or the price for which he sold it, among the poor immediately after the harvest. When a certain person endeavoured to persuade him to keep it some months that he might sell it at a better price, he answered, "I know not whether I shall be then alive to give it." Another time the same person said to him, "I have gained a fifth by keeping my corn." "But I," replied the saint, " a hundredfold by giving it immediately away." On a certain occasion when he had only one loaf in his house he ordered it to be given to the poor; but upon his vicar's complaint at this he gave him one half of it and divided the other half among the poor, reserving nothing for himself. His death happened on 19 May 1303. The greatest part of his relics are kept in the cathedral of Treguier.

The following feasts are also celebrated today:

St Basiliscus, martyred with St Lucia in 312: **St Bobo**, a gentleman of Provence, a great soldier, the father of the poor and the defender of his country against the Saracens: he died while on a pilgrimage to Rome in 985: **St Castus** and **St Æmilius**, martyrs who had at first failed to stand true in the persecution: **St Conall**, Abbot in Ireland, honoured in a large parish in the County Tyrconnel with great devotion; his church and well are visited by many pilgrims: **St Rita**, widow.

May 23
SAINT JULIA
Virgin and Martyr

St Julia was a noble virgin at Carthage who, when that city was taken by Genseric in 439, was sold for a slave to a pagan merchant of Syria. She was a Christian and he found her so diligent and faithful he could not part with her. Felix, the governor, offered him four of his best female slaves in exchange for her. But the merchant, whose name was Eusebius, replied, "No; all you are worth will not purchase her; for I would freely lose the most valuable thing I have in the world rather than be deprived of her."

However, the governor, whilst Eusebius was drunk and asleep, proffered her liberty if she would make a sacrifice to his pagan gods. The saint answered that she was as free as she desired to be as long as she was allowed to serve Jesus Christ. Felix, in a rage, struck her on the face and tore the hair from her head and ordered her to be hanged on a cross till she died. Monks of the isle of Gorgon (which is now called La Gorgona and lies between Corsica and Leghorn) carried off her body; but in 763 Desiderius, King of Lombardy, removed her relics to Brescia, where her memory is celebrated with great devotion.

The following feasts are also celebrated today:
St Desiderius, Bishop of Langres: **St John Baptist de Rosse** spent his life working among the poor and the suffering, and died in 1764.

May 24
SAINT VINCENT OF LERINS
Confessor – AD 450

St Vincent was of Gaulish extraction and was for some time an officer in the army. Having been tossed about in the storms of a bustling military life, he wanted to take shelter in the harbour of religion, which he called the safest refuge in the world.

The place he chose for his retirement was in a small remote island sheltered from the noise of the world. This was the monastery of Lerins, situated not far from the coast of Lower Provence towards Antibes. In this place he shut himself up that he might consider what is necessary to salvation. He then wrote a book which he entitled *A Commonitory against Heretics*, which he composed in 434, three years after the general council of Ephesus.

He disguised himself under the name of Peregrinus, to express the quality of being a pilgrim or stranger on earth and styled himself, "The least of all the servants of God". St Vincent died in the year 450. His relics are preserved with respect at Lerins.

The following feasts are also celebrated today:
St Donatian and **St Rogatian**, martyrs; these were two noblemen, brothers, Donatian being first baptized and Rogatian baptized in his blood by following the example of his brother in refusing to sacrifice to Jupiter and Apollo: **St John de Prado**, was sent to preach the gospel in Morocco, imprisoned, scourged and finally burnt. **St Mary Magdalen Postel**, virgin.

The gem cannot be polished without friction,
nor man perfected without trials.

May 25
SAINT GREGORY VII
Pope, Confessor, called Hildebrand – AD 1085

St Gregory was born in Tuscany and educated at Rome. He went afterwards into France to the monastery at Cluni. Pope St Leo IX ordained him subdeacon, and made him Abbot of St Paul's which church then belonged to a very small community of monks and lay at that time almost in ruins. In 1054 he was sent by Pope Victor II into France.

In 1073 he was elected Pope. Before his ordination he wrote to the pious countesses, Beatrice and Mathilda, advising them not to communicate with those bishops of Lombardy who had been buying and selling church property through King Henry.

The pope deposed Godfrey, Archbishop of Milan, for stealing from the church. He excommunicated Cencius, a rich and powerful nobleman of Rome for the same offence.

But the storm was not over. Henry wrote to the pope in the style of a humble penitent, condemning himself for having stolen from the church. The pope, on his side, sent him obliging and tender letters.

When Henry continued to repeat the same crimes, Gregory, in a council at Rome, declared the king excommunicated. Henry then set up Guibert, the excommunicated Archbishop of Ravenna, for antipope; and in 1084 entered Rome with an army and besieged St Gregory in the castle St Angelo, but was forced by Robert Guiscard the Norman, Duke of Calabria, to retreat.

His army was overthrown by the Tuscans at Lombardy. Duke Robert, having rescued him from his enemies, conducted him for greater safety from Rome to Monte Cassino and then to Salerno, where falling sick, he died.

The following feasts are also celebrated today:

St Aldhelm, Bishop, born among the West Saxons, educated by St Adrian at Canterbury and took the monastic habit under an Irish monk in a poor monastery at Malmesbury; later, as Bishop of Sherborne, a worthy successor to the apostles; his festival is kept in England on 29 May: **St Dumhade of Ireland**, abbot, who being made Abbot of St Columkille's great monastery, introduced the Roman way of celebrating Easter: **St Madeleine Sophie Barat**, virgin: **St Mary Magdalen of Pazzi**; devoted to prayer and penance from her childhood, she became a Carmelite nun in 1582: **St Maximum** and **St Venerand**, martyrs, said to have been brothers, natives of Brescia, martyred in Normandy: **St Urban**, Pope and martyr.

May 26
SAINT PHILIP NERI
Founder of the Oratorians – AD 1595

Philip, Filippo Neri, the "Apostle of Rome", was not actually a Roman at all. He was a Florentine and was born on 22 July 1515, when Florence was still a republic. His parents were proverbially honest but poor, and his education was entrusted to the Dominican friars of San Marco, who still cherished the memory of their most famous preacher Girolamo Savonarola.

He it was who had set the city alight with his lively prophecies, his warnings of coming troubles, his fierce republicanism determined to prevent the tyrannical Medici family from returning to power. But he, too, it was who taught the youth of Florence to turn away from frivolity and pride and devote themselves to prayer and helping the poor. "All the good in me," Philip was to say later, "came from the friars of San Marco."

In 1530 the Medici, supported by foreign armies, returned to power and the republic of Florence was extinguished for ever. Soon after this Philip left his home and travelled south to Monte Cassino to learn business under an uncle who was intending to make Philip his heir.

He was never to see Florence or his family again. But business was clearly not Philip's vocation. His stay in the neighbourhood of Monte Cassino was brief indeed and he was happier during his silent hours of prayer in a remote chapel, than in his uncle's counting house. He left home a second time, renounced his inheritance, and made his way alone to Rome, where he knew no one and had no prospects.

When he first settled in Rome he secured a room and a job with a Florentine compatriot, teaching his two sons in exchange for the basic necessities of life. In his spare time he would roam the streets talking to others of his age, particularly Florentines, encouraging them to look again at the practice of their religion, to consider what it was that God really required of them.

At night he would pray, spending hours in church porches or outside the city in the catacombs of San Sebastiano. It was here that he had a mysterious experience on 4 June 1544. It appeared to him, as he reluctantly told someone years later, as if a globe of fire had descended from heaven and penetrated his heart, so that ever since then he could feel his heart palpitating, enlarged throbbing with divine love. Certainly those who came close to him noticed these palpitations, and a post-mortem examination revealed that his heart was indeed grossly enlarged and had forced two ribs apart to make space.

Gradually he won a following of those who actually listened to him and began, like him, to want to do something worthwhile. In 1550 Philip's spiritual director decided it was time to persuade this remarkable youth to be ordained priest. He had attended a few lectures in Rome, and read quite a lot and prayed a very great deal, and with little further preparation he was ordained priest on 23 May 1551.

On ordination, Philip found a home in a community of priests attached to the church of San Girolamo della Carità. Philip continued much the same way of life as before his ordination, wandering the streets, meeting people, encouraging them to pray and to do something worthwhile.

They would come to his little room at San Girolamo, to listen to him talking, to pray and to sing, until Philip would send them off to the hospitals to do something worthwhile. Soon his room was not large enough, so he constructed a meeting place for them over the aisle of the church, a long room which they called the "oratory".

What was the secret that attracted so many to Philip? For many it was his unpredictability, his whimsical sense of humour, his ability to prick the bubble of self-importance. While always fastidiously clean and recognisable as a priest, he would often wear bizarre garments, a fur cape inside-out, huge white shoes, an old red shirt, a beggar's hat. What is more, he would make the more pompous and dignified of his followers do the like. For others it was his penetrative gift of spiritual direction that allured them. The people of Rome hardly knew how to react to him.

The community of Florentine merchants decided to ask him to take responsibility for their national church, San Giovanni dei Fiorentini. He agreed to send some of his followers, newly ordained priests, to live at San Giovanni and run the church. Leaving his home at San Girolamo in 1583, leading a long procession carrying all his domestic belongings through the streets (only his cat refused to move and Philip saw to it that she was looked after in San Girolamo for the rest of her life), he joined the others at San Giovanni.

Travellers from abroad would come to see the famous priest, and he would tease them by a display of eccentricity, by shaving half his beard off. Nevertheless all but the most superficial observers could see through him, and revered him as a saint while they loved him as a friend.

For the last few years he was seldom in good health, but kept his good spirits. He was well prepared and ready to die when the end came. It was the night after 25 May 1595, the feast of Corpus Christi, when his attendant came in to see why he was walking about. "Antonio," he said, "I'm on my way now," and within an hour he was dead.

The body enshrined in his own church of the Vallicella, has drawn a constant stream of pilgrims.

The following feasts are also celebrated today:
St Augustine, the Apostle of England: **St Elutharius**, Pope (176) a Greek by birth: **St Francis Geronimo**, S.J.: **St Quadratus**, Bishop of Athens, a disciple of the Apostles: **St Oduvald**, Abbot, a Scottish nobleman who entered the Abbey of Melrose.

May 27
SAINT BEDE
Confessor, Father of the Church – AD 735

Bede was sent as a young child to be educated at the monasteries of Wearmouth and Jarrow, where he studied under St Benedict Biscop and St Ceolfrith. He enrolled as a monk at Jarrow in 682 and was to spend the rest of his life there, travelling very little and little concerned with affairs of state or indeed any affairs beyond the churches and monasteries of Northumbria. He was a model brother, whose self-discipline, devotion and application were as notable as his scholarly achievements.

He was ordained in c703 by St John of Beverly: "Venerable" was a title commonly given to priests in the day and since monks were seldom ordained it became attached to Bede's name as a distinguishing feature. It was considered especially appropriate as a tribute to the saint's great learning, and was formally approved in 853 at the Council of Aachen.

Within the confines of his monastery, Bede's love of study and writing flourished and brought forth a remarkable literary harvest. He completed 25 works of biblical commentary, which he regarded as his most important work, several lives of the saints, scientific and theological treatises including a theory of music and several hymns, and works of orthography and chronology.

It is as an historian, however, that he is best remembered; his *Historic Ecclesiastic*, finished in 731, gives an account of the development of Christianity in England until Bede's day and is the single most valuable source for the history of the period, written in a highly readable style. In it Bede demonstrates a remarkably responsible historical approach, citing authorities and presenting, comparing and evaluating evidence, although it is inevitably limited as a historical document in some ways. Bede was also the first historian to use the convention "AD", signifying *anno Domini*. Unfortunately, his vernacular writings and translations, believed to have been among the first writings in Old English, are now lost.

His death was recorded by the monk Cuthbert, who tells how Bede pressed on with his translation of John's Gospel, dictating the last sentence just before his death, and he he died singing a Gloria. A cult began within five years of his death, with miracles reported at his relics, but there are few ancient dedications. After Pope Leo XIII recognized him as the only English Doctor of the church in 1899, several modern churches and schools were dedicated to him. He is shown in art studying peacefully among his books, often illuminated by light from heaven. Bede is also the only Englishman mentioned by Dante in his *Paradiso*.

The following feasts are also celebrated today:
St John, Pope, 523-526; by birth a Tuscan: **St Julius**, a veteran soldier, martyred about 302, in the reign of Diocletian.

May 28
SAINT GERMANUS
Confessor, Bishop of Paris – AD 576

St Germanus was brought up under the care of Scapilion, his cousin, a holy priest. In his youth no weather could divert him from going to church a mile from his home. Being ordained priest by St Agrippinus, Bishop of Autun, he was made Abbot of St Symphorian's in the suburbs of that city.

Fortunatus, Bishop of Poiters, who was well acquainted with our saint, tells us that he was favoured at that time with the gifts of miracles and prophecy. One night, in a dream, he thought a venerable old man presented him with the keys of the city of Paris and said to him that God committed to his care the inhabitants of that city that he should save them from perishing.

Four years after this he was made Bishop of Paris. His house was perpetually crowded with the poor and the afflicted, and he had always many beggars at his table. He took care that the souls of his guests should be refreshed at the same time as their bodies by reading from some pious book. King Childebert, in gratitude gave to the church of Paris and the Bishop Germanus the land of Celles. The good king did not long survive.

Upon the death of Charibert in 570, his three brothers divided his dominions; but not being able to agree who should be master of Paris, the capital, came to an agreement that they should hold it jointly. St Germanus found his church in great difficulties and the city divided into three different parties always plotting and counterplotting against one another.

St Germanus did not live to see the miserable end of these feuds. He died in 576. He was buried in St Symphorian's chapel, which he built at the bottom of the church of St Vincent.

The relics of St Germanus remained in the chapel until the year 754, when the abbot removed them into the body of the church.

The following feasts are also celebrated today:
St Caraunus or **Caro** (in French, **Cheron**): **St John Shirt**: **St Margaret Pole**, Countess of Salisbury: **St Robert Johnson**, English martyrs.

Life is real! Life is earnest!
And the grave is not its goal;
Dust thou art, to dust returnest,
Was not spoken of the soul.

Not enjoyment, and not sorrow,
Is our destined end or way;
But to act, that each to-morrow
Finds us farther than to-day.

Lives of great men all remind us
We can make our lives sublime,
And, departing, leave behind us
Footprints on the sands of time;

Footprints, that perhaps another,
Sailing o'er life's solemn main,
A forlorn and shipwrecked brother,
Seeing, shall take heart again.

Henry Wadsworth Longfellow

May 29
The following feasts are celebrated today:

St Conon and his Son, martyrs, of Iconia in Asia; both being stretched on a burning grid-iron, they remained steadfast to the end; their death took place about 275: **St Cyril**, a child martyr: **St Maximinus**, holy from his childhood, chosen to succeed St Agritius, Bishop of Triers; he received St Athanasius when he was banished to that place: **St Sisinnius**, **St Martyrius** and **St Alexander**, martyrs in the territory of Trent. The two last named were brothers. Beaten with clubs by the pagans, Sisinnius died in a few hours; Martyrius underwent great hardships; and Alexander, still as steadfast as the others had been, was finally burned alive in the same fire as the dead bodies of his fellow-martyrs.

May 30
SAINT JOAN OF ARC
The Maid of Orléans – AD 1431

Youngest of the five children of Jacques d'Arc, a peasant farmer, from her earliest days Joan was exceptional for her piety. She was only 13 when she first heard her famous "voices", accompanied by brilliant light, which instructed her to serve the Dauphin and save France. She identified them as messages from Saints Michael, Catherine of Alexandria and Margaret of Antioch, but despite her conviction her attempts to join the French army were met by scepticism and derision.

She persisted, and after her prophecies of defeat were fulfilled at the Battle of Herrings in 1429, Robert de Baudricourt, commander at Vaucouleurs, sent her to the Dauphin, to whom she proved herself by seeing through his disguise. A group of theologians at Poitiers cross-examined her for three weeks and finally gave their approval to this remarkable girl and her mission.

Joan's first expedition was to relieve besieged Orléans; in April 1429, clad in a suit of white armour, she led her troops and saved the city, capturing several English forts, her men inspired by her visionary courage. In June of that year she secured another important victory over the English troops, capturing Troyes. When the Dauphin was crowned Charles VII at Rheims on 17 July 1429 Joan stood at his side, but even at the pinnacle of her achievement she suffered mockery and suspicion among courtiers, clergy and soldiers.

Still Joan continued to lead the army. A mission to recapture Paris in August failed and the winter months enforced idleness, but in the following spring she set out to relieve Compiègne, besieged by Burgundy, the ally of the English. She was captured there in May and handed over to the English, as

Charles made no effort to save her. In Rouen, Joan was charged with witchcraft and heresy; although she defended herself intelligently and steadfastly she was inevitably convicted. By some means of trickery or force she was persuaded to recant (the exact terms of this are a matter for debate) but when she defiantly resumed the male attire she had promised to abandon she was declared a heretic and burnt at the stake in the market-place of Rouen on 30 May. Her ashes were thrown into the Seine.

Twenty years later the case was reopened by a commission of Callistus III. They reached a verdict of innocent, but it was not until 1920 that Joan was canonized by Benedict XV. She is venerated as a virgin rather than a martyr. Joan has appealed to secular and literary minds as well as the pious, and many attempts have been made to explain her "voices" and her significance as a patriot and as a woman in a male-dominated world. Her romantic life has inspired many artists, who usually portray her as a maiden in armour.

The following feasts are also celebrated today:
St Felix I, Pope and martyr, succeeded St Dionysius in 269: **St Ferdinand III**, King of Castile: **St Maguil** or **Madelgisilus**, a recluse in Picardy said to have been the inseparable companion of St Fursey: **St Walstan**, formerly much honoured in two villages near Norwich: **St John Nepomucen**.

May 31
MARY, BLESSED VIRGIN
The mother of God

All the factual information which we have of Mary's life is found in the New Testament, particularly in the nativity accounts in the Gospels of Matthew and Luke in which the divinity of Jesus, the virginity of Mary, and her obedience to God are all emphasized. Luke's account in particular is written from Mary's point of view. Nothing is known of her parentage or place of birth, although tradition has her as the daughter of Anne and Joachim. Although Jesus's ancestry is traced in the Gospel accounts through Joseph, it is assumed that Mary was of the same family.

Mary was living in Nazareth when she was visited by the archangel Gabriel, who announced the incredible news of the Incarnation and Mary's part in God's plan, which she accepted simply and obediently. Her fiancé, Joseph, who had planned to dissolve the engagement quietly on hearing of Mary's pregnancy, was also visited and reassured by an angel and the marriage went ahead.

Soon afterwards Mary visited Elizabeth, then pregnant with John the Baptist, and on hearing Elizabeth greet her as the mother of God, Mary expressed her thanks by singing the Magnificat.

She and Joseph were visiting Bethlehem for the census when Jesus was born; afterwards they were forced to flee to Egypt to avoid the jealous anger of King Herod, who had been told of the recent birth of a king of the Jews. After their enemy's death they settled in Nazareth, and little more is known of Jesus's early life beyond a journey to Jerusalem for Passover, when he was left behind only to be found by his distraught parents in learned discussion with the Jewish teachers in the temple.

According to John's Gospel it was Mary who prompted Jesus to perform his first miracle, the changing of water into wine at the wedding of Cana. After this she is mentioned as the mother of Jesus several times but does not feature in the gospel accounts until the crucifixion, when Jesus entrusts her into the care of John the Evangelist as they stand at the foot of his cross.

Presumably Mary lived in John's household after this. She was with the apostles at Pentecost but, as during Jesus's lifetime, her role in the early church was so much one of quiet support that it is difficult to know exactly where or how she lived, or when she died. Jerusalem and Ephesus both claim to have been the place of her death; in the eastern tradition the claim of Jerusalem is generally favoured.

The doctrine of Mary's bodily assumption into heaven (declared dogma by Pope Pius XII in 1950) is ancient, widely accepted at least from the sixth century, and from this time her role as intercessor in heaven has been increasingly emphasized. She is believed to have been the only human free from Original Sin from her conception (the doctrine of the Immaculate Conception was declared dogma in 1854 by Pope Pius IX), although this belief, unlike that of the Assumption, was challenged by various members of the medieval church including the Dominicans and Thomas Aquinas.

She is traditionally believed by Catholics to have remained a virgin after the birth of Jesus, and so is unique in her role as model of both virgin and mother. In one popular analogy she is seen as the second Eve, whose purity and obedience to God enabled the second Adam, Christ, to sacrifice himself and redeem mankind.

Mary was a figure with whom the suffering could readily identify, whose humanity they could love, and her unique position as fully human yet closer to God than any other saint or angel made her an obvious choice for intercessory prayer. The second Vatican Council provided a doctrinal statement on Mary which insists on her dependence upon and subordination to her Son, and shows her as a model for the Church.

Byzantine art characteristically presents Mary formally, as a crowned and sceptred queen, but in the Renaissance much emphasis was placed upon her humanity and compassion. The stylised medieval portraits gave way to more tender, realistic depiction of the Virgin with her child, or most poignantly, with her crucified Son. The most famous examples of these are the Pietàs of Michelangelo.

The iconography of Mary is complex and laden with significance, embracing almost the entire history of the Christian church.

Many feast-days are devoted to Mary, several of which have recently been reduced: 1 January is the celebration of Mary's part in the Incarnation and Redemption, 31 May is devoted to the Visitation, and the Annunciation is celebrated on 25 March. The purification of Christ in the Temple, commonly known as Candlemas, is on 2 February, Our Lady of Sorrows on 15 September and devotion to the Immaculate Heart of Mary falls on the Saturday following the second Sunday of Pentecost. It was under this title that Pope Pius XII dedicated the entire human race to her in 1944.

She has been claimed as patron in various capacities by countless organisations, countries and groups. There have been several reported visions of Mary, most notably at Lourdes, Fatima, Medjugorje and La Salette. Some genuine and many less reliable mystics have claimed inspiration or direction from Mary, but those who appear to have been genuinely guided tend to exhibit a tranquil strength of purpose rather than a religious hysteria. Patron saint of the entire human race.

The following feasts are also celebrated today:
St Angela Merici, virgin, founder of the Ursulines: **St Cantius** and **St Cantianus**, and their sister **St Cantianilla**, martyred together with **Protus**, their pious Christian teacher in 304 for refusing to conform to the orders of the emperor Diocletian: **St Gabriel Possenti,** C.P.: **St Petronilla**, virgin.

June 1
The following feasts are celebrated today:
St Caprais, Abbot, the spiritual guide of St Honoratus; he died soon after him in the Isle of Lerins, 430: **St John Storey**, chancellor of the Dioceses of London and Oxford under Queen Mary, martyr: **St Justin**, the philosopher: **St Pamphilus**, priest and martyr: **St Peter of Pisa**, founder of the Hermits of St Jerome: **St Wistan**, martyr, Prince of Mercia, killed by a rival claimant to his father's throne.

June 2
SAINT ERASMUS (ELMO)
AD c303

He was a bishop of Formiæ in the Campagna in Italy and was probably martyred during the persecutions of Diocletian. By confusion with another martyr, one Erasmus of Antioch, his legend claims that he was a Syrian, who fled to Mount Lebano during the persecutions to live as a hermit. His hiding place was discovered and he was brought before the Emperor, beaten, covered in pitch and set ablaze. Miraculously he survived unhurt, and was imprisoned only to be released by an angel and taken to preach in Illyricum. Here he carried on with his work of preaching and teaching. The number of his converts was so great that he was soon discovered anew and underwent more torture. Once again he was delivered by an angel, this time to Formiæ, where he died of his wounds.

As Erasmus had proved immune to the various tortures to which he had been subjected in the past, a popular legend developed which claimed that a new and particularly grisly death had been devised for him. The saint was cut open at the stomach and his entrails were wound out while he was still alive. This torture legend is the source of his patronage of those suffering from stomach pains. His relics were supposedly translated to Gaeta when Formiæ was attacked by Saracens in 842, and he is invoked as patron there.

His emblem in art is a windlass; this has been variously explained as a symbol of his patronage of sailors, which grew from a legend that he was unafraid of a violent storm, refusing to stop preaching even when a thunderbolt landed beside him, or as the instrument of torture with which his entrails were wound out which was then mistaken for a nautical capstan, whence his patronage of sailors began. The phenomenon of lights which sometimes appear at the mastheads of ships after a storm, caused by electrical discharge, was known as St Elmo's fire, by Neapolitan sailors, since it was believed to be a sign of the saint's protection through the time of danger. Patron saint of sailors, invoked against birth-pains, colic and danger at sea.

The following feasts are also celebrated today:
St Marcellinus and **St Peter**, of Rome: **St Pothinus**, Bishop, **St Sanctus**, deacon, **St Attalus**, **St Blandina** and the other martyrs of Lyons.

June 3
ST CLOTILDIS, OR CLOTILDA
Queen of France

Clotildis was daughter of Chilperic, younger brother to Gondebald, the king of Burgundy, who put him, his wife and his brothers to death in order to usurp their dominions. In this massacre he spared Chilperic's two daughters, then in their infancy. One of them became a nun; the other named Clotildis, was brought up in her uncle's court. Her wit, beauty, and piety made her the adoration of all the neighbouring kingdoms, when Clovis I, surnamed the Great, king of the Franks, asked for her in marriage. The marriage was solemnized at Soissons in 493. Clotildis made herself a little oratory in the royal palace in which she spent much time in fervent prayer. She honoured her royal husband and tried to sweeten his warlike temper by meekness.

His miraculous victory over the Alemanni and his conversion to Christianity in 496 were the fruit of our saint's prayers. He built, in Paris, at her request, about the year 511, the great Church of SS. Peter and Paul, now called St Genevieve's. He sent his royal diadem, which is called to this day The Realm, as a present to Pope Hormisdas. He died on the 27th of November in the year 511, having reigned thirty years.

As to the three sons of Clotildis, Clodomir reigned at Orleans, Childebert at Paris and Clotaire I at Soissons. This division produced wars and jealousies, till in 560 the whole monarchy was reunited under Clotaire, the youngest of these brothers.

She spent part of her life at Tours, near the tomb of St Martin, in prayer, almsdeeds, fasting and penance, seeming totally to forget that she had been a queen or that her sons sat on the throne. She foretold her death thirty days before it happened. She died in 545 and is buried in the Church of St Genevieve.

The following feasts are also celebrated today:
St Cecilius: **St Coeingen** or **Keivin**, Bishop in Ireland, baptized by St Cronin, died on this date, 618, aged one hundred and twenty years: **St Genesius**, in French **Genes**, founded a great hospital at Clermont; Bishop of Auvergne and of Clermont, 656: **St Lifard**, Abbot near Orleans; many churches about Orleans are dedicated to him.

June 4
The following feasts are celebrated today:
St Breaca of Ireland (now **Breague**), virgin, a disciple of St Patrick: **St Burian**, an Irish-woman, to honour whose relics King Athelstan built a college which enjoyed the privilege of sanctuary: **St Francis Caracciolo**, 1563(?)-1608: **St Nenook** or **Nennoca**, who directed many other holy virgins in the path of sanctity: **St Petroc**, in French **Perreuse**, a native of Wales; he passed twenty years in Ireland, then went to Rome; returning to Cornwall, he founded a monastery there: **St Optatus**, an African, bishop of Milevum: **St Quirinus**: **St Walter**, Abbot, a native of Rome and another **St Walter**, an Englishman, thirty-fourth Abbot of Fontenelle; he died in 1140.

A saint, whose name I have forgotten, had a vision, in which he saw Satan standing before the throne of God; and, listening, he heard the evil spirit say, "Why hast Thou condemned me, who have offended Thee but once, whilst Thou savest thousands of souls who have offended Thee many times?" God answered him, "Hast thou once asked pardon of me?"

Behold the Christian mythology! What matter whether the saint had or had not heard the sublime words which I have just quoted! The great point is to know that pardon is refused only to him who does not ask it.

COUNT DE MAISTRE

June 5
ST BONIFACE
Archbishop of Mainz, Apostle of Germany and Martyr – AD 755

An Anglo-Saxon peasant born in Devon and christened Wynfrith, the young Boniface (as he later called himself) attended the Benedictine school in Exeter and later at Nursling. He became director of the abbey school there, and wrote the first Latin grammar ever produced in England and was ordained at the age of 39.

But in 715 Boniface decided to leave England for the mission field; he followed Wilfred and Willisbrord into Frisia but was soon forced to return after conflict with the strong pagan tribes there. He was offered the post of abbot in Nursling in 717 but he was committed to the mission and left the next year for Bavaria and Hesse. He was consecrated bishop back in Rome in 722 and then returned to Hesse.

He continued founding monasteries and bishopics throughout Germany, including Bavaria. He and his companions were attacked on 5 June. Boniface's body was buried in the abbey he had founded at Fulda. Patron saint of brewers and tailors.

The following feasts are also celebrated today:
St Dorotheus of Tyre, martyr, suffered for the faith but survived his torments and lived to the time of Julian the Apostate: **St Dorotheus**, an Egyptian surnamed The Theban: **St Illidius**, fourth Bishop of Clermont.

June 6
The following feasts are celebrated today:
St Claude, Archbishop of Besançon: **St Gudwall**, Bishop, born in Cornwall: **St Jarlath**, who studied under St Benignus; honoured at the Patron of Tuam in Ireland: **St Norbert**, Archbishop of Madgebourg: **St Philip the Deacon**.

June 7
The following feasts are celebrated today:
St Colman, Bishop of Dromore: **St Godeschalc**, prince of the Western Vandals: **St Meriadec**, Bishop of Vannes, died about 1302: **St Paul**, Bishop of Constantinople: **St Robert**, Abbot of Newminster, a Cistercian monastery in Northumberland: **St Willibald**, brother of St Walburga.

The good we do today
becomes the happiness of tomorrow.

June 8
The following feasts are celebrated today:
St Clou or **Clodulphus**, Bishop of Metz, a son of St Arnold: **St Gildard** or **Godard**, Bishop of Rouen, commemorated with St Medard: **St Maximinus**, first Archbishop of Aix in Provence: **St Medard**, Bishop of Noyon, one of the most illustrious prelates in France in the sixth century: **St Syra** of Ireland, virgin, sister to St Fiacre: **St William**, Archbishop of York.

June 9
ST COLUMBA OR COLUMKILLE,
Abbot – AD 597

St Columba, commonly pronounced Colme, was one of the greatest patriarchs of the monastic order in Ireland, and the apostle of the Picts. To distinguish him from other saints of the same name he was surnamed Columkille, from the great number of monastic cells, called by the Irish Killes, of which he was the founder. He was of the most noble extraction from Neil, and was born at Gartan in the county of Tyrconnel, in 521.

He learned the scriptures and the lessons of an ascetic life under the bishop St Finian, in his school of Cluain-iraid. Being advanced to the priesthood in 546, he began to give lessons of piety and sacred learning, and in a short time formed many disciples. He founded, c550, the monastery of Dairmagh, now called Durrough, which original name signified Field of Oaks, and besides many smaller, those of Doire or Derry, in Ulster, and of Sord or Swords, near Dublin.

The holy abbot left his native country and went to Scotland. He took along with him twelve disciples and arrived there in 565. The Picts gave St Columba the little island of Iona twelve miles from the land in which he built the great monastery which was for several ages the chief seminary of North Britain and continued long the burying-place of the kings of Scotland. Out of this nursery St Columba founded several other monasteries in Scotland. In the same school were educated the holy bishops Aidan, Finian, and Colman.

St Columba's manner of living was always most austere. He lay on the bare floor with a stone for his pillow, and never interrupted his fast. Such was his fervour that in whatever he did he seemed to exceed the strength of man. He was of such authority that neither king nor people did anything without his consent. When King Aedhan, or Aidanus, succeeded to the throne of Scotland in 574, he received the royal insignia from St Columba. Having continued his labours in Scotland thirty-four years, he clearly and openly foretold his death. His body was buried in the island of Iona, afterwards removed to Down, in Ulster, and laid in one vault with the remains of St Patrick and St Brigit. He was honoured both in Ireland and Scotland among the principal patrons of those countries.

The following feasts are also celebrated today:
St Pelagia, virgin and martyr in Antioch: St Richard, first Bishop of Andrea in Apulia, an Englishman illustrious for eminent holiness and for miracles: St Primus and St Felicianus, brother-martyrs who escaped the dangers of many persecutions in Rome: St Vincent, probably a deacon, martyred in Agenois.

June 10
The following feasts are celebrated today:
St Getulius, his brother Amancius and St Cerealus: St Landry, Bishop of Paris about 650, buried in the church of St Germain l'Auxerrois: St Margaret, Queen of Scotland, wife of Malcolm III, famed for her boundless charity.

June 11
SAINT BARNABAS
Apostle

Barnabas was a Cypriot Jew originally named Joseph, but when he sold his possessions to live with the early Christian community in Jerusalem the apostles gave him the name "Barnabas", meaning "son of consolation".

After Paul's unexpected conversion, it was Barnabas who persuaded the nervous apostles to trust their old enemy. Barnabas was chosen to encourage and instruct the young church at Antioch, and feeling the need of assistance in this enormous task he brought Paul from Tarsus to help him.

The two spent a year at Antioch preaching and establishing the practices of the growing church along apostolic lines, and it was during this time that the adherents of the new faith became known as "Christians". From Antioch they went together on Paul's first missionary journey, beginning in Cyprus, with Barnabas's cousin, John Mark. Barnabas proposed that John Mark accompany them on a second missionary journey, revisiting several of the same cities of Galatia: as Mark had left them in Perga on their first journey to return home, however, Paul objected. A breach between the two seems to have resulted, with Paul going on to Phillippi and Corinth while Barnabas returned to Cyprus with John Mark.

He went on to preach in Alexandria and Rome, becoming bishop in Milan before martyrdom by stoning in Salamis, the Cyprian port in c61. He is traditionally believed to have been reconciled with Paul before his death.

In ecclesiastical art Barnabas is shown as a middle-aged, bearded apostle, often holding a book and an olive branch, and frequently in company with Paul. The tradition of invoking his protection from hailstorms presumably arises from his association with death by stoning.

The following feast is also celebrated today:

St Tochumra in Ireland, virgin, titular saint of Tochumra in Munster and another Irish saint of this name in Kilmore, also much honoured in Ireland and invoked by women in labour.

June 12
SAINT JOHN OF SAHAGUN
Confessor, Hermit of the Order of St Augustine – AD 1479

St John, son of John Gonzales of Castrillo, was a native of Sahagun or St Fagondez, in the kingdom of Leon in Spain. He went through the course of his studies in the schools of the Benedictine monks of St Fagondez.

He lived in the strictest evangelical poverty and mortification. Having at length obtained his bishop's consent, he went to Salamanca, where he applied himself during four years to the study of theology. After which he attended the care of souls in the parish church of St Sebastian. In 1463, as soon as he had recovered his health after an operation, he joined the hermits of St Austin, in Salamanca.

In 1471 he was chosen prior of his convent, which was a house famous for the severity of its discipline. A certain duke, whom he had exasperated by his charitable sermons, sent two assassins to murder him; but at the sight of the holy man, the assassins were struck with remorse, and casting themselves at his feet begged pardon for their crime. The duke, falling sick, repented and recovered his health. St John died in 1479.

The following feasts are also celebrated today:

St Basilides, **St Quirinus**, **St Nabor** and **St Nazarius**, martyrs; they were soldiers in the army of Maxentius: **St Eskill**, Bishop and martyr in Sweden, an Englishman by birth: **St Onuphrius**, lived in an austere monastery of one hundred monks, near Thebes, but, desiring to imitate St John the Baptist, he became a hermit and lived sixty years retired from the world: **St Ternan**, Bishop of the Picts.

Life

Life is too swift
Between the blossom and the white snow's drift,
Between the silence and the lark's uplift,
For bitter words.
In kindness and in gentleness our speech
Must carry messages of hope, and reach
The sweeter chords.

Margaret E. Sangster

June 13
SAINT ANTONY OF PADUA
Confessor – AD 1231

Son of a Portuguese knight, Antony grew up in Lisbon and was educated at the cathedral there. At 15 he enrolled with the nearby Canons Regular of St Augustine but left after only two years to finish his studies at Coimbra.

After ordination in c1220 he joined the Franciscans, and took the name of Antony. Illness compelled him to quit Morocco and the evangelizing of the Moors, and on the voyage back his ship was driven off course to Messina, Sicily. He travelled from there to Assisi, where the Franciscan General Chapter of 1221 was taking place.

At the end of the Chapter, Antony was assigned to the small hermitage of San Paolo near Forli, and his enormous talent was first discovered when he was called on unexpectedly to speak at an ordination in Forli.

Amazed by the power of his preaching, his provincial minister appointed him the first lector in theology of the Franciscans and commissioned him to preach throughout Italy.

Thousands flocked to hear this short man denouncing sin and heresy with his resounding voice, crowds broke down in penitence, churches were too small to contain the hordes and he was obliged to speak in market places, when the townsfolk would frequently close up their businesses to go and hear him.

He died at a Poor Clare convent on the outskirts of Padua, aged only 36, was canonized within the year and in 1946 was declared a Doctor of the Church by Pius XII.

His shrine at Padua is notorious for miracles, and he is frequently known as "the wonder-worker", especially as the patron saint of lost objects; one legend tells how a novice who secretly borrowed his psalter returned it in terror after a warning apparition.

The 19th-century devotion "St Antony's Bread", alms given to the poor and hungry, reflects his social concern and exists as a fund today. Modern representations of St Antony often make reference to his vision of Jesus by showing the Christ-child seated on Antony's book, or to the legend that he once preached to fish, or with sheaves of corn, recalling his traditional status as patron saint of harvests.

As patron of lower animals he is often shown with a donkey. Patron saint of Portugal.

The following feast is also celebrated today:
St Damhnade, virgin in Ireland famed for her extraordinary gift of miracles, titular saint of Fermanagh.

June 14
SAINT BASIL THE GREAT
Confessor, Archbishop of Cæsarea – AD 379

St Basil the Great was born towards the close of the year 329 at Cæsarea, the metropolis of Cappadocia. His parents were Cappadocians by birth. Our saint's father, St Basil the Elder, and his wife, St Emmelia, was blessed with ten children, four sons and five daughters. Th eldest among the boys was St Basil; the other three were Naucratius, St Gregory of Nyssa and St Peter of Sebaste. St Basil who first met St Gregory Nazianzen at Cæsarea in 352, was overjoyed to find a friend at Athens. Basil and Nazianzen applied themselves to study. St Basil excelled in philosophy and every branch of literature. Leaving St Gregory, he went from Athens in 355 to Cæsarea, where he opened a school of oratory.

In 357 St Basil travelled over Syria, Mesopotamia and Egypt, and visited the monasteries and hermits of the deserts in those countries. In 358 he returned into Cappadocia, and was ordained Reader by Dianæus, the old Bishop of Cæsarea, by whom he had formerly been baptized. The saint left Cappadocia in 358 and went to Pontus to the house of his grandmother, situated on the banks of the river Iris. His mother Emmelia and his sister Macrina had there founded a nunnery. St Basil established a monastery of men on the opposite side of the river, which he governed for five years till 362. St Basil founded several other monasteries, both of men and women, in different parts of Pontus, which he continued to superintend even when he was bishop.

The saint himself testifies that he treated his body as a slave which was ever ready to revolt unless continually kept under control. About the year 359 he sold the remainder of his estate for the benefit of the poor during a great famine. He lived in the greatest poverty possible. It was his riches to have no earthly goods.

In 362 St Basil taking with him some of his monks, returned to Cæsarea in Cappadocia. Our saint continued in the same manner of life in the city which he had led in the desert, except that to his other labours he added that of preaching. He erected there a monastery for men and another for women. Eusebius, the bishop, who stood in need of such a prudent assistant, had for that purpose raised him to the priesthood.

When violent hail and storms had destroyed the harvest, and a famine filled the country with desolation, the poor in their extreme necessity found relief in the boundless charity of Basil who opened for their supply the coffers of the rich. He distributed among them bread and other provisions.

By his prudence and charity he won the affection of Eusebius who died in 370 in the arms of Basil. Later the saint was chosen and consecrated archbishop of Cæsarea. Besides his other excessive charities he founded a vast hospital, which Nazianzen calls a new city. He frequently visited it, comforted the patients, instructed and preached to them.

St Basil fell sick in 378 and it seemed the whole city in the utmost grief resorted to his house. He died on 1st of January 379. His riches he had sent before him to heaven, and he did not leave enough for a tombstone; but the people not only erected an everlasting monument for him in their hearts, but also honoured him with a funeral magnificent to the last degree.

The following feasts are also celebrated today:
St **Docmael**, honoured in Brittany under the name of St **Töel**: St **Methodius**, Patriarch: St **Nennus** or **Nehmias** of Ireland: St **Psalmodius** of Ireland: St **Rufinus** and St **Valerius**, overseers of the imperial taxes near the river Vesle in Soissons.

June 15
The following feasts are celebrated today:
St **Germaine Cousin**, virgin: St **Landelin**, Abbot, educated under St Aubert, Bishop of Cambray: St **Vauge** of Ireland, hermit: St **Vitus** or **Guy**, St **Crescentia** and St **Modestus**.

June 16
SAINT JOHN FRANCIS REGIS
Confessor of the Society of Jesus

He was born on the 31st of January in 1597 at Foncouverte, a village in Languedoc. His parents, John Regis, who was descended from a younger branch of the noble house of Deplas, in Rovergue, and Magdalen Darcis, daughter to the lord of Segur, were distinguished amongst the nobility of Lower Languedoc by their virtue.

His first master was one of a morose, hasty temper, under whom this modest and bashful child had much to suffer. The Jesuits having opened a public school at Beziers he was one of the first whom the reputation of its professors drew to the new college. His gravity increased with his years; he scarcely allowed himself any relaxation. In his eighteenth year he developed a dangerous sickness. Soon after his recovery he joined the Society of Jesus at Toulouse. Here the spirit of prayer accompanied all his actions.

After two years, in 1618, he was sent to Cahors to finish his rhetoric and the following year to Tournon on a course of philosophy. Having finished philosophy in 1621, he was sent to teach the schools of humanity at Billom, Auch, and Puy. After he had taught the lower classes seven years, two at Billom, one at Auch and four at Puy, he began the study of divinity at Toulouse in 1628. In the beginning of the year 1630, he prepared himself for holy orders.

The same year, Toulouse being afflicted with a violent plague, Francis made pressing instances to obtain leave to serve the sick. In 1631, after the course of his studies was over, he was obliged to go to Foncouverte to settle some family affairs, where he spent his time in visiting the poor and sick. His begging for the poor, going through the streets followed by crowds of them and children, and carrying upon his shoulders a fagot, a straw bed, or such-like things for them, drew on him many insults.

F Regis entered upon his apostolical course at Montpellier in 1631, arriving there in the beginning of summer, and immediately opening his mission. Towards winter he went to Sommiers, the capital of Lavonage, twelve miles from Montpellier, living chiefly on bread and water, taking sometimes a little milk, always abstaining from fish, flesh, eggs and wine; allowing himself very little rest at night on some hard bench or floor, and wearing a hair shirt. With a crucifix in his hand he boldly stopped a troop of enraged soldiers from plundering a church.

The remaining years of his life were taken up in missions in the Velay, a mountainous country; the winters in the villages, the summer in Puy. He preached at Puy, first in the church; but this being too little, he removed to that of St Peter le Monstiers. His audience usually consisted of four or five thousand. He set out early every morning into the country amidst the forests and mountains. When storms, rains, snows, or floods made the roads seem impassable to others, nothing ever stopped or daunted him. He went the whole day from cottage to cottage.

Understanding that his death was near at hand, he went back to Puy. He suffered much in crossing the mountains and the waters, and missed his way. Overtaken by night in the woods, and quite spent, he was forced to lie in a ruinous house, open on all sides, near the village of Veirines, on the ground, exposed to a piercing wind. Here his pain grew excessive. Next morning he crawled to La Louvese. The physicians found his case past recovery. He died towards midnight on the last day of the year 1640.

The following feasts are also celebrated today:
St Aurelian, Archbishop of Arles, founded a great monastery in that city, 546: **St Ferreolus**, a priest and **St Ferrutius**, a deacon, martyrs, ordained by St Ir

anæus: **St Quiricus** and **St Julitta**, the latter a Roman lady who was killed with her little son, aged three years, Quiricus or Cyr.

A man without money
is a poor man,
a man with only money
is poorer still.

June 17
The following feasts are celebrated today:

St Avitus or **Avy**, Abbot, whose happy death occurred about the year 530: **St Botolph** and **St Adulph**, two noble English brothers who travelled into the Belgic Gaul, where St Adulph became Bishop of Maastricht and St Botolph an Abbot greatly beloved as being "humble, mild and affable": **St Molingus**, alias **Dairchilla**, one of "the four prophets of Ireland": **St Nicander** and **St Marcian**, martyrs: **St Prior**, hermit, a native of Egypt and one of the first disciples of St Anthony.

June 18
SAINT EPHREM
Decon, Confessor and Doctor – AD 375

St Ephrem was born in Nisibis in Mesopotamia of a pagan family. When Ephrem became a Christian at the age of eighteen he was cast out of his paternal home by his father who was a pagan priest. Ephrem then became a monk and was ordained deacon. His humility caused him to refuse to be ordained a priest. He passed most of his life as a hermit, and practised severe penances. He refuted several heretical errors by writing poems and Christian hymns; for this he is called "the harp of the Holy Spirit".

The following feasts are also celebrated today:

St Amand, Bishop of Bordeaux, who had served God from his infancy; "a zealous guardian of religion and of the faith of Christ": **St Elizabeth**, Abbess of Sconauge, who, at twenty-two years old, began to be favoured with heavenly visions: **St Marcus** and **St Marcellianus**, martyrs: and **St Mariana** (or **Marina**?), virgin.

Prayer moves the Hand which moves the world.

June 19
The following feasts are celebrated today:

St Boniface, Archbishop and martyr, apostle of Russia: **St Die** or **Deodatus**, Bishop of Nevers, who, dreading the charge of others, lived in a little cell: **St Gervasius** and **St Protasius**, martyrs: **St Juliana Falconieri**.

In the game of life
it is better to score by honours
than by tricks.

June 20
SAINT SILVERIUS
Pope, Martyr – AD 538

Silverius was son of Pope Hormisdas, who had been married before he entered the ministry. Upon the death of St Agapetus, Silverius being then sub-deacon, was chosen pope, and ordained on 8 June 536.

Vitiges, the Goth, returned from Ravenna in 537 with an army of one hundred and fifty thousand men and invaded the city of Rome. The siege lasted a year and nine days. The pope was accused of corresponding during the siege with the enemy; and a letter was produced which was supposed to have been written by him to the King of the Goths, inviting him into the city and promising to open the gates to him.

Knowing it to be a forged letter, the general dropped the charge of treason, but entreated the pope to leave. Upon leaving the general's house he fled for sanctuary to the basilic of the martyr St Sabina; but a few days after, was summoned to the Pincian palace. He was admitted alone, and his clergy, whom he left at the door, saw him no more. He was stripped of his papal robes and clothed with that of a monk. After this it was proclaimed that the pope was deposed and had become a monk. His enemies saw themselves again masters. Two officers took him into a little inhospitable island of Palmeruelo. Here Silverius died of hunger.

The following feasts are also celebrated today:
St Bain, Bishop of Terouann, now St Omer: **St Gobain** of Ireland, ordained by St Fursey, martyred in France: **St Idaberga** or **Edberge**, one of many saints belonging to the family of Penda, King of Mercia.

June 21
SAINT ALOYSIUS (OR LEWIS) GONZAGA
Confessor – AD 1587

Born on 9 March in the family castle in Lombardy, Aloysius was the eldest son of Ferrante, marquis of Castiglione and courtier to Philip II and Marta Tana Santena, chief lady-in-waiting to the queen. Ferrante had military aspirations for his young son, and encouraged him to participate in army parades. But the child developed a precocious piety, displaying unusual devotion and self-discipline.

In 1577 he was sent by his father to Florence, to further his education along with his brother Ridolfo. Here he was obliged to appear frequently in the court of Francesco de' Medici. He was excused from court because of a painful kidney disease which was to haunt him for the rest of his life. He now began to teach the Catechism to the boys of Castiglione.

Visiting Spain in 1581, Aloysius became a Jesuit missionary. His disappointed father was furious. The death of the Spanish infante released the family from their courtly duties and they returned to Italy in 1584. He was sent to study at Milan, where he was warned in a vision of his approaching death, and because of ill health was soon transferred back to Rome.

In 1587 when plague swept Rome he nursed the victims, disregarding his own safety. He caught the disease and died on 21 June. Patron saint of youth and students.

The following feasts are also celebrated today:

St Aaron, Abbot in Brittany in the sixth century, when St Malo came into France: **St Eusebius**, Bishop and martyr: **St Leofridus**, in French **Leufroi**, Abbot: **St Meen** (in Latin **Mevennus**, also **Melanos**) Abbot in Brittany: **St Ralph** of the royal blood of France, Archbishop of Bourges in 840.

June 22
SAINT THOMAS MORE
AD 1535

Son of the lawyer and judge St John More, at the age of 13, Thomas joined the household of the archbishop of Canterbury, John Morton, and was sent for two years to Canterbury College, Oxford, where he studied under the famous humanist scholar Thomas Linacre. He continued his education studying law at Lincoln's Inn, and in 1501 was called to the bar like his father before him. Three years later he became a member of parliament. During these years he debated various courses for his life, whether to become a Carthusian monk (he lived at the London Charterhouse for four years), a diocesan priest or to join the Friars Minor. But in 1505 he married Jane Colt, continuing with his legal career.

It is said that More had originally fallen in love with Jane's younger sister, but married the elder to spare her the humiliation of seeing her younger sister married before her. Whatever the case, their marriage appears to have been a particularly happy one, and their home became known as a centre of Renaissance learning and humanism. Sadly, Jane died young in 1511 having borne Thomas three daughters and a son.

He was appointed to a series of public posts and his reputation grew with the publication of many of his writings, most notably *Utopia* in 1516.

Thomas was married again soon after Jane's death to a widow named Alice Middleton and they moved to Chelsea in 1524. By this time Thomas had served on several diplomatic missions for Henry, speaking for him in France before Francis I and Charles V, and had been knighted two years earlier.

He was appointed Lord Chancellor after the disgrace of Wolsey in 1529. Already he was disturbed by Henry's divorce of Catherine of Aragon, which had been performed against the wishes of the Pope. He refused to sign a petition addressed to the Pope seeking his permission for the divorce and the hostility between Henry and himself developed. Finally, in 1532, More resigned the Chancellorship.

He retired to Chelsea, refusing to attend the coronation of Anne Boleyn or to sign the oath in the Act of Succession which recognised the children of Henry and Anne as heirs to the throne.

Such defiance could not be tolerated: Thomas was arrested in 1534 and imprisoned in the Tower of London for over a year, forfeiting his lands by his continued refusal to conform.

He was not alone in choosing this course; Henry was forced to execute several others, including John Fisher, John Houghton and many of the Carthusian monks in London. The execution took place on 6 July, with More memorably proclaiming himself on the scaffold "the King's good servant, but God's first". He was then publicly beheaded.

More's body was buried in the Tower of London, in the church of St Peter ad Vincula, and his head was displayed on Tower Bridge before being buried at St Dunstan's, Canterbury. He is usually represented in his chancellor's robes, often wearing a scholar's cap, together with the chalice, host and papal insignia. Patron saint of lawyers.

The following feasts are also celebrated today:
St Alban, protomartyr of Britain: **St John Fisher**, Cardinal, Martyr: **St Paulinus** of Nola, Bishop.

June 23
SAINT ETHELDREDA, OR AUDREY
Virgin, Abbess – AD 679

The five daughters born to Anna, King of the East Angles in Suffolk, are all honoured as saints: Etheldreda, Sexburga, Erconwald, Ethelburga and Withburga. Probably the most famous, however, is Etheldreda.

As a young girl she was married to Prince Tonbert of the Gryvii, and after Tonbert's early death she spent five years in solitude on the island of Ely, which had been her dowry. Another match was arranged for her in 660, a politically advantageous union with the 15-year-old king of Northumbria, Egfrith. The marriage was dissolved and in 672 Etheldreda entered the convent at Coldingham under the direction of her aunt, Ebbe. The next year she founded a double monastery at Ely, on the site of the present-day cathedral, and restored the old church there which had been destroyed by pagan Mercians.

Etheldreda spent the remaining seven years of her life in the monastery, living a life of penance, austerity and prayer. She died of a plague and was buried at Ely. She developed a tumour on her neck which she claimed was punishment for her younger, more frivolous days when she had adorned herself with necklaces. The word "tawdry" meaning cheap and showy, and the obsolete "tawdry-lace", which referred to a silk necktie, is a corruption of "St Audrey". This is said by some to refer to the frivolous necklaces on which Etheldreda blamed her tumour, but it may simply refer to the cheap jewellery sold at St Audrey's fair in Ely.

Her relics were translated into a shrine by Sexburga in 695, which soon became a popular centre for pilgrimage with many miracles attributed to her intercession as her cult developed. In art she is depicted crowned, holding a staff which may be budding and sometimes a book. Patron saint of Cambridge University.

The following feast is also celebrated today:
St Mary of Oignes; married early in life to a man remarkable for his piety; this young couple decided to serve the lepers in their own town of Nivelle in Brabant. They gave all their possessions for the relief of the poor.

June 24
SAINT JOHN THE BAPTIST
Herald of Christ – AD 30

John's father was Zechariah, a priest in Jerusalem, and his mother Elizabeth was a kinswoman of the Virgin Mary. They were both elderly at the time of John's birth, which was foretold by an angel to a disbelieving Zechariah in the Temple. No more is known of John until he appears in c27 as a wandering preacher in the desert beside the Jordan, the river in which he baptized those who came out from the towns to listen to him (this is the reason for his association with spas). He lived like an Old Testament prophet, in austerity. Because his message was "Make straight the way of the Lord!" he has recently been adopted as the patron of motorways.

Jesus came to be baptized by John, who recognised him instantly. He was outspoken and fearless. Attacking Herod Antipas, he was imprisoned. Salome, one of Herod's slaves pleased Herod so much by her dancing that she was offered any gift she named. At her mother's prompting she requested the head of John the Baptist on a dish. Herod regretted his rashness but was too proud to break his oath: John was beheaded.

Since he proclaimed the "Lamb of God", John's emblem is a lamb, and he often carries a long cross signifying his mission and Christ's sacrificial death. He is frequently shown playing alongside the Christ-child. As an adult he is shown in animal furs, preaching or proclaiming Christ, and his execution is a favourite scene. Unusually, John's principal feast celebrates his birth rather than his death. Patron saint of motorways, farriers and tailors.

The following feast is also celebrated today:
St Bartholomew a monk of the Abbey of Dunelm.

June 25
SAINT WILLIAM
Abbot – AD 1142

St William was born of noble parents at Vercelli, Piedmont. He left his family and his wealth, and built a monastery on Monte Vergine. During his life, William worked many miracles.

The following feasts are also celebrated today:
St Adelbert, a prince of Northumberland who joined St Willibrord in Lower Germany about 700: **St Agoard** and **St Aglibert** of Paris, martyred for having pulled down one of the heathen temples: **St Luan**, Abbot of Bangor in Ireland: **St Maximus**, Bishop of Turin: **St Moloc**, Bishop, a Scotsman and an assistant of St Boniface of Ross: **St Prosper of Aquitain**.

June 26
SAINT ANTHELM
Bishop – AD 1178

As a young man, Anthelm was ordained as a priest at Belley in south-east France. Just two years later, in 1139, he was appointed abbot at La Grande Chartreuse which had recently suffered damage.

In 1152 Anthelm resigned his abbacy to live as a hermit, but he soon felt called to serve his order again; from 1154 to 1156, before returning to Grande Chartreuse, he was prior at Portes. He was appointed bishop of Belley in 1163 by Pope Alexander III. He made widespread reforms among the clergy, and spent his final years caring for lepers and the poor in Belley.

Representations of Anthelm in art show him with a lamp lit by a divine hand or with a nobleman (ie Humbert) under his feet.

The following feasts are also celebrated today:
St Babolen, first Abbot of St Peter's des-Fosses: **St John** and **St Paul**, martyrs: **St Maxentius**, Abbot in Poitou: **St Vigilius**, Bishop of Trent in 385.

June 27
SAINT LADISLAS I,
Confessor, King of Hungary – AD 1095

Ladislas the First, called by the Hungarians St Lalo, and in old French Lancelot, was son of Bela, King of Hungary, and born in 1041. He became king in 1080 and restored the good laws and discipline which St Stephen had established. His life in the palace was most austere; he was frugal but liberal to the church and poor.

He added to his kingdom Dalmatia and Croatia and was preparing to command, as general-in-chief, the expedition of the Christians for the recovery of the Holy Land when he died on 30 July 1095. He was buried at Waradin.

The following feast is also celebrated today:
St John Moutier of Chinon, a native of Great Britain.

June 28
SAINT IRENÆUS
Martyr, Bishop of Lyons – AD 202

St Irenæus was a Grecian whose parents placed him under the care of St Polycarp, Bishop of Smyrna, who sent him into Gaul, perhaps in company with some priests. He was ordained priest of the church of Lyons.

In 177 Irenæus was chosen the second Bishop of Lyons. He suffered martyrdom in the general massacre of the Christians at Lyons and the martyrs who died with him amounted to nineteen thousand.

The remains of St Irenæus were buried by his priest Zachary between the bodies of the holy martyrs SS. Epipodius and Alexander. They were kept with honour in the subterranean chapel in the church of St John.

The following feasts are also celebrated today:
St John Southworth, English martyr: **St Leo II**, Pope, a Silician: **St Plutarch**, brother of **St Heraclas**, **Serenus** and **Heraclidas**, scholars of Origen: **St Potomiana** and **St Basilides**, the former a slave and the latter one of her guards deputed to carry her to execution; he protected her from the lewdness of the crowd.

The day dawns only to those who are awake.

June 29
SAINT PETER
Leader of the Apostles – AD 64

Peter was born Simon, son of John, in Bethsaida, and he worked with his brother Andrew as a fisherman by Lake Genesareth. From the account of Jesus healing his mother-in-law we know that he was, or had been, married, but nothing is known of his wife.

According to John's Gospel it was Andrew who introduced his brother to Christ, who then gave Simon the name *Cephas* (Peter), meaning "the rock", saying that Peter was the rock on which his church on earth would be built, and later that Peter would be given "the keys to the kingdom of heaven". It is upon this foundation that the Catholic church's teaching on the supremacy of the papacy, the line following from Peter as first bishop of Rome, is based.

In lists of apostles, Peter is always named first and he is mentioned more frequently than any other disciple in the gospels. He was one of the three present at Jesus's transfiguration, the raising of Jairus's daughter and the agony in Gethsemane and witnessed most of Jesus's miracles, yet he deserted him in the Garden and betrayed him in the courtyard of Pontius Pilate.

Christ had predicted this betrayal, as he had predicted Peter's subsequent repentance. After the resurrection and ascension Peter was acknowledged as the head of the Christian community in Jerusalem. It was he who first preached to the Gentiles leading many to conversion at Pentecost, and who performed the first of the apostles' miracles recorded in Acts, healing the lame beggar at Jerusalem's Beautiful Gate.

Imprisoned by Heron Agrippa in c43, Peter was miraculously freed by an angel but the New Testament gives little further information on his movements. He appears to have preached in Samaria, Antioch and elsewhere, and to have been rebuked by Paul at Antioch for his unwillingness to be seen eating with Gentile believers. According to a very early tradition he went on to become the first bishop of Rome and was martyred there under Nero.

Peter has been venerated from the earliest days of the church, regarded as its powerful patron and as the doorkeeper of heaven (he is usually shown in art holding a set of keys), or an inverted cross. Patron saint of fishermen, invoked for a long life.

*Take care of your thoughts
and the deeds
will take care of themselves.*

and
SAINT PAUL
The Apostle to the Gentiles – AD 66

Born of a Jewish family in the Roman province of Cilicia (modern-day Turkey), Saul of Tarsus was a fervent follower of the Jewish law. At the age of 14 he studied as a Pharisee under the famous rabbi Gamaliel of Jerusalem and, following the rabbinic tradition of studying a trade as well as the law, learnt tent-making also. Although Aramaic was his mother tongue he had a strong Hebrew education. Saul's birth in Tarsus automatically gave him the status of a Roman citizen and he spoke Greek fluently; he was eminently qualified for his later role as apostle to the Gentiles.

As a Pharisee, Paul persecuted the early Christian church relentlessly. His concern was for strict application of the Jewish law which this new sect appeared to be flouting. His conversion took place as he travelled from Jerusalem to Damascus intent on further persecution of the church when he experienced a mystical vision of the risen Christ speaking the famous words, "Saul, Saul, why do you persecute me?"

After his conversion, Paul spent three years in prayer and solitude in Arabia and then preaching back in Damascus, where opposition against him became so violent that he was forced to flee to Jerusalem, escaping in a basket let down over the city walls. In Jerusalem he met Peter, James and the other apostles who were understandably nervous until convinced by Barnabas of Paul's sincerity. Preaching in Jerusalem, Paul again faced much opposition; he finally returned to Tarsus for some years until introduced by Barnabas to the church at Antioch. From Antioch, Paul began the spread of Christianity throughout the world.

He was beheaded on the Ostian way at Tre Fontane, just outside Rome (hence he is often represented in literature by a sword as well as the book symbolising his writings). His body is now in the Basilica of San Paolo fuori le Mura there. Although it is claimed that he was martyred on the same date as Peter, this probably originates in the fact that the two share a feast-day, 29 June.

Depicted in art with a sword and book. Patron saint of tent makers and saddlers.

The following feast is also celebrated today:
St Emma, founded the monastery of Gurk.

June 30
The following feast is celebrated today:
St Martial, Bishop of Limoges, one of the first apostles of France (about the year 250).

July 1
The following feasts are celebrated today:
St Calais, first Abbot of Ancille in France: **St Cybar**, a recluse in Angouleme: **St Gal**, Bishop of Clermont: **St Julius** and **St Aaron**, Britons, martyrs at Carleon about 303: **St Leonorus**, in French **Lunaire**, Bishop of a noble family in Wales, he was educated under St Iltud: **St Oliver Plunkett**, the last to be martyred under the English penal laws: **St Rumold**, Bishop and martyr, patron of Mechlin or Malines: **St Simeon**, surnamed **Salus**, a native of Egypt, born about 522, lived twenty-nine years in the desert: **St Thierri**, Abbot of Mont d'Hor, near Rheims: **St Theobald** or **Thibault**.

The best gift is a good example.

July 2
SAINT SWITHIN
Bishop of Winchester, – AD 862

As a child in Wessex he was educated at the Old Minster in Winchester, and in the early ninth century he was appointed personal chaplain to Egbert, the king of Wessex.

In 852 Ethelwulf appointed Swithin bishop of Winchester, the capital of Wessex. Swithin was energetic in founding new churches and was renowned for his compassion and charity towards the needy. Before his death on 2 July he had asked to be buried in the cemetery of the Old Minster, and his grave was placed by the west door of the cathedral and marked by a tomb. It was planned that Swithin's relics should be translated to a shrine inside the cathedral.

The translation was scheduled to take place on 15 July 971, but it was delayed by an exceptionally heavy rainfall. When finally accomplished, it was accompanied by a number of miraculous cures. This is probably the origin of the famous superstition which states that rain on 15 July means rain for the following 40 days.

The following feasts are also celebrated today:
St Monegondes, a recluse in Tours: **St Otho**, Bishop of Bamberg: **St Oudoceus**, third Bishop of Landaff: **St Processus** and **St Martinian**, converted by the preaching of Saints Peter and Paul.

You can mould a mannerism,
but you must chisel a character.

July 3
SAINT THOMAS
The Apostle of India

Thomas was surnamed Didymus, the twin. He was probably born in Galilee where he lived until he became a disciple of Jesus. When told by the other disciples that Jesus had appeared to them while he was absent, he asserted that "unless I put my hands in his side ... I will not believe." When however he saw Christ, and was invited to touch his wounds, Thomas fell before him and cried "My Lord and my God!", the first confession of Christ's divinity after his resurrection.

Thomas went on to found the Christian church in Parthia and another ancient and more prevalent tradition holds that he preached in India. He was martyred near Madras, killed by a spear where his grave is now marked by a stone cross.

In art he is usually shown either doubting the word of the apostles or before the wounded Christ. Sometimes he carries the spear of his martyrdom (occasionally portrayed as a sword or dagger) and often a builder's rule, from a legend that he built a heavenly palace for an Indian king. The story tells that Thomas promised to build King Gundafor a beautiful palace, but spent all the money he had been given for the work upon the poor. When challenged by the irate king, Thomas answered that he would see his new palace in the next world.

He is invoked against blindness because of his own lack of spiritual sight. Patron saint of builders, architects and theologians.

The following feasts are also celebrated today:
St **Bertran**, Bishop of Mans: St **Guthagon**, recluse, an Irishman: St **Gunthiern**, Abbot in Brittany in the sixth century: St **Leo II**, Pope in the seventh century: St **Phocas**, a gardener in Sinope, a city of Pontus.

July 4
SAINT ELIZABETH OF PORTUGAL
Queen – AD 1336

Named after her grand-aunt Elizabeth of Hungary, Elizabeth was the daughter of King Peter III of Aragon. At the age of only 12 she was married to King Denis of Portugal, establishing educational and religious communities to meet the needs she saw around her. These included a hospital, a hostel for women in need or in danger and an orphanage: in addition she provided shelter for pilgrims and money for alms to the poor.

Her own marriage was unhappy: despite Denis's undoubted capabilities as a ruler he was a jealous, unfaithful and inconsiderate husband. They had two children.

Denis died in 1325 after a long illness. With her husband gone, she spent the rest of her life in retirement near the Poor Clare convent which she had founded at Coimbra, living simply and devoting herself to serving the needs of the surrounding community.

Her emblem in art is the rose, either worn in a crown or carried in wintertime, from a legend that the bread she carried would miraculously turn to roses. Invoked in time of war.

The following feasts are also celebrated today:
St Bertha, widow, Abbess of Blangy in Artois: **St Bolcan**, a disciple of St Patrick: **St Finbar**, Abbot in Ireland and founder of a monastery between Kinselech and Desies: **St Odo**, Archbishop of Canterbury, a Dane: **St Sissoes** or **Sissoy**, an anchorite in Egypt: **St Ulric**, Bishop of Augsburg, born 893, educated in the Abbey of St Gal.

July 5
SAINT PETER OF LUXEMBURG
Confessor, Cardinal, Bishop of Metz – AD 1387

He was son to Guy of Luxemburg, count of Ligny, and Maud, countess of St Pol; and was born at Ligny, a small town in Lorrain, Toul, in 1369. His father died when he was thee years of age and his mother a year after, but his aunt, countess of Orgieres and countess dowager of St Pol, took care of his education. At ten years of age he was sent to Paris, where he studied Latin, philosophy and the canon law. Upon the news that his brother was made prisoner and sent to Calais, Peter, in 1381, interrupted his studies, went over to London, and delivered himself up a hostage for his brother till his ransom should be paid.

In 1383 his brother, the count of St Pol, obtained for him a canonry in Our Lady's at Paris. In the year 1384, Clement VII, soon after he had nominated him bishop, created him cardinal under the title of St George, and in 1386 called him to Avignon. Ten months after his promotion to cardinal, for the sake of his health, he was advised to retire to Villeneuve, a town near Avignon. He died on 2 July 1387 being eighteen years old. On account of many miracles, the citizens of Avignon built a chapel over his grave.

The history of the miracles which have been wrought at his tomb fills whole volumes. A famous one in 1432 moved the city of Avignon to choose him for its patron. It is related as follows:

A child about twelve years old fell from a high tower in the palace of Avignon upon a sharp rock, by which fall his skull was split, his brains dashed out.

The father of the child, distracted at this accident, ran to the place, and falling on his knees, implored the intercession of St Peter. Then gathering up the scattered bloody pieces of the child's skull, he carried them with the body in a sack, and laid them on the saint's tomb. The people and the Celestine monks joined their earnest prayers; and after some time the child returned to life, and was placed upon the altar that all might see him wonderfully raised from the dead. This miracle happened on 5 July on which day the festival of the saint has ever since been celebrated at Avignon.

The following feasts are also celebrated today:
St Anthony Mary Zaccaria, in Italy in the sixteenth century: **St Edana** or **Edaena**, virgin in Ireland where a famous holy well bears her name: **St Modwena**.

July 6
The following feasts are celebrated today:
St Goar, priest in Triers: **St Julian**, hermit: **St Laurence of Brindisi**: **St Moninna**, of Mount Cullen: **St Palladius**, bishop and Apostle of the Scots: **St Sexburgh**, Abbess, a niece of St Hilda.

July 7
SAINT PANTÆNUS

He was by birth a Sicilian, by profession a philosopher. He was head of the Christian school at Alexandria in Egypt some time before the year 179. The Indians who traded to Alexandria asked him to pay their country a visit, whereupon he left his school and went to India.

The following feasts are also celebrated today:
St Benedict XI, Pope, born in 1220, a native of Treviso: **St Cyril** and **St Methodius**, Bishops, Apostles of Moravia, Bohemia and other Sclavonic countries in the ninth century: **St Edelburga**, a daughter of the King of the East Angles: **St Felix**, Bishop of Nantes: **St Hedda**, a monk of the monastery of St Hilda, Bishop of the West Saxons in 676: **St Willibald**, Archbishop of Aichstadt.

The tree is known by its fruits;
not by its roots.

July 8
SAINT WITHBURGE
Virgin – AD 743

She was the youngest of four sisters, daughters of Annas, the King of the East-Angles. As a child she led an austere life in close solicitude at Holkham, near the coast in Norfolk, where a church, afterwards called Withburgstow, was built. After the death of her father she changed her home to another estate of the crown, called Dereham.

Withburge laid the foundation of a great church and nunnery, but did not live to finish the buildings. Her death happened on 17 March 743. Her body was interred in the churchyard at Dereham, and fifty-five years after found uncorrupt and translated into the church.

The following feasts are also celebrated today:
St Grimbald, a native of St Omer, the first professor of divinity at Oxford: **Saints Kilian**, Bishop, **Olman**, priest and **Totnam**, deacon, martyrs: **St Procopius**, martyr, a native of Jerusalem.

July 9
SAINT EPHREM OF EDESSA
Confessor, Doctor of the Church – AD 378

St Ephrem was born in the territory of Nisibis, a city on the banks of the Tigris, in Mesopotamia. His parents lived in the country and earned their bread with the sweat of their brows. They consecrated Ephrem to God from his cradle, but he was eighteen years old when he was baptized. Soon after he joined a monastery and put himself under the direction of a holy abbot. It was a rule observed in all the monasteries of Mesopotamia and Egypt that every religious man should perform his task of manual labour. The profits from their work were always given to the poor.

He was naturally irritable but so perfectly did he subdue this passion that he was called "The meek". Once, when he had fasted several days, the monk who was bringing him a mess of pottage, made with a few herbs for his meal, let fall the pot and broke it. The saint, seeing him in confusion, said cheerfully, "As our supper will not come to us, let us go to it." And sitting down on the ground by the broken pot, he picked up his meal as well as he could.

St Ephrem lived at Edessa, but from time to time returned into his desert. In his last sickness he told his disciples and friends: "Sing no funeral hymns at Ephrem's burial. Wrap not my carcase in any costly shroud: erect no monument in my memory." He died at a very advanced age c378.

> **The following feasts are also celebrated today:**
> **St Everildis**: **St Veronica de Julianis**, virgin.

> *July 10*
> **The following feasts are celebrated today:**
> **The Seven Brothers** and **St Filicitas**, their mother, martyrs in the second century: **St Rufina** and **St Secunda**, two sisters, martyrs in Rome.

July 11
SAINT JAMES
Bishop of Nisibis, Confessor – AD 350

James was a native of Nisibis in Mesopotamia and chose the highest mountains for his home, sheltering himself in a cave in the winter and the rest of the year living in the woods, continually exposed to the open air. He lived only on wild roots and herbs which he ate raw, and had no other garments other than a tunic and cloak, both made of goat's hair. By his personal merit and great reputation he became Bishop of Nisibis; but here he still followed the same course of life.

One day as he was travelling he was accosted by a gang of beggars with the view of taking money from him on pretence to bury their companion, who lay stretched on the ground as if he had been dead. The holy man gave them what they asked.

As soon as he was gone, his companions, calling the other to rise and take his share of the booty, were strangely surprised to find him really dead. Seized with sudden fear and grief, they immediately ran after James, confessed the cheat, begged forgiveness and asked him to restore their unhappy companion to life, which the saint did.

When the Persians invaded the territories of the Romans in 348 they lay siege to Nisibis in 350. St Ephrem, deacon of Edessa, being present asked James to go upon the walls to take a view of the Persians, and pray to God that He would defeat the infidel army. Going to the top of a high tower, and seeing the multitude of men and beasts which covered the whole country, he said: "Lord, defeat these multitudes by an army of gnats."

For scarce had the saint spoken those words when whole clouds of gnats and flies came pouring down upon the Persians, got into the elephants' trunks and the horses' ears and nostrils, which made them chafe and foam, throwing their riders, and putting the whole army into confusion and disorder.

The citizens of Nisibis attributed their preservation to St James.

The following feasts are also celebrated today:
St Droatan, Abbot, a royal prince of Scotland, educated under St Columba: **St Hidulphus**, Bishop: **St Pius I**, Pope and martyr.

July 12
SAINT JOHN GUALBERT
Abbot – AD 1073

St John Gaulbert was born at Florence. Hugo, his only brother, was murdered. John happened to be riding home when he met his brother's murderer in so narrow a passage that it was impossible for either of them to avoid the other. John drew his sword and was going to kill him, but the other, lighting from his horse, fell upon his knees and besought him to spare his life. They parted, and John went to the monastery of St Minias.

Not long after, he left and went in search of solitude. He arrived at a shady valley covered with willow-trees, commonly called Vallis-Umbrosa, half a day's journey from Florence, in Tuscany. There he found two hermits with whom he built a small monastery of timber and mud-walls to form together a little community. From this foundation came the Order of Vallis-Umbrosa.

St John was chosen the first abbot. He also founded the monastery of St Salvi, of Moscetta, of Passignano, another at Rozzuolo, and another at Monte Salario. He reformed some other monasteries and left about twelve houses of his Order at his death.

The following feast is also celebrated today:
St Nabor and St Felix, suffered martyrdom in Milan about the year 304. A church was built over their tomb.

July 13
The following feasts are celebrated today:
St Anacletus, Pope; he governed the Church after St Clement: **St Eugenius**, Bishop of Carthage: **St Turiaf,** Bishop of Dol in Brittany.

It is not every bad man that will ever be good,
but there will be no good man
who was not at some time bad.

ST AUGUSTINE

July 14
SAINT CAMILLUS DE LELLIS
Confessor

He was born in 1550 at Bacchianico in Abruzzo, in the kingdom of Naples. He lost his mother in his infancy, and six years after his father, who had been an officer in the French troops in Italy. Camillus entered in the army and served first in the Venetian and afterwards in the Neapolitan troops till, in 1574, his company was disbanded. He had a passion for cards and gaming. At length he was reduced to such straits that for a subsistence he was obliged to work at a building which belonged to the Capuchin friars.

With their help he broke his gambling addiction and went to Rome, and there served the sick in St James's hospital. In 1585 his friends hired for him a large house to serve people infected with the plague, prisoners, and the dying. In 1586, the church of St Mary Magdalen was bestowed on him for the use of his congregation. He founded religious houses at Bologna, Milan, Genoa, Florence, Ferrara, Messina, Palermo, Mantua, Viterbo, Bocchiano, Theate, Burgonono and Sinuessa. He died on 14 July 1614.

The following feasts are also celebrated today:
St Bonaventure, Cardinal-Bishop and Doctor of the Church, surnamed "The Seraphic Doctor" 1274: **St Idus**, disciple of St Patrick.

July 15
SAINT HENRY II
Emperor – AD 1024

St Henry, surnamed the Pious and the Lame, was son of Henry, Duke of Bavaria, and of Gisella, daughter of Conrad, King of Burgundy and was born in 972. In 995 he succeeded his father in the duchy of Bavaria, and in 1002, upon the death of his cousin Otho III, he was chosen emperor. He was the same year crowned King of Germany, at Mainz. He procured a national council of the bishops at Dortmund, in 1005, Frankfurt in 1006 and another of Bamberg in 1011.

Two years later, he quelled a rebellion in Italy, when Ardovinus of Hardwic, a Lombard lord, had crowned himself king at Milan. Henry marched into Italy, vanquished him in battle, and deprived him of his territories, but did not take away his life, and Ardovinus became a monk. After this victory, St Henry went in triumph to Rome where, in 1014, he was crowned emperor with great solemnity by Pope Benedict VIII. The protection of Christendom obliged St Henry to lead armies to Poland, Sclavonia and Italy. His death happened at the castle of Grone, near Halberstadt in 1024. His body was interred in the cathedral at Bamberg.

The following feast is also celebrated today:
St Plechelm, Bishop.

July 16
The following feasts are celebrated today:
St Elier or **Helier**, hermit in the Isle of Jersey: **St Eustathius**, Patriarch of Antioch.

July 17
SAINT ALEXIUS
Confessor in the fifth century

St Alexius or Alexis was the only son of a rich senator of Rome, born and educated in that capital in the fifth century. In disguise he travelled in extreme poverty, and resided in a hut adjoining a church. After some time there, he returned home, and being received as a poor pilgrim, lived unknown in his father's house, bearing the ill-treatment of the servants with invincible patience and silence. A little before he died, in a letter he disclosed himself to his parents.

The following feasts are also celebrated today:
St Ennodius, Bishop of Pavia: **St Marcellina**, virgin, eldest sister to St Ambrose: **St Speratus and his Companions**, called **The Scilitan Martyrs**: **St Turninus** an Irish monk who with St Folian, came to the Netherlands.

July 18
SAINT SYMPHOROSA AND HER SEVEN SONS
Martyrs – AD 120

This lady lived with her seven sons, upon a plentiful estate which they enjoyed at Tivoli. She was widow of St Getulius or Zoticus. Symphorosa had buried the bodies of her husband and brother, who were martyrs, in her farm and prepared herself to follow them by the exercise of all good works. Adrian ordered her and her sons to be seized and brought before him. The emperor then had her carried to the temple of Hercules, where she was first buffeted on the cheeks and afterwards hung up by her hair until she died. Her seven sons were tortured and stretched. Orders were given next day for a deep hole to be dug, and all the bodies thrown into it. Between Tivoli and Rome, still to be seen are some remains of a church erected in memory of them, in a place called, "The Seven Brothers".

July 19
SAINT VINCENT OF PAUL
Confessor, Founder of the Lazarites, or Fathers of the Mission – AD 1660

St Vincent of Paul was a native of Poui, a village near Acqs, in Gascony, not far from the Pyrenæan mountains. His parents, William of Paul and Bertranda of Morass, had a very small farm. They brought up a family of four sons and two daughters. Vincent, the third son, spent a great part of his time in the fields keeping cattle. His schooling was with the Franciscan friars, at Acqs. At twenty years of age, in 1596 he was qualified to go to the university of Toulouse, where he spent seven years in the study of divinity. He joined the priesthood in 1600.

Vincent went to Marseilles in 1605, to receive a legacy of five hundred crowns which had been left him by a friend. Returning, he was set upon by pirates who took the vessel and passengers to Tunis. There Vincent was sold as a slave to an old physician. He lived with this old man from September 1605 to August 1606.

Upon the physician's death, Vincent escaped. He crossed the Mediterranean sea in a small light boat and landed at Aigues-Mortes, near Marseilles on 28 June 1607 and proceeded to Rome. After a short stay at Rome, he returned to Paris where he served as curate in the parish of Clichi.

In 1617 with five other priests he formed a little community in the parish of Chatillon. In 1633 the community were given the Priory of St Lazarus, which being a spacious building was made the chief house and from it the fathers of the mission were often called Lazarites or Lazarians.

He lived to see twenty-five similar communities founded in France, Piedmont and Poland. He procured and directed the foundations of several great hospitals in Paris and Marseilles.

He died in his eightieth year and is buried in the Church of St Lazarus, in Paris.

July 20
The following feasts are celebrated today:
St Aurelius, first Archdeacon and then Archbishop of Carthage, a friend of St Augustine: **St Ceslas**, of the Order of St Domenic: **St Jerome Æmiliani**: **St Joseph Barsabas**, one of the seventy-two disciples of our Lord: **St Justa** and **St Rufina**, martyrs, two Christian women who maintained themselves and many poor by selling earthenware: **St Margaret**, martyred at Antioch in Pisidia: **St Ulmar** or **Wulmar**, Abbot of Samer, three miles from Boulogne.

July 21
The following feasts are celebrated today:
St Arbogastus, Bishop of Strasburg: **St Barhadbesciabus**, martyr: **St Praxedes**, daughter of Pudens, a Roman senator, and sister to St Pudentiana: **St Victor of Marseilles**, martyr: **St Zoticus**, Bishop of Comana, martyred about 204.

July 22
SAINT MARY MAGDALENE
First Century

Mary came from Magdala, a town on the west coast of the Sea of Galilee, and when Jesus began his ministry in Galilee she was one of the women who followed and supported him. Mary was one of the group of women who stood at the foot of Jesus's Cross and it was she, together with Joanna and Mary, the mother of James and Salome, who discovered the empty tomb and heard the angel proclaim Christ's resurrection.

Most memorable of all, however, she was the first to see the risen Lord who appeared to her in the garden of his burial later that day; blinded by her tears, she at first supposed him to be the gardener.

The enormous popularity of Mary is attested by the many ancient and modern dedications of churches and of colleges at both Oxford and Cambridge. In art she is usually shown with long hair and holding a jar of ointment and she is often included in scenes of the Passion and Resurrection. Patron saint of repentant sinners and the contemplative life.

The following feasts are also celebrated today:
St Dabius or **Davius** of Ireland, preacher in Scotland: **St Joseph of Palestine**, commonly called Count Joseph, a title given to him by Constantine in 323: **St Mineve**, Abbot, related to the emperor Charlemagne: **St Vandrille** or **Wandre Gisilus**, Abbot of Fontenelle in Normandy.

July 23
The following feasts are celebrated today:
St Apollinaris, disciple of St Peter, first Bishop of Ravena: **St Liborius**, Bishop of Mans (348)

July 24
SAINT LUPUS
Confessor, Bishop of Troyes – AD 478

St Lupus was born at Toul. He married Pimeniola, sister of St Hilary of Arles. After six years of marriage, they parted by mutual consent. Lupus joined the abbey of Lerins.

After the first year he went to Macon in Burgundy and was preparing to return to Lerins when he was chosen bishop. He continued the same practices of poverty. He wore no garments other than a sackcloth and a single tunic, lay upon boards and allotted every second night to prayer. He often passed three days without taking any nourishment.

In 471 Attila, with a numberless army of Huns, overran Gaul. Troyes was threatened. Lupus, putting on his bishop's attire, followed by a procession of clergy, went out to meet Attila at the head of his advancing army. Attila, hearing his words, admired his boldness and spared the city, turning his army from Troyes.

He governed his church for fifty-two years, dying in the year 479. The chief part of his body is kept in a rich silver shrine: His skull and part of his head in another far more precious, in the figure of a bishop, formed of silver, adorned with jewels and diamonds, said to be the richest in France.

The following feasts are also celebrated today:
St Christina, a Tuscan martyr: **St Declan**, first Bishop of Ardmore: **St Francis Solano**: **St Kinga** or **Cunegundes**: **St Lewine**, a British virgin, martyred under the Saxons before their conversion: **St Romanus** and **St David**, martyrs, patrons of Muscovy: **St Wulfhad** and **St Ruffin**, two brothers, martyrs.

Life

Life is too great
Between the infant's and the man's estate.
Between the clashing of earth's strife and fate,
For petty things.
Lo! we shall yet who creep with cumbered feet,
Walk glorious over heaven's golden street,
Or soar on wings.

Margaret E. Sangster

July 25
SAINT JAMES THE GREAT
AD c44

The Gospels agree that James was the son of Zebedee and brother of John, a fisherman who worked with them in his native Galilee. When he was called by Jesus, James was mending nets with his brother by Lake Genesareth.

After this calling, James and his brother stayed with Jesus throughout his years of teaching and miracles and appear to have been among his closest friends. James is specially mentioned in the Gospel accounts of the healing of Peter's mother-in-law and the raising of the daughter of Jairus, and was one of the three who witnessed the Transfiguration on the Mount of Olives and the agony of Jesus in Gethsemane. Jesus nicknamed the brothers "Boanerges" (sons of thunder), traditionally because of their impetuous desire to strike the Samaritan village down with lightning because it refused Jesus hospitality. It was James and John who requested that Jesus reserve them seats in Heaven at his left and right hand.

James was the first of the apostles to be martyred. The shrine at Santiago de Compostela was one of the great centres of pilgrimage in the Middle Ages, and James became the rallying figure of Christian opposition to the Moors. Numerous stories of visions and miracles developed to support this view of James and the shrine remains popular in Spain even today.

The shrine was so significant that in art James is associated with a pilgrim's hat and staff and the cockle-shell representing Compostela, and occasionally at his martyrdom. He is regarded as the patron saint of Spain, and many churches are dedicated to him.

Reading Abbey claims to possess the relic of James's hand, presented as a gift by Empress Matilda. He is known as the Great to distinguish him from the other apostle named James, called the Younger. Patron saint of Spain.

The following feasts are also celebrated today:
St Cucufas, a martyr of Spain, who is called **St Cougat** in Barcelona, **St Quiquenfat** at Ruel, near Paris and **St Guinefort** in other parts of France: **St Nissen**, whom St Patrick baptized, Abbot of Mount Garret in Wexford: **St Thea** and **St Valentine**, virgins and **St Paul**, martyrs.

Truth
In order that all men may be taught to speak truth, it is necessary that all likewise should learn to hear it.

SAMUEL JOHNSON

July 26
SAINT ANNE
Mother of Mary – First century BC

Anne was the childless wife of Joachim, but she was visited by an angel as she prayed and was promised that she would have a child. Anne vowed to dedicate the child to God and so the Virgin Mary was born.

Anne is frequently pictured holding Mary and Jesus (on her lap or in her arms), at her betrothal to Joachim, or teaching the young Mary to read Scripture. Patron saint of miners.

The following feast is also celebrated today:
St Germanus, Bishop of Auxerre, born about 380, titular saint of many churches in England and of the Abbey of Selby in Yorkshire.

July 27
SAINT PANTALEON
Martyr – AD 303

St Pantaleon was a physician who lost his faith. Brought back to his faith by Hermolaus, a zealous Christian, St Pantaleon wished to make amends to God by his own martyrdom. When persecution broke out in Nicomedia in 303 his wish was granted when he was tortured and beheaded. His relics are now kept in the abbey of St Denys, near Paris, but his head is at Lyons.

The following feasts are also celebrated today:
St Congall, Abbot of Iabhnal-Livin, in the upper part of Lough Erne: **St Luican**, titular saint of Kil-luican in Ireland: **Saints Maximian, Malchus, Martinian, Dionysius, John, Serapion** and **Constantine**, young martyrs, commonly called "the seven sleepers".

July 28
SAINT NAZARIUS AND SAINT CELSUS
Martyrs – AD 68

St Nazarius's father was a high-ranking officer in the Roman army. St Nazarius zealously followed his mother, Perpetua, in her Christian faith. He left his home-town Rome to preach and it was in Milan that he was beheaded together with Celsus, a young man who accompanied him on his travels. Their bodies were buried separately in a garden outside the city, and when they were discovered by St Ambrose in 395 AD, a vial of St Nazarius's blood was found in his tomb as fresh and as red as the day he died.

The following feasts are also celebrated today:
St Innocent I, Pope 402: **St Nazarius** and **St Celsus**, about the year 68, honoured with **St Victor** and **St Innocent**: **St Sampson**, Bishop, born 496 in that part of Wales now called Glamorganshire; educated by St Itultus: **St Victor**, Pope.

July 29
SAINT MARTHA
Virgin

She was the elder sister to Mary and Lazarus and when Jesus preached in the region of Judea he often stayed at their home. St Luke tells us that on Jesus's first visit, Martha was very busy preparing everything for her holy guest while Mary sat at his feet listening to his teaching. Martha complained to Jesus, asking him to tell Mary to get up and help, but, although Jesus was pleased by the devotion Martha was showing by serving him so attentively, he said, "Martha, Martha, Mary has chosen the better part."

St Martha seems to have been one of the holy women who was with Christ during his crucifixion. Her body lies in a chapel of the collegiate church at Tarascon. King Lewis XI had a bust of gold made, in which the head of the saint is kept.

The following feasts are also celebrated today:
St Felix, Pope and martyr: **St Olaus**, King of Norway: **St Olaus**, King of Sweden: **St Simplicius**, **St Faustinus**, two brothers, and **St Beatrice**, their sister, martyred: **St William Pinchon**, Bishop of St Brieuc in Brittany.

The sun, with all those planets revolving around it
and dependent upon it,
can still ripen a bunch of grapes
as if it had nothing else in the universe to do.

GALILEO GALILEI

July 30
The following feasts are celebrated today:
St Abdon and **St Sennen**, Persians who, coming to Rome, confessed their faith in Christ in the persecution in 250. The images of these martyrs with Persian bonnets and crowns are still seen in ancient sculpture: **St Julitta**, a rich lady of Cæsarea in Cappadocia.

July 31
SAINT IGNATIUS LOYOLA
Confessor Founder of the Society of Jesus – AD 1556

Born in the family castle in the Basque province of Guipúzcoa (modern-day Spain), Iñigo de Recalde de Loyola was the youngest of the 13 children of his noble parents. As a youth he spent some time as page in the court of King Ferdinand. He then trained to become a soldier, but his military career in the service of the duke of Nagara was cut short when he received a shot to the leg during the siege of Pamplona, 1521. His right leg was broken and was incompetently set, which meant that it later had to be rebroken and set again. This traumatic experience left Ignatius with a pronounced limp for the rest of his life.

It was while he was incapacitated, however, and convalescing slowly, that he began to read the lives of Christ and the saints which so impressed him that he converted to Christianity.

As soon as he had recovered in 1522 he went on pilgrimage to Monserrat, where he dedicated his soldier's life to the service of God by symbolically hanging his sword over the altar, and lived for a year in prayer and penance at nearby Manresa, tending to the needs of the sick at the hospital there with devoted selflessness until he attracted such attention that he withdrew to a solitary life of austerity. It was then that he began to write his famous *Spiritual Exercises*, not published until 1548. In 1524 Ignatius began to study, learning Latin and philosophy and going on to gain a Master of Arts from the University in Paris.

It was at Paris that Ignatius collected around him the group of students (one of whom was Francis Xavier) who practised his Spiritual Exercises and pledged themselves to the work of the Gospel, by mission to Palestine or in any other capacity dictated by the Pope. Three years later in 1537 the group met again in Venice, all ordained as priests by this time, and since war prevented them from going to Jerusalem they determined to found a new religious order in Rome.

They received the official approval of Paul III in 1540, and in 1541 the group took their final vows as the Society of Jesus, with Ignatius as superior-general despite his initial reluctance.

Ignatius died suddenly in Rome on 31 July. He left behind a well-established order with over 1,000 members, operating in nine different areas of Europe and with additional missions throughout the world, to carry through his vision of reform, education and mission.

Patron saint of retreats and spiritual exercises.

The following feasts are also celebrated today:
St Helen of Skofde, in Sweden: **St John Columbini**, founder of the Order of the Jesuate, the first magistrate of Siena.

August 1
The following feasts are celebrated today:
St Ethelwolf, Bishop of Winchester: **Saints Faith**, **Hope** and **Charity**, virgins and martyrs, three sisters who suffered death under Adrian in Rome: **The Seven Macchabean Brothers** with their mother, Jewish martyrs: **St Pellegrini** or **Peregrinus**, a young Irish prince.

August 2
SAINT STEPHEN
Pope and Martyr – AD 257

Saint Stephen was by birth a Roman and was made archdeacon by St Cornelius and St Lucius. He was chosen pope on 3 May 253.

and
SAINT ALPHONSUS MARY DE LIGUORI
Bishop, Confessor and Doctor

St Alphonsus was born near Naples in 1696. He was the founder of the Order of the Redemptorists. He made a vow never to lose a moment of time, and during most of his ninety-one years of life he laboured without ceasing for the church and Her people.

The following feasts are also celebrated today:
St Gamaliel, a doctor of the law: **St Nicodemus**, senator of Jerusalem: **St Walthen**, Abbot of Melrose.

August 4
SAINT DOMINIC
Confessor, Founder of the Dominicans – AD 1221

Born in Old Castile, Spain, Dominic was educated by his uncle, and then at the University of Palencia where he was probably ordained priest at Osma cathedral in 1199.

In c1204 Dominic left the community with his bishop Diego de Avezedo on a mission to the Albigensia heretics of Languedoc. Here in 1206, Dominic established a house of nuns. He attached to this nunnery a house for friars. The leader of the Pope's troops, Count Simon IV of Montfort, gave Dominic a castle in recently-conquered Casseneuil in 1214 in which Dominic, with six followers, founded his Friars Preachers.

Over the next few years, Dominic worked tirelessly to establish his order throughout Europe, with great success. Dominic died in Bologna. His emblem in art is a dog, from a pun on the Latin *domini canis*, Dominicans. The dog holds in its mouth a torch, symbolizing truth, and is often accompanied by a lily, star or book. Occasionally Dominic is shown receiving a rosary from the Virgin, from a tradition that he first invented it.

The following feast is also celebrated today:
St Luanus or **Lugid**, Abbot in Ireland.

August 5
SAINT OSWALD OF NORTHUMBRIA
King and Martyr – AD 642

The son of Æthelfrith, King of Northumbria, Oswald was forced to flee to Scotland when his father was killed in battle by Redwold of East Anglia and Edwin of Deira became King of Northumbria. Oswald was converted to Christianity at Iona, and on Edwin's death in 633 he and other exiled royals returned to Northumbria. The kingdom was now in the hands of the Christian king of Gwynedd, Cadwallon, against whom Oswald successfully led his greatly inferior army at Hevenfelt near Hexham in 634. He slew Cadwallon and succeeded to the throne, attributing his victory to a vision of St Columba and a wooden cross around which he had led his army in prayer before the battle.

One of his first actions as king was to send for help from Iona missionaries to aid in the task of evangelism among his new subjects. First he received a harsh bishop, whose inflexible rule met with little sympathy or success among the Northumbrians and who soon returned to Iona declaring that the English were unteachable. The next missionary sent from Iona was a close personal friend of Oswald's, the more kindly and charismatic Aiden who spoke little English. According to Bede, the king himself interpreted Aidan's sermons to the people and he gave him the island of Lindisfarne on which to establish a monastery.

Penda, the pagan king of Mercia, led a large army against him at the battle of Maserfelth (Old Oswestry) and he was defeated and killed there on 5 August, aged only 38. The various limbs were recovered and venerated in diverse places. The head is buried at Lindisfarne.

In art he is usually shown with a raven and a jar of sacred oil.

The following feasts are also celebrated today:
St Afra and **her Companions**, martyrs: St Memmius in French **Menge**, first Bishop and apostle of Chalons on the Marne.

August 6
The following feasts are celebrated today:
St Juatus and **St Pastor**, martyrs, titular patrons of the Collegiate Church at Alcada: **St Xystus** or **Sixtus II**, Pope and martyr, a Grecian by birth and a deacon under St Stephen.

August 7
SAINT CAJETAN OF THIENNA
Confessor – AD 1547

St Cajetan was son of Gaspar, Lord of Thienna, and Mary Porta, of Vicenza, in Lombardy. The saint was born in 1480. He built and founded a chapel at Rampasso. After this he went to Rome. Pope Julius II compelled him to accept the office of lawyer in his court. Upon the death of Julius II, he resigned and returned to Vicenza. There he entered the confraternity of St Jerome, which consisted only of men in the lowest stations of life, taking up his lodgings in their new hospital.

In 1524 the plan of a new institute was drawn up. Cajetan made it a rule of the new institute that clergy should possess no annual revenues, and be forbidden to beg or ask for necessary subsistence, content to receive voluntary contributions. They lived at first in a house in Rome which belonged to Boniface de Colle; but, their number increasing, they took a larger house on Monte Pincio. Shortly after, he was called to Naples to found a convent of his Order. He died worn out by labours.

The following feasts are also celebrated today:
St Donatus, Bishop and **St Hilarinus**, martyrs, the former Bishop of Abrezzo and the latter a monk who was beaten to death with clubs.

August 8
The following feasts are celebrated today:
St Cyriacus, **St Largus**, **St Smaragdus** in 303: **St Hormisdas**, martyred in Persia.

August 9
The following feasts are celebrated today:
St Fedlimid or **Felimy**, Bishop of Kilmore, in the sixth century: **St John Baptist Vianney**, known as The Cure D'Ars: **St Nathy** or **David**, priest in Ireland, patron of the diocese of Achonry: **St Romanus**, martyr, a soldier in Rome at the time of the martyrdom of St Laurence.

August 10
SAINT LAURENCE
Martyr – AD 258

Historians cannot place his birth or education but the Spaniards call him their countryman. In his youth St Xystus, then archdeacon of Rome, took him under his protection. When St Xystus became pope in 257, he ordained Laurence deacon. The Emperor Valerian, in 257, commanded all bishops, priests and deacons to be put to death, consequently Pope St Xystus was apprehended. As he was led to execution, his deacon, St Laurence, followed him weeping; and said to him "Where are you going, O holy priest, without your deacon?" He could not watch the pope go to martyrdom and himself left behind. The pope answered "I do not leave you, my son: you shall follow me in three days."

Laurence full of joy, hearing that he should be so soon called to God, set out immediately to seek all the poor widows and orphans and gave them all the money which he had. The church at Rome at that time possessed considerable riches.

The prefect of Rome was informed of these riches and sent for St Laurence, to whose care these treasures were committed, and said to him, "I am informed that your priests offer in gold, that the sacred blood is received in silver cups, and that in your sacrifices you have wax tapers fixed in golden candlesticks. Bring to light these concealed treasures; the prince has need of them for the maintenance of his forces." St Laurence replied, "The church is indeed rich; I will show you a valuable part; but allow me a little time."

Laurence went all over the city, seeking out in every street the poor whom he gathered together in great numbers before the church. Then he went to the prefect and invited him to come and see the treasure of the church. The prefect, astonished to see such a number of poor wretches who made a horrid sight, turned to the holy deacon and asked him what all this meant and where the treasures were which he had promised to show him.

St Laurence answered, "What are you displeased at? Behold in these poor persons the treasure which I promised to show you; they are the church's crown, it has no other riches; make use then of them for the advantage of Rome, of the emperor and yourself." "Do you mock me? I know that you desire to die; but you shall not die immediately. I will protract your tortures, that your death may be the more bitter as it shall be slower. You shall die by inches."

Laurence was stripped, and bound with chains upon an iron bed over a slow fire which broiled his flesh little by little. Having suffered a long time and slowly roasting to death, he turned to the judge and said to him, "Let my body be now turned; one side is broiled enough."

Noblemen took up the martyr's body on their shoulders and gave it an honourable burial in the Veran field, near the road to Tibur.

The following feasts are also celebrated today:
St Blaan of Ireland, a disciple of St Congall, afterwards Bishop among the Picts in Scotland died about 446: **St Deusdedit**, a poor labouring man who distributed to the poor every Saturday all he could save from what he earned in the week.

August 11
The following feasts are celebrated today:
St Equitius, Abbot: **St Gery** or **Gaugericus**, Bishop: **St Susanna**, said to have been a niece of Pope Caius; she suffered martyrdom with heroic constancy: **St Tiburtius**, martyr and **St Chromatius**, his father.

August 12
SAINT CLARE
Virgin, Abbess, Founder of the "Poor Clares"– AD 1253

Born into the noble Offreducia family, Clare dismayed her parents when she refused to marry at the age of 12 and horrified them six years later when, after hearing a Lenten sermon of St Francis, she ran away from home to take the veil from him at Portiuncula, renouncing all her possessions; Francis put her under the care of the Benedictine nuns at St Paul's convent in Bastia. The strenuous attempts of her family to persuade her to return home proved fruitless, and in fact soon after her removal to Sant'Angelo de Pazo, Clare was joined by her younger sister Agnes, who also took the veil from St Francis. It is said that their father sent a dozen men to forcibly fetch Agnes back, but Clare's prayers made her sister so heavy that they could not shift her.

In 1215 Francis offered Clare a house next to the church of St Damiano in Assisi, and she became abbess of the first community of women living under the Franciscan rule. Upon the death of her father, Clare was joined by her mother, another sister Beatrice, and members of the wealthy Ubaldini family of Florence. She spent her entire life at the convent at Assisi. After the death of Francis in 1226, by her prayers she twice saved Assisi from the armies of Emperor Frederick II. Following 27 years of poor health, Clare died in 1255.

A legend that she once clearly saw a Christmas service which she could not attend because of illness led to her patronage of television.

The following feasts are also celebrated today:
St Euplius: **St Muredach**, first Bishop of Killala, appointed by St Patrick about 440.

August 13
SAINT HIPPOLYTUS
Martyr – AD 252

A most illustrious martyr who suffered in the reign of Gallus, one of the twenty-five priests to have been apprehended and interrogated on the rack in Rome; then dragged by horses until the ground, the thorns, trees and stones were sprinkled with their blood. The crowds that followed gathered together all the mangled parts of flesh and limbs which lay scattered about. They brought these precious relics to Rome and buried them in the subterranean caverns called catacombs.

The following feasts are also celebrated today:
St Cassian, a Christian schoolmaster at Imola: **St John Berchmans**, S.J.: **St Radegundes**, a saintly Queen of France: **St Wigbert**, Abbot.

August 14
SAINT EUSEBIUS
Priest, Martyr – about the end of the Third Century

St Eusebius was a Roman Priest, who was imprisoned in his own room where he died after seven months of prayers and sufferings, probably in Palestine.

August 15
The following feasts are celebrated today:
St Alipius, Bishop, born at Tagaste in Africa: **St Arnoul** or **Arnulphus**, Bishop of Soissons: **St Mac-cartin**, called **Ard** or **Aed**, Bishop of Clogher in Ireland.

August 16
SAINT HYACINTH
Confessor – AD 1257

St Hyacinth was born in 1185 in the castle of Saxony in Silesia. During his studies at Cracow, Prague and Bologna, he took the degree of doctor of law and divinity. Yvo of Konski, Chancellor of Poland, going to Rome took with him his two nephews, Hyacinth and Ceslas. There, Hyacinth joined St Dominic in his convent of St Sabina, in March 1218. Hyacinth, then thirty-three years old, was appointed superior of their mission. He travelled on foot and without provisions through Eastern Europe. He founded numerous convents in Cracow, Sendomir and Plocsko, upon the Vistula, in Moravia. Seeing one day an assembly of people on their knees worshipping a tree on an island in the river Boristhenes, he walked over the water to them. At this sight they felled the tree and became Christians. He regularly visited converts and communities in Denmark, Sweden, Germany and Russia.

Primislava, a noble lady, sent her son to invite Hyacinth to come and preach at her home, but the young man was drowned on his return crossing a river. The mother carried the corpse to Hyacinth who took him by the hand and restored him to life. This is the last miracle recorded in his life. His relics are preserved in a chapel built in his honour at Cracow.

The following feast is also celebrated today:
St Roch, who devoted himself to the sick and died about 1327.

August 17
The following feasts are celebrated today:
St Liberatus, Abbot and Six Monks, summoned to Carthage and martyred there: **St Mamas**, about 275, ranked by the Greeks among the great martyrs.

August 18
SAINT HELENA
Empress – AD 328

St Helena was the mother of the Emperor Constantine, the first Christian emperor of Rome. Helped by her son, St Helena succeeded in discovering the true Cross at Jerusalem. She was outstanding for her almsdeeds, faith and zeal.

The following feasts are also celebrated today:
St Agapetus, a young Roman, martyred at Palestrina: **St Clare of Montefalco**, virgin, born near Spoletto about 1275.

August 19
The following feasts are celebrated today:
St Cumin, Bishop in Ireland, entered the monastic state early in life: **St Lewis**, Bishop of Toulouse, grand-nephew to Louis, King of France and nephew on his mother's side to St Elizabeth of Hungary: **St John Eudes**: **St Mochteus**, Bishop, a Briton, a disciple of St Patrick, first Bishop of Louth in Ireland: **St Timothy**, **St Agapius** and **St Thecla**, martyrs in 304.

August 20
SAINT BERNARD
Abbot – AD 1153

The son of a nobleman of Burgundy, Bernard was born in the family castle near Dijon and educated in Châtillon-sur-Seine. As a young man he was known for his wit and charm, living a brilliant but dissipated life, but in 1113 he joined the original Cistercian monastery at Cîteaux, along with four of his brothers and 27 other companions whom he persuaded to join him.

The recently founded order was floundering, but this large novitiate revived it, and in 1115 Cîteaux sent out Bernard as abbot with 12 other monks to form a daughter house at Langres. Its name was changed from Vallée d'Absinthe to Clairvaux, and it in its turn founded a further 68 Cistercian monasteries, including several in Britain. His treatise *On the love of God* and his sermons *On the Song of Songs* have remained classic works.

Bernard died at Clairvaux on 20 August. In art, his emblem is a beehive, symbolizing eloquence and he is often shown with the Virgin Mary.

Patron saint of Gibraltar, bee-keepers and wax-melters.

The following feast is also celebrated today:
St Oswin, King and martyr, who founded the kingdom of Northumberland.

August 21
SAINT JANE FRANCES DE CHANTAL
Widow and Abbess – AD 1641

Widow of the Baron de Chantal, St Jane left her father and four children, and entered the religious congregation which she founded with the assistance of St Francis de Sales. So becoming the "mother" of innumerable nuns of the Order of the Visitation.

The following feasts are also celebrated today:
St Bernard Ptolemy, founder of the Olivetans, born at Siena, 1272: **St Bonosus** and **St Maximilian**, martyrs in 363: **St Richard**, Bishop of Andria, an Englishman by birth.

Learning
Wear your learning, like your watch, in a private pocket: and do not merely pull it out and strike it, merely to show that you have one.
EARL OF CHESTERFIELD

August 23
SAINT ROSE OF LIMA
The Flower of Lima – AD 1617

Born to Spanish parents of moderate means, Rose was christened Isabel de Santa Maria de Flores but at her confirmation by St Toribie, archbishop of Lima, she took the name by which she had been popularly known since childhood.

Renowned for her beauty, Rose took pains to disfigure her good looks in an attempt to repel possible suitors and to guard against any sensual pride of her own. It is said that she rubbed pepper into her face to make the skin blotchy, and that she once covered her hands with lime, disabling herself for a month, because she had been complimented on their smoothness.

Her parents' financial situation worsened after an unsuccessful mining venture, and Rose worked to help support the family, labouring in the garden and plying her needle late into the night to produce works of embroidery and other stitching. The hardness of this life suited Rose well.

She lived as a recluse in a hut at the bottom of the garden in which she worked, and her reputation for mystical experiences, visions and suffering spread throughout the city. Although she lived a reclusive life, Rose was greatly concerned with the care of others in need and she is regarded as the founder of Peru's social service.

When earthquakes hit Lima many in the city attributed its survival to the intercession of its beautiful recluse.

For the last three years of her life, plagued by illness, Rose lived in the house of the government official Don Gonzalo de Massa and his wife. She died after one last painful illness, aged only 31. Because of her deep attachment to her parents' garden and also because her name itself recalls a flower, Rose is unofficially recognized as the patron saint of florists and gardeners. Patron saint of Peru, New World, India.

The following feasts are also celebrated today:
St Apollinaris Sidonius, Bishop of Clermont, 431: **St Claudius**, **St Asterius**, **St Neon**, **St Domnina** and **St Theonilla**, martyrs: **St Eugenius**, first Bishop of Derry: **St Justinian**, hermit: **St Philip Beniti** or **Benizi**: **St Theonas**, Archbishop of Alexandria.

There is but one law for all,
namely, that law which governs all law,
the law of our Creator, the law of humanity, justice, equity
– the law of nature, and of nations.

EDMUND BURKE

August 24
SAINT BARTHOLOMEW
Apostle – First century

It is believed that St Bartholomew is the same person mentioned in the Gospel as Nathanael and whom our Lord praised for his innocence and simplicity of heart. He was martyred in Armenia. Some say he was crucified, others say he was flayed alive. His remains are enshrined in the church of St Bartholomew in Rome.

He has come to be known as the patron saint of tanners and all workers with leather, including such associated trades as shoemaking, bookbinding and dyeing.

> **The following feasts are also celebrated today:**
> **St Irchard or Erthad** in Scotland, Bishop: **The Holy Martyrs of Utica**, called **The White Mass**, because their ashes, taken from the furnace wherein they were burned, had cemented with the lime: **St Ouen** or **Audoen**, Bishop, also called **Dadon**.

August 25
SAINT LOUIS IX
King – AD 1270

Twelve-year-old Louis succeeded to the throne of France after the death of his father, Louis VIII, in 1226. In 1234 Louis married Margaret of Provence, sister-in-law to King Henry III of England, by whom he had 11 children. At home he was obliged to defend himself against rebellions in southern France in 1242-3, and in 1242 he defeated Henry III of England in battle at Taillebourg, conquered Poitou, and the following year defeated Raymond VII of Toulouse. Later, by two judicious treaties with ambitious England and Aragon, he established peace in his kingdom.

After an illness in 1244 Louis had determined to go on Crusade, so in 1248 he sailed for the Holy Land. He captured Damietta in 1249 but was defeated by the Saracens at Mansura the following year, and he and his men were held to ransom. He contracted typhoid in Tunis and died on 25 August.

He left behind an enduring legacy in France; in addition to many religious and educational establishments founded by him, he had built the famous church of Sainte Chapelle in Paris to house a relic believed to be Christ's crown of thorns, presented by Emperor Baldwin of Constantinople in 1239.

In art Louis is often shown carrying a model of the Sainte Chapelle, which has led to his patronage of stonemasons and sculptors. Patron saint also of French monarchs and soldiers.

The following feasts are also celebrated today:
St Ebba or in English, **Tabbs**, sister to St Oswald, founded an abbey near Durham: **St Gregory**, Abbot of Utrecht.

August 26
SAINT NINIAN (NYNIA, RINGAN)
The earliest known Christian leader in Scotland – AD 432

Ninian was born near the Solway Firth, the son of a Christian king, and after being instructed in Rome was sent to evangelize Britain by the Pope.

He is said to have established his centre for evangelism at Whithorn in Galloway, where a stone church which he built may have given rise to the name by which Bede knows it, "Candida Casa" ("white house").

The following feasts are also celebrated today:
St Genisius, martyr, a comedian and the patron saint of the stage: **St Zephyrinus**, Pope and martyr, a native of Rome.

August 27
SAINT CÆSARIUS
Archbishop of Arles, Confessor – AD 542

St Cæsarius was born in 470 in the territory of Challons on the Saone. At eighteen years of age he joined the monastery of Lerins, where he was ordained deacon and afterwards priest and later abbot of a monastery built on an island in the Rhone. In 501 he became a bishop. Knowing that the church puts the poor under the special protection of the bishops, he gave them almost his whole revenue and built many hospitals.

In 508 a great number of prisoners were brought into Arles and the churches were filled with them. St Cæsarius, moved exceedingly at their condition, gave them both clothing and food using the whole treasury of his church. He took the utmost care of the sick, whom he provided with a very spacious house. The poor had easy access to him, and he gave strict instructions to the servant who waited on him to see there was not some poor at the door afraid of coming in. He died in Arles amid the poor whom he loved.

The following feasts are also celebrated today:
St Hugh of Lincoln, a child aged eleven, killed in 1255: **St Joseph Calasanctius**: **St Malrubius**, lived as a hermit in Scotland, martyred: **St Pœmen** or **Pastor**, retired into the wilderness of Sceté in Egypt: **St Syagrius**, Bishop of Autun.

August 28
SAINT AUGUSTINE
Bishop, Confessor, Doctor – AD 430

A native of Roman North Africa, Aurelius Augustinus was brought up as a Christian by his mother, St Monica, although his father Patricius was a pagan Roman officer. At the age of 16 he left for Carthage to study rhetoric, hoping to become a lawyer, but then abandoned law to devote himself to literature, teaching and philosophical study. It was at this point too that he abandoned his Christianity and took a mistress. They lived together for 15 years and in 372 she bore him a son Adeonatus. Much of his energy throughout his life was spent grappling with the problem of the existence of evil. He taught for some time in Carthage and Tagaste, and in 384 he moved to Milan where he met Ambrose, the bishop of Milan, who introduced him to Christian Neoplatonism and whose preaching forced him to reconsider his lost faith.

After reading a Bible passage from Romans in his garden one evening, he experienced a firm spiritual certainty and turned back to God. He was baptized on the day before Easter in 387, along with a friend Alipius and his son Adeonatus. Later that year he returned to Africa where he founded a community organized along semi-monastic lines, based on prayer and study. Bishop Valerius ordained him as priest and encouraged him to preach. Only four years later he was appointed coadjutor to Valerius, and on the bishop's death the following year he succeeded to the full bishopric, which he held for the rest of his life.

Augustine died at Hippo while the city was being besieged by Genseric's Vandal army. In art, Augustine is frequently represented in his bishop's robes holding a book as one of the four Latin Doctors of the Church. Because of his later penitence, his emblem is usually a broken, pierced or flaming heart. Patron saint of theologians.

The following feasts are also celebrated today:
St Hermes, martyred in Rome about 132: **St Julian**, martyr at Brioude.

August 29
The following feasts are celebrated today:
St Merri, in Latin **Medericus**: **St Sebbi** or **Sebba**: **St Sabina** martyr.

August 30
The following feasts are celebrated today:
St Agilus or **Aile**, Abbot: **St Felix** and **St Adauctus**: **St Fiaker** of Ireland: **St Pammarchius**, a Roman senator, a schoolfellow in youth of St Jerome.

August 31
SAINT AIDAN
AD 651

Beyond his Irish origin, little is known of Aidan's early life until we hear of him as a monk at Iona. Aidan was consecrated bishop and settled on Lindisfarne. From Lindisfarne, Aidan made countless missionary journeys on foot into the surrounding area, founding monasteries and churches.

In art he is frequently depicted with a stag, after a legend that he once rendered a stag invisible by prayer to protect it from its hunters. Aidan died at the church he had founded at Bamburgh. He was buried in Lindisfarne's cemetery.

The following feasts are also celebrated today:
St Cuthburge, Queen, virgin and Abbess, sister to King Ina: **St Isabel**, a daughter of Louis VIII of France: **St Raymond Nonnatus**, made Cardinal by Pope Gregory IX; but he neither changed his mode of dress nor left his poor cell after that honour.

September 1
SAINT GILES
Abbot – AD 710

The scanty facts known of Giles's life are that he was born during the seventh century, lived for some time as a hermit and that he founded a monastery near Arles in Provence on land given by King Womba. The neighbourhood of the monastery was later known as Saint-Gilles.

This rough outline was coloured and elaborated by a famous early medieval legend, which claimed that Giles was born in Athens and performed a miracle there which brought him unwanted attention: he is said to have cured a sick beggar by giving him his own cloak. In addition to the acclamation which he received for the miracle, Giles dreaded the approval of his fellow men occasioned by his generosity, and he fled to the area around Marseilles. He studied with the celebrated St Cæsarius of Arles and after two years became a hermit near Nines, at the mouth of the Rhône river.

The most famous incident of Giles's life (according to his legend) occurred when King Womba was out hunting one day and he or one of his men shot into a thicket at a stag. They then discovered Giles, himself wounded by the arrow while he protected the hind in his arms.

Some versions of the legend add that this hind was a pet who had supplied Giles with milk throughout his seclusion. He is popular as protector of the crippled and of nursing mothers.

In art he is usually shown with a hind in his arms and the arrow in his hand. He was also known as patron of blacksmiths and his churches can often be found at busy junctions where the smithies would also ply their trade, the one serving the spiritual needs and the other the practical needs of travellers. Patron saint of beggars, and cripples.

The following feasts are also celebrated today:
St Fiacre of Ireland: **St Firminus II**, the third Bishop of Amiens: **St Lupus** or **Leu**, Archbishop of Sens.

September 2
SAINT STEPHEN OF HUNGARY
King – AD 1038

Son of Geza, the duke of the Magyar community recently settled in Hungary and at least partly Christianized, Stephen was baptized along with his father by St Adalbert of Prague in 985. Ten years later he married Gisela, sister to Duke Henry III of Bavaria (later an emperor and saint) and in 997 succeeded Geza as ruler of the Magyars.

In 1031 tragedy struck when Stephen's son and heir Emeric died in a hunting accident. His last years were marred by ill health and by the succession squabbles which broke out well before his death.

His successors were to undo much of Stephen's extraordinary achievement, and this no doubt contributed to his reputation as a national hero along with the miracles reported at his tomb. His relics were enshrined at the church of Our Lady in Buda in 1083.

In art Stephen is usually represented holding a sword with a banner of the cross, and he is sometimes shown with his son St Emeric, whose relics were enshrined at the same time as those of his father. Patron saint of Hungary.

The following feasts are also celebrated today:
St Justus, Archbishop of Lyons: **St William**, Bishop of Roschild, chaplain to King Canutus.

I shall pass through this world but once.
Any good therefore that I can do, or any kindness that I can show to any
fellow creature let me do it now.
Let me not defer or neglect it, for I shall not pass this way again.

STEPHEN GRELLET

September 3
SAINT SIMEON STYLITES THE YOUNGER
AD 592

This saint was born at Antioch in 512 and went as a child into the monastery of Thaumastore situated in the deserts of Syria, near Antioch. For several years he served a holy hermit who was a monk and lived not far from the community upon a pillar. Simeon one day met a young leopard, and not knowing what it was, he put a rope about its neck and brought it to his master, saying he had found a cat. The good hermit, seeing the furious beast tamely obeying a child knew there was something special about this child. Not long after in 526 the old monk told Simeon to make a pillar and to live upon it. The youth obeyed and lived successively upon two pillars, within the grounds of the monastery for 68 years.

The saint fell ill about the year 592 and Gregory, the patriarch of Antioch, being informed that he was at the point of death, went in haste to assist at his last moments; but before he arrived St Simeon had died.

and
SAINT PIUS X
Pope – AD 1914

Joseph Sarto was born in very humble surroundings in the small town of Riese, Italy. Starting out as a poor parish Priest, he rose to be a Bishop, then a Cardinal, and finally Pope, without ever losing his profound humility and love for poverty. Pope Pius X, however, is also known for his marvellous gifts of insight and practicality which enabled him to lead the Church over a most difficult period.

The following feasts are also celebrated today:
St Macnisius, first Bishop of Connor in Ireland: **St Mansuet**, first Bishop of Toul in Lorraine: **St Remaclus**, first Abbot of the monastery and seminary at Solignac and later Bishop of Maestricht.

September 5
SAINT LAWRENCE JUSTINIAN
Bishop and Confessor – AD 1455

St Lawrence was born in Venice in the fifteenth century. While still a youth he entered the Order of the Canons of St George of Alga. He was made the first Patriarch of Venice, and his diocese was a model to all Christendom. St Lawrence died in 1455 after having led a very austere life.

The following feasts are also celebrated today:
St Alto of Ireland, a Scottish monk who travelled into Germany:
St Bertin.

September 6
SAINT PAMBO OF NITRIA
Abbot – AD 385

St Pambo took himself in his youth to the great St Antony in the desert and became one of his disciples. After he left St Antony, he settled in the desert of Nitria on a mountain where he built a monastery; but he lived some time in the wilderness of the Cells. St Athanasius asked St Pambo to come out of the desert to Alexandria. Our saint, seeing in that city an actress dressed up for the stage, wept, and being asked the reason of his tears, said he wept for the sinful condition of that unhappy woman, and also for his own because he did not take so much pains to please God as she did to ensnare men.

He died seventy years old, without any sickness or pain as he was making a basket, which he bequeathed to Palladius, who was at that time his disciple, the holy man having nothing else to give him.

The following feasts are also celebrated today:
St Bega or **Bees**, an Irish virgin, founded a nunnery near Carlisle in the middle of the seventh century: **St Eleutherius**, Abbot: **St Macculindus**, Bishop of Lusk, died in 497.

September 7
SAINT CLOUD
Confessor – AD 560

St Cloud is the first saint among the princes of the royal family of France. He was son of Chlodomir, King of Orleans, the eldest son of St Clotilda, and was born in 522. He was three years old when his father was killed in Burgundy in 524; his grandmother Clotilda brought him up in Paris.

He left his home whilst still very young to put himself under the discipline of St Severinus, a holy recluse who lived near Paris and became a monk. But Paris being a trouble to him, he withdrew secretly to Provence. Seeing he gained nothing after his hermitage was once made public he at length returned to Paris and was ordained priest by Eusebius, Bishop of Paris, in 551. He afterwards retired to Nogent, on the Seine, now called St Cloud, where he built a monastery.

The following feasts are also celebrated today:
St Alchmund and St Tilberht, both Bishops of Hedham: St Eunan, Bishop of Raphoe: St Evurtius, Bishop of Orleans in the reign of Constantine the Great: St Grimonia or Germana, an Irish maiden, martyred in Picardy: St Madelberte, Abbess, niece to St Aldegundis: St Regina, called in France St Reine, beheaded at Aliza.

September 8
The following feasts are celebrated today:
St Adrian, an officer of the Roman army: St Corbinian, a native of France, lived as a recluse for seven years; later made Bishop of Frisingen in Upper Bavaria: St Disen or Disibode, an Irish monk who laboured in France and in Germany,: St Eusebius, St Nestorius, St Zeno and St Nestor, martyrs in the time of Julian the Apostate: St Sidronius, martyr, Rome.

September 9
SAINT PETER CLAVER
Confessor – AD 1654

A native of Catalonia in Spain, Peter studied at the University of Barcelona and enrolled with the Jesuits at the age of 20 at Tarragona. He continued his studies in Majorca, at the Montesione College in Palma, and it was here that he met St Alphonsus Rodriguez who encouraged his desire for missionary work in the New World. He left Spain as a missionary to New Granada, landing at Cartagena (modern Columbia) in 1610. Five years later he was ordained as a priest there.

The city was a centre for the ubiquitous slave trade; blacks from West Africa were shipped to the port in appalling conditions and kept in enclosures like animals before being distributed to traders or their new masters. Peter worked alongside the Jesuit Father Alfonso de Sandovel, who had already spent 40 years trying to relieve the sufferings of the slaves both practically and spiritually.

When the slaves were sold to mines and plantations Peter followed up his care by paying regular visits to check on their conditions, ensuring at least that the basic laws for their protection were fully observed.

In addition to his work among the slaves, Peter spent much of his time visiting the inmates of the city jail and patients in the local hospitals. When plague struck Cartagena in 1650 Peter was one of those infected, and he never fully recovered. He carried on with his work as best he could, but spent much time alone in his cell, apparently neglected and mistreated by the black slave appointed to look after him and died alone.

The following feasts are also celebrated today:
St **Bettelin** or **Beccelin**, hermit, who served St Guthlac: St **Kiarin** or **Kierin**, Abbot: St **Gorgonius**, St **Dorotheus** and **Companions**, martyrs: St **Omer**, Bishop: St **Osmanna**, virgin.

September 10
SAINT NICHOLAS OF TOLENTINO
Confessor – AD 1306

St Nicholas was a native of St Angelo, a town near Fermo, in the Marca of Ancona and was born about the year 1245. He had a tender love for the poor and would take home those that he met in order to share with them whatever he had for his own subsistence. He entered the convent at Tolentino when he was eighteen years of age, and was sent successively to several convents at Recanati, Macerata and Cingole where he was ordained priest by the Bishop of Osimo. The last thirty years of his life he resided at Tolentino where his body is buried in the church.

The following feasts are also celebrated today:
St **Finian**, called **Winin** by the Welsh, born in Ireland early in the sixth century: St **Macanisius** in the diocese of Connor: St **Pulcheria**, Empress: St **Salvius**, Bishop.

September 11
The following feasts are celebrated today:
St **Paphnutius**, an Egyptian who, after spending several years in the desert under the great St Antony, was made Bishop of Upper Thebais; he was one of those who, under Maximin Daia, lost the right eye and was afterwards sent to work in the mines: St **Patiens**, Archbishop of Lyons: St **Protus** and St **Hyachinthus**, brothers, martyred in the third century.

*It is always wise
to keep your words soft and sweet,
because you never know when you will have to eat them.*

HAROLD PYNE

September 12
SAINT EANSWIDE
Virgin, Abbess

Eanswide was the daughter of Eadbald whose father was St Ethelbert, the first Christian King of England. She founded a monastery of nuns near Folkestone, in Kent. The sea having afterwards swallowed up part of this priory, the nunnery was removed into Folkestone itself and the saint's relics were deposited in that church which had been built by her father, King Eadbald.

The following feasts are also celebrated today:
St Albeus, Bishop and chief patron of Munster: **St Guy**, in Latin **Guido**, called the poor man of Anderlect.

September 13
SAINT JOHN CHRYSOSTOM
AD 407

Fatherless as a baby, John was brought up as a Christian by his mother. He studied oratory under the famous pagan rhetorician Libanius and theology under Diodorus of Tarsus, was baptized as a young man and then abandoned a promising legal career in c373 to live as an ascetic in a mountain community near Antioch. The austere life ruined his health, and in 381 he returned to Antioch to be made deacon.

Five years later he was ordained as a priest by Bishop Flavian of Antioch, whom he served for the next 12 years. His powerful sermons soon gained him the nickname Chrysostom, "the golden-mouthed".

John's primary concern was the misuse of wealth by the rich: in his reforms he made huge personal donations to the poor, cutting back on clerical pomp and extravagance, and funding missions to the East.

He travelled to Armenia, where he wrote many extant letters describing his sufferings and was then moved on to Pontus where he died of exhaustion, treated harshly by his captors. His body was returned to Constantinople 31 years later, to be buried at the Church of the Apostles there. In art his emblem is a beehive, symbol of eloquence. Patron saint of preachers, invoked against epilepsy.

The following feasts are also celebrated today:
St Amatus or **Ame**, Abbot in Lorraine: **St Eulogius**, a Syrian Bishop, Patriarch of Alexandria, 608: **St Maurilius**, Bishop.

September 15
The following feasts are celebrated today:
St Aicard or **Achard**, seventh Bishop of Troyes, about 486: **St Aper** or **Evre**: **St John the Dwarf** (from his low stature) anchoret of Sceté: **St Nicetas**, martyr: **St Nicomedes**, a priest of Rome, beaten to death with clubs for assisting the martyrs and for burying their bodies.

September 16
SAINT CYPRIAN
Bishop, Martyr – AD 258

Until the age of about 46, Cyprian enjoyed a successful career in Carthage as orator, and lawyer. but after conversion to Christianity he turned his attention and his studies exclusively to the Bible and Christian writings. He was soon ordained as a priest, and was popularly elected bishop of Carthage in 248.

During his life Cyprian inspired great devotion among his flock, and the accounts we have of him, including a biography by Pontius, show him as a conscientious pastor, greatly concerned with the condition of the church as a whole and of each individual under his care. His writings are many and varied.

and
SAINT CORNELIUS
Martyr – AD 253

Nothing is known of Cornelius's early life, but when St Fabian was martyred in 250 Cornelius was elected his successor as Pope, after a gap of a year.

He was banished to Civita Vecchia (Centumcellae), where he died. Some traditions claim that he was beheaded but it seems more likely that his death was caused by harsh conditions in exile.

Cornelius is closely associated with Cyprian, and they share a feast-day. In art he is usually represented in papal vestments, holding a triple cross or a horn, or occasionally with bulls, and this association has led to his patronage of cattle and other domestic animals. Patron saint of cattle and domestic animals, invoked against earache, epilepsy, and fever.

The following feasts are also celebrated today:
St Editha or **Eadgith** (961), the natural daughter of King Edgar. **St Euphemia**, virgin, martyr: **St Lucia**, a noble widow and **St Germianus**, martyrs: **St Ninian** or **Nynias**, Bishop, the apostle of the Southern Picts.

September 17
SAINT ROBERT BELLARMINE
AD 1621

Born near Siena on 4 October, Roberto Francis Romulus Bellarmine, known for his prowess in literature, music and rhetoric as a youth, enrolled with the Jesuit order at 18, against the wishes of his father. He spent some years teaching classics in Piedmont and Florence and studying theology in Padua and Louvain.

In 1570 he was ordained at Ghent, and elected to the chair of theology at Louvain, where he promoted the study of Hebrew. In 1576 he was appointed professor of controversial theology at the new Roman College. Over the next 11 years, Bellarmine drafted his great work *Disputations on the Controversies of the Christian faith*.

In 1592 he became rector of the Roman College and two years later was appointed provincial of Naples. In 1597 he became theologian to Pope Clement VIII, and produced two catechisms which remained in use until quite recently. When he was appointed cardinal in 1599, against his own wishes, he refused to give up the life of austerity to which he was accustomed, and continued to live almost exclusively on bread, water and garlic. He was made archbishop of Capua in 1602 and died at the age of 79.

The following feasts are also celebrated today:
St Columba, a nun in the monastery of Tabanos, beheaded by the Moors, 853: **St Hildegardis**, Abbess, born 1098: **St Landebert**, later called **St Lambert**, Bishop of Maestricht and patron of Liége: **St Peter Arbues**, martyr: **St Rouen**, in Latin **Rodingus**, first Abbot of Beaulieu in Argonne: **St Socrates** and **St Stephen**, martyrs.

September 18
SAINT JOSEPH OF COPERTINO
Confessor – AD 1563

St Joseph was born of poor parents at Copertino, near Naples. He entered the Order of St Francis as a lay-brother, but because of his spirit of sacrifice, humility and charity, he was ordained a priest.

He found it extremely difficult to study and it took him many years to reach the priesthood. Invoked by students for help with examinations.

Tis well for us to toil, and strive to win
All that our comfort and our health require,
But let the angel still within us reign,
That we may aid the world to something higher.

Anon

The following feasts are also celebrated today:
St Ferreol, martyr, a tribune in Gaul, who was secretly a Christian:
St Methodius, Bishop of Tyre.

September 19
SAINT THEODORE OF TARSUS
AD 690

A native of Tarsus, Theodore was educated in Athens and took his monastic vows as a Basilian monk in Rome. In 668, at the age of 66, Theodore was appointed archbishop of Canterbury by Pope Vitalian. The post was unexpectedly vacant following the death of Wighard, archbishop-elect, in Rome, and when Vitalian had asked the African monk Adrian to accept the appointment he had declined, suggesting instead his Greek friend Theodore.

When Theodore sailed for England he was accompanied by Adrian as an adviser. With them was Benedict Biscop, later founder of the monasteries at Wearmouth and Jarrow.

Theodore died on 19 September; he was buried in the monastery of St Peter and St Paul in Canterbury, close to the bones of St Augustine, and his incorrupt body was translated into a shrine in 1091.

The following feasts are also celebrated today:
St Eustochius, Bishop of Tours: St Januarius, Bishop of Benevento, and his Companions, martyrs, 305; St Januarius is greatly honoured in his relics in Naples: St Lucy, virgin, a daughter of a king of the Scots, who retired to France: St Peleus, St Pa-termuthes, and their Companions, martyrs: St Sequanus or Seine, Abbot.

September 20
SAINT EUSTACE AND HIS COMPANIONS
Martyrs

St Eustace a Christian officer of the Roman army, refused to offer incense to the gods after a great victory. He, his wife, and two children were therefore burned at the stake.

The following feast is also celebrated today:
St Agapetus, a native of Rome who succeeded Pope John II.

September 21
SAINT MATTHEW
Author of the first Gospel

Our information about Matthew comes almost exclusively from the Gospel accounts, beyond which little is known except his highly probable authorship of the Gospel that bears his name, written between the years 60 and 90. He was probably born in Galilee, the son of one Alpheus, and worked as a tax-collector until he was called by Jesus. He is traditionally thought to have been called Levi before his conversion.

His profession would have made him a man despised by other Jews: tax-collectors (or publicans) served the oppressing Romans and it was widely recognized that they supplemented their pay by extortion. They were banned from religious communion in the temple and avoided in the social and business spheres. When he heard Jesus's summons, Matthew abandoned his despised yet lucrative life-style, but in the list of disciples in his own gospel he uniquely places Thomas (the Doubter) above himself and adds to his own name "the publican".

Among the four evangelists, the other three of whom are linked with symbolic beasts, Matthew is represented by the figure of a winged man in recognition of the human concerns expressed in his Gospel, especially the family of Christ.

The later life and death of Matthew are unknown, although one strong tradition claims that he preached in Judaea, Ethiopia and Persia where he is said to have been martyred.

Matthew is a popular figure in art, shown as an evangelist writing his Gospel at his desk aided by an angel or as an apostle carrying either an instrument of martyrdom (usually a spear or sword) or a money-box, recalling his earlier profession. In later representations he sometimes wears glasses, presumably the distinguishing mark of an accountant or financial clerk. He was declared patron saint of Italian accountants and of tax-collectors and customs officials.

The following feasts are also celebrated today:
St Lo, in Latin **Laudus**, Bishop of Coutances in Normandy: **St Maura**, virgin, nobly born at Troyes.

September 22
The following feasts are celebrated today:
St Emmeran, Patron of Ratisbon, he was Bishop of Poitiers, 653: **St Maurice and his Companions**, martyrs, soldiers of the famous Thebean Legion: **St Thomas of Villanova**, Bishop of Valentia, an Augustinian, died 1555.

September 23
SAINT ADOMNAN
AD 704

Also known as Adomnan, he was an Irishman traditionally descended from the grandfather of Columba. He enrolled as a novice at Iona under abbot Seghine at the age of about 28, whom he went on to succeed as ninth abbot in 679. At Iona Adomnan received and taught Aldfrith, son of King Oswiu of Northumberland, who was seeking sanctuary after his father's death had embroiled him in a violent dispute over succession.

Adomnan died on 23 September at Iona. He is usually depicted praying with the moon and seven stars about him, and occasionally writing his *Life of St Columba*.

The following feasts are also celebrated today:
St Linus, Pope, the immediate successor of St Peter: **St Thecla**.

September 24
The following feasts are also celebrated today:
St Chuniald or **Conald** of Ireland, one of the most eminent Scottish or Irish missionaries who carried the faith into Germany: **St Gerard**, Bishop of Chonad, martyr: **St Germer** or **Geremar**, Abbot, who, whilst yet a layman, built a monastery in honour of St Peter, where his only son was afterwards buried: **St Rusticus**, commonly called **St Rotiri**, lived as a hermit for five years, Bishop of Auvergne; there were in his age two other bishops of this name, one of Lyons and the other of Narbonne.

September 25
SAINT FINBAR (BARR)
Founder of Cork – AD 630

An illegitimate child of the clan of Ui Briuin Ratha, whose father was a metal worker and mother of royal extraction, Finbar was born in Co Cork, baptized at Lochan and educated by monks at Kilmacahil, Kilkenny. It was here that he received his nickname Fionnbharr, meaning "white-head". He is said to have journeyed to Rome on pilgrimage with several of the monks, visiting St David in South Wales on the way, and legend has it that when the Pope wanted to consecrate him as bishop he was divinely prevented.

On return to Ireland he lived for some years as a hermit by Lake Gougane Barra, quickly attracting a number of followers and establishing the monastery of Etargabail which was to become a school renowned throughout Ireland. His more famous foundation, however, was that which began as a monastery on the river Lee, and which developed into the city of Cork. Finbar is traditionally believed to have been consecrated as the first bishop of Cork in c600, and is thought to have died at Cloyne between 10 and 30 years later. His body was removed to Cork for burial.

Many fantastic miracles have been accredited to Finbar, perhaps the most poetic claim being that he crossed the Irish sea on horseback. It was said that for two weeks after his death the sun refused to set at Cloyne. Although he is venerated throughout Ireland and Scotland, and especially in Cork, the true centre of devotion to Finbar is his monastery at Gougane Barra. Patron saint of Barra in Scotland and Cork, Ireland.

The following feasts are also celebrated today:
St Aunaire, Bishop of Auxerre about 570: **St Ceolfried**, Abbot, 716; this is the same Teutonic name as Geoffroy and means "Joyful", this saint was related to St Bennet Biscop: **St Firman**, Bishop of Amiens.

September 26
The following feasts are celebrated today:
St Colman Elo, Abbot, born in Meath; built there the great monastery of Land-elo in which he trained many to religious perfection: **St Cyprian**, surnamed the Magician, devoted by his parents to the worship of the devil; he found Christian women proof against his spells: **St Justina**, who suffered martyrdom with him: **St Eusebius**, Pope, who succeeded St Marcellus: **St Nilus the Younger**, Abbot, of Grecian extraction, who, after the death of his wife took himself to a monastery; he died, aged ninety-six in 1005.

It doesn't pay to be too good –
Just good enough will do;
It answers pretty well for me,
And it will serve for you.
Don't fret about your neighbours' faults –
It isn't right you should;
And bear in mind they try as hard
As you do to be good.

Anon

September 27
The following feasts are celebrated today:
St Cosmas and **St Damian**, martyrs, about 303, two brothers born in Arabia: **St Elzear** and **St Delphina**, his wife, a noble couple, he was Count of Arian.

September 28
SAINT WENCESLAS
Duke of Bohemia – 929

The education of young Wenceslas, son of Duke Wratislaw of Bohemia, was left largely in the hands of his Christian grandmother, St Ludmilla. In c920 Wratislaw died in battle against the Magyars and Wenceslas's mother Drahomira took the opportunity to seize power. Her rule ended with popular revolt in c922 and Wenceslas succeeded to the duchy.

The young duke proved a fair if strict ruler, who wasted no time in suppressing rebellion among his discontented nobles and in redressing the pagan policies of his mother.

Wenceslas was murdered at the hands of Boleslav and his followers on 20 September, traditionally believed to have been attacked and overcome on his way to Mass during a visit to his brother's estate. He was immediately venerated as a martyr, and Boleslav had his relics translated to the church of St Vitus in Prague.

The church quickly became established as a popular destination for pilgrims and Wenceslas himself was soon regarded as the patron saint of Bohemia, with his image stamped on the country's coins. The crown of Wenceslas came to be regarded as a potent symbol of nationalism for the Czechs. Because of the region's reputation for producing fine beer, its patron naturally became associated with the brewing industry, although in life he was in fact more closely associated with the wine trade; he used to produce the wine for Mass from his own vineyards. In Britain, the familiarity of his name is due mainly to the famous carol by J. M. Neale, *Good King Wenceslas*, a reworking of the medieval carol *Tempus adest floridum*. Patron saint of Czechoslovakia and brewers.

The following feasts are also celebrated today:
St Eustochium, virgin: **St Exuperius**, Bishop of Toulouse: **St Lioba**, an Englishwoman, born in Dorset and trained in the monastery of Wimborne.

September 29
SAINT MICHAEL – THE ARCHANGEL

One of only three angels to be venerated by the Western church (the other two are Gabriel and Raphael, whose feast began only in this century). He appears in Judaeo-Christian traditions as the deputy of God himself, carrying out the Almighty's commands in relation to mankind.

He is mentioned twice in the Old Testament by Daniel (10:13 and 12:1) as the protector of the chosen people Israel and a chief prince of the heavenly host, and in the New Testament he features in Revelation, as the conqueror of the satanic dragon and is mentioned by Jude (v9) arguing with the Devil for possession of Moses's body.

Michael was thought to have appeared during a plague in Rome and in some tradition is regarded, Charon-like, as the receiver of the souls of the dead. In the West he is best known as a warrior saint, whose care was the protection of soldiers and victory over the forces of evil. Unsurprisingly, he was often invoked by military leaders as a sign of the right on their side.

In art he is most frequently shown with a sword, either battling with or standing in triumph over a dragon or the prostrate Satan.

He is also depicted, especially in medieval art, weighing the souls of the dead, a reference to the widely-held belief that he was entrusted with the power of judgement over them. Patron saint of Brussels, the sick and battle. Invoked when tempted or when storm-tossed at sea.

The following feast is also celebrated today:
St Theodata, martyr.

September 30
SAINT JEROME
Confessor and Doctor – AD 420

Jerome was born in Dalmatia, and in his early years was educated at home by his father and brought up as a Christian. Later he went on to study under the famous pagan grammarian Donatus in Rome, and became learned in rhetoric and classical literature. It was in Rome, too, that he was baptized, by Pope Liberius in c360.

By now Jerome was in the habit of making regular visits to the churches and catacombs of Rome, and after some travelling through Italy and Gaul, in 370 he decided to join a religious community at Aquileia, along with some friends. This was a scholarly group led by Bishop Valerian.

A few years later there was a quarrel within the community; Jerome travelled east and in 374 arrived in Antioch, where two of his companions died. He lived for five years as a hermit in the Syrian desert.

On his return to Antioch and against his wishes, Jerome was ordained by Paulinus, but in fact he never said a Mass.

In 382 Jerome went to Rome to serve as interpreter to Paulinus, who was aspiring to the see of Antioch. He remained there as secretary to Pope Damasus I and began the major task of revising the Latin version of the Bible to create a standard text.

On the death of his protector Damasus, Jerome left Rome under something of a cloud to return east with several of his disciples, including Paula and Eustochium; in 386 they settled in Bethlehem. Paula began a community of nuns and Jerome founded a monastery where he lived for the rest of his life; they also founded a hospice to serve travellers and a free school for the local children in which Jerome taught Latin and Greek.

Jerome died in Bethlehem and his body was buried at the Church of the Nativity there, near the site traditionally believed to have been the birthplace of Christ. He is regarded as one of the four Latin Doctors of the Church and his contribution to biblical scholarship is unequalled.

His emblem, appropriately enough, is a lion, which appears throughout the various representations of him as cardinal, scholar, Doctor and founder. This was because of a popular tradition that Jerome had once plucked out a thorn from a lion's foot and that afterwards the grateful beast followed him everywhere as a tame pet. Patron saint of librarians.

The following feasts are also celebrated today:
St Gregory, Bishop of Cæsaria in Cappadocia, surnamed the Apostle of Armenia and the Illuminator: **St Honorius**, Archbishop of Canterbury, one of those sent by St Gregory to convert the English nation to Christ; he died 30 September 753.

October 1
SAINT THÉRÈSE OF LISIEUX
The little flower – AD 1897

Thérèse, born Marie Françoise Martin was the youngest daughter of the watchmaker Louis Martin and his wife Zélie Guérin who died when she was only four or five years old. When the family moved to Lisieux in 1877 she was cared for by her aunt and her older sisters and educated by Benedictine nuns. Five of the sisters were eventually to join the Carmelite convent at Lisieux. Although the youngest, Thérèse was the third to enrol at the age of only 15, taking the name Thérèse of the Child Jesus.

For the next nine years, Thérèse lived quietly at the convent. Her aim was a simple, unselfconscious obedience, her "little way" as she called it. In 1895 she died at the age of 24, after silently and patiently suffering enormous pain, and suddenly the young unknown nun was accredited with interceding in innumerable miracles, attracting almost universal veneration. A great part of her popularity was her very simplicity; Thérèse had demonstrated that one need not accomplish great deeds or possess enormous talent to attain sanctity.

In 1925 a large church was built in Lisieux for the hordes of pilgrims visiting her shrine there. Patron saint of France, mission and florists.

The following feasts are also celebrated today:
St Bavo, hermit, a model of penance, patron of Ghent: St Fidharleus of Ireland, Abbot of Raithin, died in 762: St Piat, apostle of Tournay, where he suffered tortures, finishing his martyrdom at Seclin: St Remigius, the apostle of the French, called by many in his lifetime a second St Paul: St Wasnulf or Wasnon, one of the many Scottish monks invited by St Vincent, Count of Haynault, to preach in the Netherlands.

October 2
The following feast is celebrated today:
St Leodegarius in French St Leger, martyr.

October 3
SAINT THOMAS OF HEREFORD
Thomas de Cantelupe – AD 1282

Baron William de Cantelupe, chief steward in the household of King Henry III a member of a noble Norman family, married the countess of Gloucester. Their son Thomas was born in Buckinghamshire, and his education was entrusted to an uncle, Bishop Walter of Worcester. He was sent first to Oxford and then to Paris.

Thomas attended the Council of Lyons with his father in 1245 and probably received ordination then. He continued his legal studies in Orléans and Paris, where he gained his licence in canon law, and returned to Oxford as a lecturer. Around 1262 he was appointed Chancellor of the University and in 1264 he was named Chancellor of England.

In 1265 Thomas was dismissed from this post and retired to France. After several years of lecturing in Paris, Thomas returned to England to be elected Bishop of Hereford in 1275. His energetic and combative approach made him unpopular with many of the lay lords he confronted, but the common people of his parish generally loved this large-hearted holy man. During 1282 Thomas went to Rome but the journey exhausted him and he died near Orvieto. His heart and some bones were returned to Hereford and many miracles were reported at his shrine.

The following feasts are also celebrated today:
St Dionysius who is said to have been named Bishop of Athens by St Paul and to have been burnt alive in that city: Two St Ewalds, brothers, both priests who for distinction and because of the colour of their hair, are called The White Ewald and the Black Ewald: St Gerard, Abbot, to whom the inspection and reformation of all the abbeys in Flanders was committed.

October 4
SAINT FRANCIS OF ASSISI
AD 1226

While Pietro di Beradone, a wealthy silk trader from Assisi, was away from home on business in France his wife gave birth to a son whom she christened Giovanni. On his return, the boy's father insisted that he be renamed Francesco, "the French one", struck by the coincidence that he had been in France at the time of the boy's birth and that his mother was from Provence.

The young Francis followed his father into business, spending his spare time in extravagance until his capture as a prisoner of war in 1202, when fighting against the Perugians. He was held for a year, and soon after his release underwent a long period of serious illness: the experience was a sobering one. In 1205 he returned to the wars, and on his return to Assisi the young man, already displaying a more serious and spiritual aspect, entered the run-down church of San Damiano.

As he prayed, he saw a vision of Christ speaking to him, saying "Repair my home, which is falling into disrepair." Ever literally-minded, Francis began to raise the money to pay for the rebuilding of San Damiano by selling a bale of cloth from his father's warehouse. A fiery conflict ensued between father and son, which ended only when Francis dramatically renounced his inheritance, throwing down even the clothes he was wearing, and left empty-handed to espouse "Lady Poverty".

Begging around the town he raised enough money to complete the rebuilding of San Damiano, and lived otherwise as a homeless pilgrim, owning nothing, caring for the sick and always preaching. Within a few years he had attracted several followers. They settled at the Portincula chapel near a leper colony in Assisi, forming a community dedicated to poverty. The brothers studied little as they did not even own books; simplicity rather than learning was the concern of the new community. They were known as the Friars Minor, an indication of their humility.

By 1212, Francis had founded the Poor Clares with St Clare, a community of women living by his Rule, and then he headed east. His aim was to convert the Saracens, but he was thwarted by shipwreck. He tried again the following year but fell seriously ill in Spain and was forced to return to Italy. By now the number of monks had grown to almost uncontrollable proportions. 5,000 friars, with 500 more clamouring for admission.

Many of Francis's most famous doings belong to the last period of his life, after his official leadership of the Franciscans. He built the first Christmas crib at Grecchia in 1223, beginning a custom still celebrated across the Christian world. Even more famous perhaps was his experience of the stigmata while praying on Mount La Verna in 1224, wounds on his body corresponding to those inflicted on Christ in his Passion; these were said to be visible until his death, although Francis usually kept them covered. He died at the age of 45 at the Portincula. Buried at San Giorgio in Assissi, Francis's relics were translated to the New Basilica specially built by Elias in 1230. His remains now lie in a modest shrine built in 1931, which is a centre of worldwide pilgrimage.

He is a favourite with artists, usually shown as a small Franciscan, bearded and bearing the stigmata, surrounded by animals and birds, together with St Clare, St Dominic and the Virgin or contemplating a skull, and in 1980 was named patron saint of ecology. Patron saint also of merchants, animals, animal and welfare societies.

The following feasts are also celebrated today:
St Ammon, hermit, founder of the Hermitages of Nitria: St Aurea, Abbell: St Edwin, King who was baptized in the eleventh year of his reign, killed in battle in 633, after he had governed his people with wisdom and justice for seventeen years: St Marcus, St Mercian (said to have been brothers) and their Companions, martyrs, killed in 304.

October 5
The following feasts are celebrated today:
St Galla, widow; being married very young, she lost her husband during the first year and gave the revenues of her great estate to be the patrimony of the poor, and gave herself up to a life of prayer and suffering: St Placidus, St Eutychius and thirty other martyrs.

October 6
SAINT BRUNO
Founder of the Carthusian Order – AD 1101

Born into a noble family of Cologne, Bruno was sent to be educated at the famous cathedral school in Rheims. He returned to Cologne after his studies to be ordained and was appointed canon at St Cunibert's in c1055, but he left the next year to return to Rheims as professor of theology and grammar and remained there for nearly 20 years, teaching such illustrious pupils as the future Pope Urban II.

In 1074, Archbishop Manasses obtained for him the post of chancellor of Rheims, and in c1084 with six companions founded a monastery at Grenoble based on the precepts of solitude, austerity and manual labour on land in the untamed mountains. So successful was it that in 1090, much against his will, Bruno was called to Rome by Urban II as his adviser in church affairs and clergy reform. Urban also offered him the archbishopric of Reggio, but Bruno managed to persuade his former pupil to allow him the seclusion he craved. He left Rome to found a community, St Mary's at Della Toeer in Calabria, and here he died. His emblem in art is a ray of light, which illuminates the saint and the book which he holds.

The following feast is also celebrated today:
St Faith of Fides, virgin, suffered under Dacian a terrible death by burning; Dacian apprehended a number of spectators who pitied her; refusing as she had done, to sacrifice to the heathen gods, they were also beheaded.

October 7
The following feasts are celebrated today:
St Justina of Padua, virgin and martyr, suffered death under Diocletian about 304: **St Marcellus** and **St Apeleius**, martyrs, honoured at Placentia in Italy: **St Mark**, Pope, 336, a Roman by birth, succeeded St Silvester: **St Osith**, virgin: **St Sergius** and **St Bacchus**, martyrs.

October 8
The following feasts are celebrated today:
St Bridget of Sweden, widow, 1373: **St Keyna**, called by the Welsh "the virgin", lived as a recluse in a wood in Somerset: **St Pelagia**, of Antioch, shut herself up in a grotto on Mount Olivet.

October 9
SAINT DENIS
First bishop of Paris – AD c250

An Italian by birth, Denis was sent to Gaul as a missionary from Rome in the middle of the third century. On his arrival in Paris he established a centre for Christianity on an island in the Seine, but this success aroused opposition from the Roman authorities and he was arrested along with two companions, a priest named Rusticus and Eleutherius, a deacon. The three are believed to have been beheaded on the hill now known as Montmartre, "hill of martyrs".

A legend claimed that Denis was a "cephalophore", a martyr believed to have carried his own head to his burial place (in this case the site of the abbey of St Denis) after execution.

This is the basis of the most common representations of St Denis, shown carrying his head on a book before him or preparing to catch it as he is beheaded. Patron saint of France, invoked against headaches and strife.

What saint has ever won his crown
without first contending for it?
(St Jerome)

The following feasts are also celebrated today:
St **Domninus**, an officer of Maximian Herculeus, beheaded in 304 on the Claudian Way: St **Guislain**, Abbot who founded a monastery in honour of St Peter and St Paul: St **Lewis Bertrand**, 1526.

October 10
The following feasts are celebrated today:
St **Francis Borgia**, Duke of Gandia, the third general of the Jesuit Order; he died in Rome in 1572: St **John of Bridlington**, an eminent comtemplative, whose study ever was to know himself and God, 1397: St **Paulinus**, one of the second band of missionaries sent by St Gregory the Great to England, first Archbishop of York, died 644.

October 11
SAINT PETER OF ALCANTARA
AD 1562

The son of the governor of Alcantara, in Estremadura, Spain, Peter Garavito was educated locally and then followed in the footsteps of his father by going on to study law at the University of Salamanca. At the age of 16 he became a Franciscan. Following the ascetic regime there he performed extreme penances and austerities. He won such respect that in 1521 he was sent to found a new monastery at Badajoz, although he was not ordained for another three years.

In 1538 he became minister provincial of the Observants' province of Estremadura; it was already renowned for its severity, and Peter's attempts to reform it even further were a failure. He resigned in 1540 and left for Arabida near Lisbon, where he lived as a hermit.

Peter died kneeling in his monastery. In art his extraordinary penances and his mysticism are recalled in the visual representation of a radiant Franciscan levitated before a cross. He is also shown walking on water with a friend, a star shining above his head, or with an inspirational dove at his ear.

The following feasts are also celebrated today:
St **Ethelburge** or **Edelbirge**, Abbess of Barking in Essex, an English Saxon princess, sister to St Erconwald, Bishop of London: St **Canice**, **Canicus**, or **Kenny**, connected by holy friendship with St Columkille, patron of Kilkenny (Church of Kenny), a disciple of St Finian; he founded the monastery of Achadbho or "Ox's Field" and died in 599: St **Gummar**, called **Gomer** by the French: St **John Leonardi**: St **Tarachus**, St **Probus** and St **Andronicus**, 304.

October 12
SAINT WILFRID
Bishop – AD 709

Wilfrid's father was a nobleman whose close connections with the court of Northumbria secured his child a place in the household of King Oswiu at the age of 13. Here he became a particular favourite of Queen Enfleda, and to secure the best education for him she arranged his departure for Lindisfarne, the great centre of Celtic Christianity in the north of Britain. He left for Canterbury and studied briefly under St Honorius, developing a taste for Roman practices of the church before going on to visit Rome itself with Benedict Biscop in 654.

In Rome, Wilfrid studied under Boniface. He arrived back in his native country in about 660, and was asked by Alcfrith, king of the Northumbrian province of Deira, to take on the abbacy of Ripon. He was made bishop of York in 669 and set about reforming his diocese. He improved the great Minster at York, built a magnificent church at Hexham and gained large areas of land for his monasteries.

It was while visiting his monasteries in Mercia that Wilfrid died. He was buried at Ripon, when both Canterbury and Worcester claimed his relics. In art he is usually represented as a bishop either baptizing or preaching, holding his pastoral staff.

The following feasts are also celebrated today:
St Salvinus, Bishop of Verona.

October 13
SAINT EDWARD THE CONFESSOR
AD 1066

The son of King Æthelred the Unready and Emma, sister of a Norman duke, the young Edward was educated in Ely. At the Danish invasion of 1013 he was sent with his mother to Normandy where he remained after the death of his father and his mother's return to England to marry Cnut, now king of England. Edward ascended the throne in 1042. Two years later he married Edith, daughter of the powerful Earl Godwin. Edward's rule was peaceful and prosperous; he was popular with the poor for his generosity, gentleness and sound government.

Near the end of his life Edward rebuilt St Peter's Abbey at Westminster, site of the modern Westminster Abbey in which English monarchs are traditionally coronated and buried. Edward spent vast sums on the Romanesque church, but was too ill to attend its consecration. He was buried there, and there his body has remained up to the present day.

The following feasts are also celebrated today:
St Colman martyr, tortured and hanged near Vienna in 1012:
St Comgan, Abbot, said to have been the son of Cellach, King of
Ireland; unjustly dethroned and banished, he fled to Scotland where
he became a monk; after his death his body was taken to Iona:
St Faustus, **St Januaris** and **St Martialis**, called "the three crowns
of Cordova", martyred there in 304: **St Gerald** of Upper Auvergne,
born in 955.

October 14
The following feasts are celebrated today:
St Burckard, first Bishop of Wurtzburg, invited from England by
St Boniface to work in his missionary field of Germany: **St Callistus**
or **Calixtus**, the Pope who succeeded St Zepherin; he governed the
Church in a time of great difficulty: **St Dominic**, surnamed Loricatus:
St Donatian, Bishop of Rheims and patron of Bruges.

October 15
SAINT TERESA OF ÁVILA
First female Doctor of the Church – AD 1582

The daughter of aristocratic Castilian parents, Teresa exhibited a lively and
pious disposition from an early age. On the death of her mother in c1529
she was sent to be educated by Augustinian nuns in Ávila but was obliged
to quit the convent after three years because of her poor health. Despite
initial opposition from her father she entered the Carmelite house in Ávila,
in 1533. After only a year her health failed again and she was forced to
retire temporarily, but after recuperating with her family she returned to the
convent in 1540.

During middle-age Teresa resolved to found a religious house which
would adhere more strictly to the original Carmelite rule, distressed by the
laxity of life within her unreformed convent. Her new foundation in 1562,
the first community of Discalced (barefoot) Carmelite nuns was
St Joseph's at Ávila, distinguished from the unreformed movement by the
personal poverty of the nuns, the enclosed and disciplined spiritual life,
and a regime of simple manual work that made the convent practically
self-sufficient. She was to found another 16 such convents in the course
of her life.

The Discalced Carmelites, both male and female houses, faced much
opposition from their unreformed counterparts. It was during these troubled
years that Teresa wrote her famous letters and books, most notably her
own *Life* in 1565. *The Way of Perfection* written for nuns in 1573 and the
Interior Castle (1577) a classic work on contemplative prayer.

On her way back to Ávila after founding a new house at Burgos in 1582, Teresa died and was buried at Alba de Tormes.

In art she is usually represented with a dove above her head or a fiery arrow which pierces her heart, a reference to one of her most famous mystical experiences. Patron saint of lace-makers.

The following feasts are also celebrated today:
St Gregory of Tours: **St Hospicius**, hermit in French **Hospis**, who devoted his life to penance: **St Tecla** a holy English nun at Wimborne in Dorset who being invited by Boniface to Germany was made Abbess of Kilzingen.

October 16
SAINT GALL
The apostle of Switzerland – AD 645

Probably born in Leinster, Gall was educated at Bangor Abbey under Saints Comgall and Columban and was ordained there. He accompanied Columban into voluntary exile on the Continent in c585 along with 11 other companions, and helped to found the monasteries of Annegray and Luxeuil.

During his life he attracted many followers and undoubtedly ranks as one of the most important and pioneering Christian missionaries in Switzerland. It is difficult to be certain why Gall has traditionally been acknowledged as the patron saint of birds. Suggestion comes from the legend of his activities as an exorcist: it was thought that when he cast the demon out of King Sigebert's betrothed it flew out of her mouth in the form of a blackbird. Patron saint of birds.

The following feasts are also celebrated today:
St Lullus or **Lullon**, Archbishop of Mainz, an Englishman, probably one of the West Saxons, who pursued his studies under the Venerable Bede: **St Mummolin** or **Mommolin**, Bishop of Noyon: **St Gerard Majella**, born near Naples, 1726.

When the cares of life are many,
And its burdens heavy grow
For the ones who walk beside you,
If you love them tell them so.
What you count of little value
Has an almost magic power,
And beneath that cheering sunshine
Hearts will blossom like a flower.

Anon

October 17
SAINT MARGARET MARY ALACOQUE
Saint of the Sacred Heart – AD 1690

Born in Burgundy on 22 July, Margaret Mary was the fifth of the seven children of Claude Alacoque, a royal notary, and Philiberte. Her father died when Margaret was only eight and she was sent to school at the Poor Clares in Charolles. But after only two years at the school she was forced to leave through ill-health and between the ages of 10 and 15 was bedridden with rheumatic fever. Even after partial recovery, she remained weak and heavily dependent on her mother and relatives.

Margaret rejected the possibility of marriage and in 1671 enrolled in the Visitation Order at Paray-le-Monial, where after a year as a somewhat clumsy but likeable novice she made her profession as a nun.

Over the next three years she experienced her most famous series of visions. She faced much opposition from theologians and members of her community.

One course of unfailing support was the Jesuit confessor to the convent, Claude la Colombière, who made her visions more widely known and insisted on their genuineness. Margaret died in the convent.

The following feasts are also celebrated today:
St Andrew of Crete, a zealous defender of holy images in the reign of Constantine Copronimus: **St Anstrudis**, commonly called Anstru, Abbess: **St Hedwiges**, Duchess of Poland, entered a Cistercian nunnery after the death of her husband, died in 1243.

October 18
SAINT LUKE
Evangelist – First century

Practically all the information we have about Luke comes from the New Testament. A doctor believed to be of Greek origin, he accompanied Paul on his second missionary journey and stayed on in Philippi to lead the church there until c57. He was with Paul during the shipwreck on Malta and under house arrest in Rome, and after Paul's death is traditionally believed to have gone to Antioch in Greece to lead the Christian community there until his death as an old man.

In art Luke's evangelistic emblem is an ox, perhaps because he mentions Zechariah's sacrifice in the temple at the beginning of his Gospel, and this has led to his patronage of butchers. He is often shown painting the Virgin or holding his book, dressed in his doctor's robes and cap. Patron saint also of bookbinders, doctors, painters, sculptors, glassworkers and surgeons.

> **The following feasts are also celebrated today:**
> **St Julian**, hermit, called **Sabas** for his wisdom and prudence:
> **St Justin** or **Justus**, martyred: **St Monon**, martyr, a native of
> Scotland who led a holy life in the Forest of Ardennes in the
> seventh century; killed in his cell by robbers, his tomb was made
> famous by many miracles; a church near St Andrews in Scotland is
> called Monon's Kirk in his honour.

October 19
SAINT PAUL OF THE CROSS
AD 1775

The eldest son of a father whose ancestry was noble but whose
circumstances were reduced to that of a businessman, Paul Francis Danei
was born near Genoa in Piedmont, Italy on 3 January. His family were
devout and from an early age Paul committed himself to a life of austerity
and religion, renouncing the chance of both a sizeable inheritance and an
advantageous marriage. At the age of 20 he volunteered to fight with the
Venetian army against the Turks but within a year found that he was not
suited to the soldier's life. He was discharged from the army, and spent the
next few years living as a hermit in prayer and penance at Castellazzo,
searching for a direction for his religious zeal.

Finally in 1720 he received the enlightenment he had sought; he
experienced a vision in which the Blessed Virgin, wearing a black habit
with a cross and the name of Jesus in white, instructed him to found a
congregation whose mission should be centred on the cross and passion
of Christ. He secured approval from the bishop, and Paul began his new
order at Monte Argentaro, Tuscany in 1727, with his brother John and a few
companions, after being ordained as a priest in Rome.

Many of those who enrolled with the congregation left, claiming that its
regime was excessively harsh, but nevertheless the order expanded, with
the founding of a convent for Passionist nuns and a few other houses by
the time of Paul's death in 1771. Paul died in Rome and was buried in the
church of St John and St Paul.

> **The following feasts are also celebrated today:**
> **St Ethbin** or **Egbin**, Abbot; he lived twenty years in a cell in the midst
> of a forest, famed for austerities and miracles: **St Frideswide**, virgin,
> patroness of Oxford, who learned from childhood the most important
> Christian maxim that "whatever is not God is nothing"; she desired to
> consecrate her life to God in the cloister, and her father founded a
> nunnery at Oxford in honour of St Mary and all the saints and
> committed its direction to her care: **St Ptolomy** and **St Lucius**,
> martyrs in Rome under Marcus Aurelius in 166.

October 20
The following feasts are celebrated today:

St Aidan, Bishop of Mayo, died in 768: **St Artemius**, an officer of the Romans appointed as general of Europe, summoned to appear before Julian at Antioch and condemned for having broken the idols; beheaded for the faith in 362: **St Barsabias and his Companions**, martyrs in Persia; Barsabias was an abbot, having under him ten monks whom he had educated with great care in the path of Christian perfection; they were marked out among the first to suffer under Sapor; a noble Magian passing by the scene of their martyrdom joined them and gave his life with this heroic band: **St Sindulphus of Sendou**, a priest of Rheims: **St John Cantius**, died in 1473: **St Zenobius**, Bishop of Florence, patron, protector and principal apostle of that city.

October 21
SAINT HILARION
Abbot – AD 371

Hilarion was born near Gaza of pagan parents. He converted to Christianity while studying at Alexandria, was baptized and journeyed to visit St Antony in his desert retreat, with whom he stayed for some time. On his return to Gaza he found that his parents had died; he gave away all that he owned to the poor and retired to become a hermit at Majuma in about 306.

His lifestyle emulated that of St Antony, characterized by austerity and holiness, and he quickly attracted large numbers of disciples and sightseers, who had heard reports of his marvellous miracles. Soon he found himself in possession of land and goods, practically the leader of a community, and to regain the solitude he so desired he was forced to flee Palestine.

He lived first in Egypt but his fame had reached even there and he was soon obliged to move on to Sicily. After three years there his retreat was discovered by Hesychius, a faithful disciple who had pursued him westwards. Again the crowds began to arrive and again Hilarion fled before them to Epidaurus in Dalmatia on the Adriatic coast, and then on to Cyprus. He settled with Hesychius near Paphos but when the islanders discovered his identity he withdrew further inland to a remote spot. There he was visited by Bishop Epiphanius of Salamis in about 403 and died in relative seclusion at the age of 80.

The following feasts are also celebrated today:
St Fintan, surnamed Munno; **St Ursula and companions**, virgins and martyrs.

October 22
The following feasts are celebrated today:
St Donatus, Bishop of Ficosole in Tuscany: **St Mark**, Bishop of Jerusalem: **St Mello**, Bishop of Rouen: **St Nunilo** and **St Alodia**, virgins, martyred in Spain: **St Philip**, Bishop of Heraclea and his companions, martyred under Diocletian.

October 23
SAINT JOHN OF CAPESTRANO
Priest – AD 1456

Born at Capestrano in the Abruzzi in the year 1386. He studied law at Perugia and for a time held the office of judge. Then he entered the Order of Friars Minor, was ordained priest, and went throughout Europe leading an apostolic life. He died at Villach in Austria.

The following feasts are also celebrated today:
St Ignatius, Patriarch of Constantinople: **St John Capistran**: **St Romanus**, brought up at the Court of Clotaire II, became chancellor and later Archbishop of Rouen: **St Severin**, Archbishop of Cologne: **St Theodoret**, priest and martyr.

October 24
SAINT ANTONY MARY CLARET
Bishop – AD 1870

Born at Sallent in the year 1807. After becoming a priest he spent several years preaching to the people throughout Catalonia. He founded a society of missionaries (Claretian Fathers) and was made a bishop in the island of Cuba. Coming back to Spain he had to endure many trials for the sake of the Church. He died at Fontfroide in France.

The following feasts are also celebrated today:
St Felix, Bishop of Thiabara, Africa, martyred for his refusal to give up the books and writings belonging to his church, was beheaded in 303: **St Magliore**, a fellow disciple of St Sampson under St Iltutus in Wales, he resigned his bishopric and retired to a desert on the continent, but later still he governed a monastery of sixty monks in Jersey: **St Proclus** and **St Raphael**, archangel, known to us from the Book of Tobias, his name means "medicine of God" and his special task is to help and pray for those in distress.

October 25
SAINT MARGARET CLITHEROW
AD 1586

Her father was Thomas Middleton, a candle-maker in York who later became sheriff there. She was married to a wealthy butcher named John Clitherow in 1571. As Margaret became more outspoken and active in her faith she was imprisoned for two years, and profited from the confinement by learning to read. On her release she set about establishing a small school in her house for the benefit of her own children and those of the neighbourhood.

In 1586 John Clitherow was brought before a court to explain his son's absence; the boy was in fact studying at a Catholic college on the continent. The house was searched, and Margaret was brought to trial. Wanting to spare her friends and children the ordeal of testifying against her, Margaret stolidly refused to plead, insisting that "Having made no offence, I need no trial." She held to her refusal, and was therefore sentenced to the penalty, death, by pressing. On 25 March in the Tolbooth at York she was crushed to death under a 800-pound weight, killed within 15 minutes.

The following feasts are also celebrated today:
St Boniface, Pope and Confessor, a priest well versed in the discipline of the Church and advanced in years when he succeeded Zosimus, Dec. 29, 418: **St Chrysanthus** and his wife **St Darias**, martyrs: **St Crispin** and **St Crispinian**: **St Gaudentius of Brescia**, ordained Bishop by St Ambrose about 387: **St John of Beverley**, a monk of Whitby, afterwards Archbishop of York: **St Thaddeus Machar**, Bishop.

October 26
The following feasts are celebrated today:
St Bean, an Irishman, first Bishop of Murthlach: **St Evaristus**, Pope and martyr: **St Lucian** and **St Marcian**.

October 27
The following feasts are celebrated today:
St Abban, Abbot in Ireland, son of Cormac, King of Leinster; trained in the monastery of Beg-erin: **St Elesbaan**, King of Ethiopia: **St Frumentus**, Bishop and Confessor, apostle of Ethiopia: **St Otteran**, Bishop, a brother of St Medrain, he died in the middle of the sixth century.

October 28
SAINT JUDE THADDEUS
First century

Luke's Gospel includes the name of Jude but in Matthew and Mark it is replaced by the name Thaddeus; it is widely accepted that the two names refer to the same apostle, believed to be the brother of James the Younger and author of the epistle of Jude.

Jude is best known in modern days as the patron saint of hopeless cases, a familiar name in the personal columns of The Times for appeals for help or expressions of gratitude. This is said to have originated from the uncomfortable similarity of Jude's name to that of Jesus's betrayer, Judas Iscariot; the faithful avoided seeking his help for fear of confusion and hence he was only resorted to in desperate situations, when prayer to all other saints had failed.

In art he is generally represented with the club of his martyrdom, occasionally holding his book, and sometimes holding a ship. Patron saint of hopeless causes.

The following feasts are also celebrated today:
St Faro, fourteenth Bishop of Meaux, who lived rather as a recluse than a courtier at the Court of King Theodobert II: **St Neot**, hermit, first adviser to King Alfred, said to have been related to him, he took the monastic habit at Glastonbury, where the king frequently visited him while he lay concealed in Somerset.

October 29
The following feasts are celebrated today:
St Bede, Doctor of the Church: **St Chef**, in Latin **Theuderius**, Abbot: **St Colman**, patron of Kilmacduagh: **St Narcissus**, Bishop of Jerusalem.

October 30
The following feasts are celebrated today:
St Alphonsus Rodriguez, S.J., 1531-1617: **St Asterius**, Bishop of Amasea in Pontus: **St Germanus**, Bishop of Capua: **St Marcellus the Centurion**, martyr.

Nothing is so strong as gentleness,
nothing so gentle as real strength.
(St Francis de Sales)

November 1
The following feasts are celebrated today:
St Austremonius, who planted the faith in Auvergne in the third century: **St Benignus**, priest and martyr, apostle of Burgundy: St Cæsarius, martyred because he protested against a young man sacrificing his life to Apollo, a Christian priest was, with him, put into a sack and cast into the sea (300): **St Fortunatus**, Bishop: **St Harold VI**, King of Denmark, martyr: **St Marcellus**, Bishop of Paris: **St Mary**, a humble slave to Tertullius.

November 2
The following feasts are celebrated today:
St Marcian, hermit: **St Victorinus**, Bishop, martyred 304: **St Vulgan**, who preached the faith in Lens in Artois and died in a cell there.

November 3
SAINT HUBERT
Bishop – AD 727

Thought to have been the son of the duke of Guienne. He is traditionally believed to have been out hunting one Good Friday instead of attending church. It is said that the stag he was pursuing suddenly turned towards him, and Hubert clearly saw the emblem of a cross between its antlers, and heard a voice calling him to repentance.

He became a priest under St Lambert, bishop of Maastricht, and on the bishop's assassination in about 708, Hubert was appointed his successor. Hubert is said to have been warned of his death a year before it happened. He died on 30 May near Brussels after journeying to consecrate a new church at Brabant, and his body was returned to Liège and buried in the church of St Peter.

Patron saint of hunting and huntsmen, invoked against rabies and hydrophobia.

The following feasts are also celebrated today:
St Flour, apostle of and first Bishop of Lodeve in Languedoc, his relics are kept in the cathedral there: **St Malachy**, Archbishop of Armagh: **St Papoul** or **Papulus**, priest and martyr, after whom a town in Languedoc is called: **St Rumwald**, patron of Brackley and Buckingham: **St Winefride**, virgin and martyr, patron of North Wales, who served God in a small nunnery near Holywell, where miracles still attest her sanctity.

November 4
SAINT CARLO BORROMEO
Bishop/Confessor – AD 1584

Carlo, son of Count Gilbert Borromeo, was born on 2 October at the family castle of Arona on Lake Maggiore. He was educated at the Benedictine abbey at Arona, before going on to further education in Paris and Milan, where despite his speech impediment he proved a hard-working, intelligent and devout pupil.

By the age of 22, with a doctorate in civil and canon law, he was appointed secretary of state, administrator of Milan and cardinal by his uncle, Pius IV, despite the fact that he had not even been ordained as a priest. He was one of the motivating forces in initiating the final part of the famous Council of Trent, which had been suspended in 1552.

His influence can be seen in many of the decrees for reform which it passed, especially in the *Catechismus Romanus,* in the composing of which he played a prominent part. In 1563 he was consecrated Bishop of Milan. Carlo's reforming zeal made him many enemies, but all attempts to remove him from his post and even to assassinate him failed.

He continued working tirelessly until his dedication and commitment wore him out by the age of 46, and he died on 3 November.

The following feasts are also celebrated today:
St Brinstan, Bishop of Winchester in 941: **St Clarus**, martyr, a noble Englishman: **St Joannicius**, Abbot, who, after a dissolute youth, became one of the most illustrious saints of the monastic order: **St Vitalis** and **St Agricola**, martyred at Bologna in 300, the latter a gentleman of that place and the former his slave.

November 5
The following feast is celebrated today:
St Bertille, Abbess of Chelles.

November 6
The following feasts are celebrated today:
St Iltutus or **Iltyd**, a noble Briton, kinsman to King Arthur, who founded and governed the most famous monastery and school then in Britain: **St Leonard**, hermit, a French nobleman, converted by St Remigius, he lived only on wild herbs and fruit: **St Winoc**, Abbot, famed for many miracles.

November 7
The following feasts are celebrated today:
St Presdecimus, first Bishop of Padua: **St Willibrord**, first Bishop of Utrecht, 738: **St Werenfrid**, priest, an English monk who followed St Willibrord into Friesland, preaching the Gospel.

November 8
The following feasts are celebrated today:
St Godfrey, Bishop of Amiens: **St Willehad,** Bishop of Bremen and apostle of Saxony.

November 9
The following feasts are celebrated today:
St Benignus of Benen, Bishop, a disciple of St Patrick, eminent for his gentle disposition: **St Mathurin**, who, embracing the Christian faith, sold all his goods and renounced the world, becoming a priest: **St Theodorus Tyro**, martyr: **St Vanne** or **Vitonius**, Bishop of Verdun.

November 10
SAINT LEO THE GREAT
Pope – AD 461

Nothing is known of Leo's early years, although it is thought that he was born in Tuscany or of Tuscan parents in Rome. We first heard of him as a deacon under Popes Celestine and Sixtus III, obviously a figure who commanded respect within the church since he corresponded with Cyril of Alexandria. He was called to act as peacemaker between Aetius and Albinus, quarrelling generals whose enmity was laying Gaul open to barbarian attacks, and it was while he was still in Gaul that Leo learnt that he had been appointed Pope.

In 452 Italy was attacked by the Huns under Attila, and it seemed that defenceless Rome would inevitably fall, but Leo secured a personal interview with Attila and persuaded him to accept tribute rather than plunder the city. He had less luck three years later with Genseric, leader of the Vandals; despite Leo's intercession Rome was sacked and looted for a fortnight. Leo did obtain a promise that the city would not be burnt, and after its devastation he was able patiently to set about rebuilding the city and its churches and restoring the stricken population. Leo died in Rome, and was buried at St Peter's where his relics were enshrined.

The following feasts are also celebrated today:

St Andrew Avellino, a native of Naples, born 1520: **St Justus**, first Bishop of Rochester, sent to England by Pope Gregory in answer to St Augustine's appeal for workers, Justus was afterwards consecrated Archbishop of Canterbury: **St Milles**, Bishop, **St Ambrosimus**, priest, and **St Sina**, deacon, martyred in Persia, educated at the Persian Court, they suffered death together: **St Trypho** and **St Respicius**, martyrs, natives of Bithnia, commemorated with St Nympha, virgin martyr, because her body lies with theirs at Rome, she was of Palermo, in Sicily.

November 11
SAINT MARTIN OF TOURS
Bishop and Confessor – AD 400

Born in Pannonia (modern Hungary), the son of a pagan Roman army officer, Martin was brought up in Pavia. He joined the army, probably as a conscript, but his life changed in c337, when he tore his cloak in two and gave half to a freezing beggar. That night Christ appeared to him in a dream, wearing the half of the cloak he had given away. Martin was converted to Christianity, refused to continue fighting, was imprisoned and eventually discharged. It is said that when accused of cowardice, Martin offered to stand unarmed between the warring lines.

He lived for some time as a recluse on a small island off the coast of Liguria. Even as bishop he lived in a cell close to his cathedral at Tours and then at Marmoutier, where a community of 80 monks soon grew up. After Martin's death near Tours, his cult spread quickly. Hundreds of villages and churches in France are dedicated to him and his shrine at Tours became the major centre for French pilgrimage.

He is most frequently represented in art dividing his cloak with a beggar, a symbol of charity and hospitality which has associated him with innkeepers. His emblem is a ball of fire over his head.

The popularity of his feast is demonstrated by a second, later emblem, a goose; his feast-day often coincides with the migration of geese. Similarly, the phrase "St Martin's Summer" refers to the spell of good weather which frequently occurs around this time. Patron saint of France, soldiers, beggars and innkeepers.

The following feast is also celebrated today:

St Mennas, an Egyptian, a soldier in the Roman army, martyred after boldly confessing himself a Christian.

November 12
The following feasts are celebrated today:
St Lebwin, Archbishop, patron of Daventer: **St Livin**, Irish bishop, preached in Flanders and was martyred: **St Martin**, Pope and martyr, 655: **St Nilus**, hermit.

November 13
SAINT FRANCES XAVIER CABRINI
AD 1917

Francesca Maria was born on 15 July, the thirteenth and last child of an Italian farmer. She was brought up strictly, much under the influence of her elder sister Rosa, and educated like her to become a schoolteacher, but in 1870 she was orphaned and turned instead to the religious life. After two years, during which time she qualified as a teacher, Frances applied to two convents, only to be rejected by both on the grounds of poor health.

Her potential was recognised, however, by the local parish priest of Codogno, who appointed her to teach in and reorganize a badly-managed orphanage there, the House of Providence. The foundress, Antonio Tondini, who was violently opposed to any interference, made life almost impossible for Frances and the pupils.

In 1880 Antonio Tondini was excommunicated and the orphanage dissolved. Frances left with seven of her pupils to found the Missionary Sisters of the Sacred Heart, which flourished eventually in an abandoned Franciscan friary at Codogno to become an order with houses throughout Northern Italy. In 1889, conquering her childhood fear of water, Frances sailed for America with six sisters to found an orphanage there at the invitation of Archbishop Corrigan.

Frances succeeded in establishing the orphanage and moved it to West Park on the Hudson river, which became the central house of her American congregation. For over 25 years she travelled throughout the Americas and Europe; by the time of her death there were 67 houses devoted to nursing, care of orphans and education. Patroness of immigrants.

The following feasts are also celebrated today:
St Brice, Bishop: **St Chillen** or **Killian** of Ireland, priest, a near kinsman of St Fiaker: **St Constant**, priest, hermit: **St Didacus** or **Diego** (in Spanish, **James**), a native of Seville: **St Mitrius**, martyr: **St Stanislaus Kostka**, son of a Polish senator.

No man should praise poverty but he who is poor. (St Bernard)

November 14
SAINT DUBRICIUS
AD 612

He was probably born at Medley near Hereford and went on to become a monk, whose first foundation was at nearby Ariconium (modern Archenfeld). Later foundations included Henllan and Moccas (in the Wye Valley), which attracted countless novitiates, and having studied there for some time he moved on to found and populate new monasteries and churches.

Geoffrey of Monmouth, who is not renowned for his accuracy, reports that it was Dubricius who crowned Arthur King of Britain and Tennyson takes up the legend in his *Idylls of the King*, Dyfrig is the High King in *The Coming of Arthur.* In art he is represented holding two croziers and the archbishop's cross.

The following feasts are also celebrated today:
St Josaphat, Bishop: **St Laurence**, Archbishop of Dublin 1180: **St Erconwald**, an English prince who governed the monastery of Chertsey in the seventh century.

November 15
SAINT ALBERTUS MAGNUS (ALBERT THE GREAT)
Bishop – AD 1280

Albertus's titles of "great" and "universal" both refer to the phenomenal extent of his learning; he spoke so authoritatively on so many subjects that he was sometimes accused of magic by his bewildered contemporaries. He was born in Swabia, the eldest son of the Count of Bollstadt, but while studying at the University of Padua in 1223 he overthrew his family's objections, rejected his inheritance and joined the recently-founded Dominican Order. The next few years were spent teaching theology, mainly in Cologne where he tutored Thomas Aquinas. Albertus early recognized and loudly proclaimed the genius of his pupil Aquinas; the two men were close friends and intellectual soulmates until Aquinas's death in 1274.

In 1254 Albertus was appointed prior provincial of the Dominican Order and for a time as personal theologian to the Pope in Rome. At the Council of Lyons in 1274 he called for reconciliation between the Greek Church and Rome, and when Aquinas's teaching was attacked by theologians from the University of Paris in 1277 Albertus spoke brilliantly in his defence. But in the next year he suffered a memory lapse; it was the beginning of a degenerative illness that was to lead two years later to his death in Cologne on 15 November 1280. In art he is usually represented lecturing from a pulpit, usually dressed in the robes of a Dominican bishop, or in discussion with Thomas Aquinas.

The following feasts are also celebrated today:
St Eugenius, a disciple of St Dionysius: **St Gertrude**, 1292, chosen Abbess of the Benedictine nunnery of Rodalsdorf: **St Leopold**, marquis of Austria: **St Malo** or **Maclou**, first Bishop of Aleth in Brittany, an Englishman.

November 16
SAINT MARGARET OF SCOTLAND
AD 1093

During the rule of the Danes in England, the ousted Anglo-Saxon royal family lived in exile in the court of St Stephen of Hungary and it was here that Margaret was born and educated, grand-daughter of Edmund Ironside and daughter of Prince Edward d'Outremer and Agatha, a German princess.

In 1057 she was brought back to England, to the court of Edward the Confessor, but her family found themselves in danger yet again after the Norman Conquest of 1066 and fled England a second time arriving under the protection of Malcolm III (Malcolm Canmore) at his court in Scotland.

Malcolm married the beautiful, pious Margaret at Dunfermline castle in 1070, and their marriage seems to have been an exceptionally happy and fruitful one. Eight children were born of the marriage of Malcolm and Margaret; David became one of the best-loved of Scottish kings and was canonized like his mother. Alexander also became king, and Matilda, who married Henry I of England, is the link in the English royal family between the ancient Anglo-Saxon and the Norman lines. Another son was killed along with his father in a rebel attack on Alnwick Castle in 1093.

Broken-hearted and worn out by a life of austerity and childbearing, Margaret herself died at Edinburgh Castle and was buried beside her husband in Dunfermline Abbey.

She is usually represented in art carrying a black cross as she goes about her charitable work visiting the sick. Patron saint of Scotland.

The following feasts are also celebrated today:
St Edmund of Canterbury (Edmund Rich), son of a tradesman, became a monk at Evesham and afterwards Archbishop of Canterbury. After many difficulties with Henry III he died in exile, 1242: **St Eucherius**, Bishop.

No one is suddenly made perfect.
(Bede the Venerable)

November 17
SAINT GREGORY THAUMATURGUS
Bishop – AD c270

Born of wealthy pagan parents in Pontus, he was originally named Theodore and studied for a career in law. He happened to meet Origen in Palestine and was so attracted by Origen's personal example and his teaching that he gave up all thoughts of a legal career, was converted and began studying theology under him.

Gregory returned to Neocaesarea in about 238. There were only 17 Christians in the city, but they unanimously elected him their bishop and he took up the appointment with energy and vision.

Faced with persecution in 250 under Decius, Gregory advised his disciples to follow his example and flee the city. He left for the desert in the company of his deacon (an ex-pagan priest) but his hiding-place was betrayed. The soldiers sent to find him came back, reporting that they had seen only a couple of trees; their informer visited the spot himself to see Gregory and his deacon at prayer.

By the time Gregory died, it is said that Neocaesarea contained only 17 people who did not profess the Christian faith. Because of the legend that he moved the mountain and another that he once stopped the flooding of the Lycus, he is frequently invoked at scenes of natural disasters such as floods and earthquakes, and his reputation for miracles naturally endeared him to those in desperate situations. Patron saint of those in desperate situations, invoked against earthquake and flood.

The following feasts are also celebrated today:
St Anian, in French **Agnan**, Bishop of Orleans: **St Dionysius** called The Great, by St Basil and called the Doctor of the Catholic Church by St Athanasius: **St Gregory of Tours**, Bishop: **St Hugh**, first bishop of Lincoln: **St Hilda**, Abbess and Patron of Whitby.

St Jerome in his study kept a great big cat,
It's always in his pictures, with its feet upon the mat.
Did he give it milk to drink, in a little dish?
When it comes to Fridays, did he give it fish?
If I lost my little cat, I'd be sad without it;
I should ask St Jerome what to do about it;
I should ask St Jerome, just because of that,
For he's the only saint I know who kept a pussy cat.

Anon

November 18
SAINT ODO OF CLUNY
Abbot – AD 942

The son of Abbot of Maine, a knight of Tours, Odo spent his childhood in the households of Count Fulk II of Anjou and Duke William of Aquitaine. He enrolled as a canon of St Martin's in Tours and studied music in Paris and it was here that he first read the Rule of St Benedict; he was so impressed by it that he resigned his canonry and became a monk at Baume-les-Messieurs in 909. Odo became director of the monastery school there and in 924 became abbot of Baume.

When he died at the monastery of St Julian in Tours soon after celebrating the feast of his patron, St Martin, he was a respected and influential figure in both monastic and popular opinion.

> **The following feasts are also celebrated today:**
> **St Alphæus**, **St Zacæus**, **St Romanus** and **St Barulus**, martyrs:
> **St Hilda** or **Hild**, who ruled over a double monastery of monks and nuns in Whitby.

November 19
SAINT ELIZABETH OF HUNGARY
Queen – AD 1231

As befitted a daughter of King Andrew II of Hungary, a suitable marriage had been arranged for Elizabeth in her infancy and at the age of four she was taken to live at the court of Landgrave Herman I of Thuringia, as fiancée to his son Louis (later Louis IV). The marriage of political experience proved to be a love-match too, and when the two were married 10 years later, after the succession of Louis, they appear to have been extraordinarily happy. They lived comfortably at the Wartburg castle near Eisenach with their three children, and Elizabeth was able to give full rein to her impulsively generous nature in building hospitals, giving money to the poor and caring for the needy and especially the orphans.

Elizabeth's romantic history captured the imagination of artists and she is frequently depicted wearing her crown and sheltering or tending beggars. Patron saint of bakers, beggars, Sisters of mercy, charities and lace-makers, invoked against toothache.

> **The following feasts are also celebrated today:**
> **St Balaam**, martyr: **St Pontian**, Pope and martyr.

November 20
SAINT EDMUND
King – AD 870

An Anglo-Saxon who had been brought up as a Christian, Edmund is traditionally believed to have been chosen king of East Anglia whilst still a youth, as the adopted heir of the famous Offa of Mercia. He ruled wisely and peacefully for several years, but disaster came with the invasion of Ingwar from Denmark in 865. In 870 Ingwar led his enormous army down into East Anglia, capturing Thetford in Norfolk. Edmund set out against them with as great an army as he could muster, but he proved no match for the Vikings. His troops were defeated, and he himself captured at Hoxne in Suffolk and imprisoned. His captors demanded that he renounce his Christianity and pay tribute of land and homage to Ingwar, both of which Edmund staunchly refused to perform, despite horrific torture.

In art, Edmund's emblem is usually an arrow or occasionally the wolf which was believed to have guarded his head after execution. He is also famously portrayed on the Wilton Diptych along with Edward the Confessor, as the patron of England who presents Richard II to the Virgin Mary and Child. Patron saint of Richard II, invoked against plague.

The following feasts are also celebrated today:
St Bernward, Bishop of Hildesheim, chaplain to Otho III, King of Germany: **St Felix of Valois**: **St Humbert**, Bishop of the East-Angles, martyr: **St Maxentia** of Ireland, virgin, martyr.

November 21
SAINT COLUMBAN
AD 615

Despite his mother's objections, Columban dedicated himself to the religious life from an early age. His family were noble and he probably received an excellent education before deciding to become a monk. He lived first on an island at Lough Erne called Cluain Inis, and then went on to Bangor as a disciple of St Comgall. After many years in c590, he obtained permission from Comgall to leave with 12 companions on a mission to Gaul, one of the many Irish monks to enter voluntary exile on the Continent.

The Irish group founded three centres of monasticism, Annegray, Luxeuil and Fontaine. Columban then founded a monastery at Bobbio, participating in the building himself. It became the greatest centre for monasticism and spiritual life in the area and it was there that he died on 23 November. His emblem in art is a bear.

The following feast is also celebrated today:
St Gelasius, Pope, of an African family.

November 22
SAINT CECILIA
The Virgin Martyr of music – Second/Third century

Cecilia was born into a Christian patrician family in Rome and early consecrated her virginity to God. Against her will she was betrothed to one Valerian, and on her wedding night told him of her vow and persuaded him to respect it. Cecilia was apprehended burying the bodies of Christian martyrs and she was brought before the prefect, Almachius. Almachius tried to overthrow her faith by debate; when this failed he gave orders that she was to be suffocated. Cecilia was miraculously unharmed and Almachius sent a soldier to despatch her by beheading. Unfortunately for Cecilia, the soldier proved to be an incompetent executioner; three blows failed to kill her and she lingered on for three agonized days, still singing to God, before finally dying.

After her death her house became a church, possibly the St Cecilia in Rome's Trastevere quarter, and her body was buried in the Cemetery of Callistus. She is usually represented with an organ, lute or other musical instrument, but ancient art shows her without an emblem. Patron saint of poets, singers, music and musicians.

The following feasts are also celebrated today:
St Philemon and St Appia: St Theodorus the Studite, Abbot.

November 23
SAINT CLEMENT I
Pope and Martyr – AD c101

St Peter was succeeded as bishop of Rome by Linus and Cletus and according to legend Cletus's successor in c91 was Clement, a freedman of the imperial household. The Emperor Trajan however found the extensive apostolic activity of the new bishop intensely galling, and according to the fourth century Acts, Clement was sentenced to labour in the Crimea.

Undaunted, he is said to have created a spring there and preached with such success to the miners that 75 new churches were built among the Christian community. At this, the imperial displeasure was roused to such a pitch that Clement found himself lashed to an anchor and drowned.

Seven hundred years later Cyril and Methodius, the apostles to the Slaves, claimed to have discovered the pieces of his body together with the anchor. The relics were translated to the church of San Clemente in Rome in 868.

The following feasts are also celebrated today:
St Amphilochius, Bishop of Iconium, a friend of St Basil and St Gregory Nazianzen: St Daniel, bishop of Bangor.

November 24
The following feasts are celebrated today:
St Chrysogonus: St Ceanan or Kenan, Bishop of Duleek in Ireland: St Flora and St Mary, virgins and martyrs.

November 25
SAINT CATHERINE OF ALEXANDRIA
AD c310

Catherine was born of a wealthy, possibly even a royal, family in Alexandria, and that after her conversion by a vision at the age of about 18 she denounced the emperor Maxentius for his persecution of the Christians.

Thinking to silence this upstart girl, the emperor confronted her with 50 pagan philosophers; instead of exposing the fallacies of her faith through reason, however, they were unable to answer her arguments and the furious Maxentius had them executed. He then tried to bribe Catherine into silence with the offer of a royal marriage, and was further enraged when she refused, calmly declaring herself "the bride of Christ".

Catherine was imprisoned, but not silenced. On returning home from a camp inspection one day Maxentius found that his wife, his chief soldier Porphyrius and 200 of his imperial guard had been converted to Christianity. By now almost insane with anger, Maxentius executed them and prepared a spiked wheel on which Catherine was to be broken, but he was thwarted again when the wheel burst leaving Catherine unharmed, although several spectators were killed by flying splinters. Finally he had the troublesome saint beheaded, at which it is said milk rather than blood ran from her veins.

She is frequently depicted in paintings, tapestries and manuscripts, identified by the wheel of her martyrdom or shown confounding the pagan philosophers. Patron saint of philosophers, preachers, librarians, young girls and craftsmen working with a wheel (eg potters, spinners, etc.).

The following feast is also celebrated today:
St Erasmus or Elme, lived as a hermit on Mount Lebanus.

Be not anxious about what you have, but about what you are.
(Pope St Gregory)

November 26
The following feasts are celebrated today:
St Conrad, Bishop of Constance, "a saint from the cradle": **St Leonard of Port Maurice**: **St Nicon**, surnamed Metanoite: **St Peter**, martyr, Bishop of Alexandria: **St Sylvester Gozzolini**, Abbot of Osimo.

November 27
The following feasts are celebrated today:
St Cungar, also known as Docunus, Abbot, died in 711: **St James**, surnamed **Intercisus**, martyr, a Persian: **St Maharsapor**, a noble Persian prince, martyr: **St Maximum**, Bishop of Riez about 460: **St Secundin** or **Seachnal**, bishop in Ireland, nephew and disciple of St Patrick: **St Virgil**, Bishop of Saltzburg, born in Ireland.

November 28
The following feasts are celebrated today:
St James of La Marca of Ancona: **St Stephen** the Younger.

November 29
The following feasts are celebrated today:
St Cuthbert Mayne, martyr: **St Radbod**, Bishop of Utrecht: **St Saturninus**, martyr, Bishop of Toulouse.

November 30
SAINT ANDREW
Apostle – AD c60

A native of Bethsaida, by Lake Genesareth in Galilee, Andrew was born into a family of fishermen. His father, Jona, and brother Simon, worked on the lake with him, but it appears that by the time of Jesus's ministry the brothers were living in Capernaum, since Jesus stayed in their house while visiting the town. Andrew was an early follower of John the Baptist.

After baptizing both Andrew and Simon Peter in the Jordan, Jesus called them from their nets to full-time discipleship with the famous words "Come, follow me, and I will make you fishers of men." Andrew is also mentioned at the feeding of the five thousand, and in the Upper Room at Pentecost.

The distinctive saltire (X-shaped) cross associated with Andrew and used in the Scottish flag was an innovation of the 10th century; ancient art depicts him bound to a regular cross from which he is said to have preached for two days before dying. He is also frequently depicted with a fishing net, obvious symbol of his occupation as both fisherman and evangelist. Patron saint of Scotland, Russia, Achaia, fishermen and old maids, invoked against gout and sore throats.

The following feasts are also celebrated today:
St Narses, Bishop: **St Sapor**, **St Isaac** (Bishops), **St Mahanes**, **St Abraham** and **St Simeon**, martyrs.

December 1
SAINT ELOI (Eligius)
Bishop – AD c658

Born near Limoges in Gaul of Gallo-Roman parents, he was apprenticed by his metal-working father to a goldsmith named Abbo, master of the mint at Limoges.

Having learnt his trade Eloi worked under the royal treasurer Bobon and gained a name for himself as a goldsmith of exceptional skill who was unusually economical with his materials.

This thriftiness attracted the attention of King Clotaire II who took him into his personal service on learning that he had managed to make two exquisite thrones out of the gold allocated for only one.

He became master of the mint in Paris and was commissioned by both Clotaire and his successor, Dagobert I, to work on various royal projects such as shrines, crosses, chalices and plaques. Naturally Eloi gained great personal wealth from his sudden elevation; this he used to help the needy, free slaves and establish a number of churches and other foundations.

In 640 he was ordained as a priest and the following year was consecrated bishop of Noyon and Tournai. He died in his monastery at Noyon, a popular figure whose craftsmanship and holiness alike were revered.

Not surprisingly he was claimed as patron by metalworkers and goldsmiths in particular; his emblems in art are more frequently a hammer, anvil and horseshoe than the goldsmith's hammer, although this does occur, because of a legend which tells how he detached the leg of a horse in order to shoe it more easily and then restored it to the animal.

The following feasts are also celebrated today:
St Edmund Campion, S. J., **St Ralph Sherwine**, **St Thomas Ford**, **St William Filby**, priests, martyrs: **St Didacus**: **St Eligius**, Bishop of Noyon: **St Nessan**, Patron of Cork, a disciple of St Finbar.

December 2
The following feasts are celebrated today:

St Bibiana, virgin and martyr (363), daughter to Flavin, a Roman knight: **St Finian**, Bishop of Cluain-iraird (called Clonard) in Meath, 552.

December 3
SAINT FRANCIS XAVIER
Confessor – AD 1552

Born of a wealthy Spanish Basque family, Francis left home to study at the University of Paris. While he was there he met and befriended Ignatius Loyola, and with five others they took monastic vows together at Montmartre in 1534, becoming the first Jesuits, and were ordained together as priests three years later in Venice. Francis visited Rome in 1538 and two years later he was sent along with Fr Simon Rodriguez to the East Indies, the first of countless Jesuit missionaries.

The voyage took 13 months; when Francis finally arrived he made his base at Goa. He spent the next seven years living alongside the peasants in India, Ceylon and Malaysia. In c1548 he moved further east to Japan, travelling to Hirado then on to Yamaguchi and the capital, Miyako. After returning briefly to Goa, Francis embarked on his final journey, a mission of which he had long dreamed, to China. He never reached the shore.

On the island of San-chian, near the mouth of the river Canton, he fell ill waiting for the ship that was to drop him secretly on the mainland and died, accompanied only by a young Chinese Christian from Goa named Antony. His body was taken in quicklime to Goa, where it is still enshrined. In art Francis is usually represented as a young bearded Jesuit together with a torch, flame, cross and lily, and sometimes in company with Ignatius Loyola.

The following feasts are also celebrated today:

St Birinus, first Bishop of Dorchester in the seventh century: **St Lucius**, King: **St Sola**, hermit.

December 4
The following feasts are celebrated today:

St Anno, Bishop: **St Barbara**, virgin and martyr: **St Peter Chrysogonus**, Archbishop of Ravenna and Doctor of the Church, 450: **St Osmund**, Bishop of Salisbury, 1099: **St Siran**, Abbot, in the seventh century.

December 5
The following feasts are celebrated today:
St Birinus, a Roman priest sent to England about 625: **St Nicetius**, Bishop of Triers: **St Sabas**, Abbot in Capadosia.

December 6
SAINT NICHOLAS
Bishop of Myra – Fourth century

He is thought by some to have been born at Patara in Lycia into a wealthy family, and on becoming bishop transformed it with his piety, energy and miracles. Perhaps the most famous legend is that of his intervention to save the honour of three poverty-stricken sisters; their father could not afford their dowries and in desperation was about to give them over to prostitution. Hearing of this, Nicholas secretly came by the house at night and threw a bag of gold, sufficient for one sister's dowry, through the window on three different occasions. This is the source of the traditional sign for pawnbrokers, three golden balls. Frequent representation of the story, with the three rounded money bags, may have led to a different version of the legend in which the three balls became the severed heads of three murdered children, whom Nicholas found and restored to life.

The mystical number three recurs in Nicholas's legends; he is also said to have saved three prisoners who had been falsely condemned from execution by warning Emperor Constantine of their innocence in a dream, and to have miraculously rescued three sailors off the coast of Turkey. As patron of children, Nicholas's feast-day became associated with the giving and receiving of presents. Nicholas is usually shown in art with the three balls of gold. Patron saint of Russia, children, pawnbrokers, unmarried girls, perfumiers and sailors.

The following feasts are also celebrated today:
St Dionysia, **St Dativa** and other martyrs: **St Nicholas**, Archbishop of Myra in Asia: **St Peter Paschal**, Bishop.

December 7
SAINT AMBROSE
Bishop, Confessor and Doctor – AD 397

Ambrose senior was praetorian prefect of Gaul, and on his death his young son was taken back to Rome to be educated. After distinguishing himself at his studies in rhetoric and poetry, he became a lawyer renowned for his oratory skills, and his success paved the way in c369 to a commission from the emperor; governorship of Liguria and Aemilia. Based at the capital of his province, Milan, he proved an industrious and popular ruler. One of the best-loved bishops of the church, Ambrose has also had an enormous influence on the history of western Christianity, not least for his part in the conversion of Augustine whom he baptized in 387.

Patron saint of Milan, bee-keepers, wax refiners and domestic animals.

The following feast is also celebrated today:
St Fara, Abbess, in the seventh century.

December 8
The following feast is celebrated today:
St Romaric, Abbot, in the seventh century.

December 9
The following feasts are celebrated today:
St Felix of Valois: St Leocadia, martyr, a native of Toledo: **St Peter Fourier**, known as "the good father of Mattaincourt", his birth place, of which he became the parish priest. He instituted a mutual help bank as well as pious societies and founded the Order of Notre Dame to teach poor girls: **The Seven Martyrs of Samosata** (297), these were **St Hipparchus**, **St Philothea**, **St James**, **St Paragrus**, **St Habebus**, **St Romanus** and **St Lollianus**: **St Wulfhilde**, Abbess (990).

December 10
The following feasts are celebrated today:
St Erconwald: **St Melchiades**.

December 11
SAINT DANIEL THE STYLITE
AD 493

The son of Christian parents in Mesopotamia, Daniel entered a nearby monastery at the age of 12. He spent the next 30 years there, during which time he accompanied his abbot to Antioch.

On the journey they visited St Simeon Stylites, aloft on his pillar at Telanissus, and Daniel was inspired. When the abbot died some time later Daniel refused the abbacy, going instead to revisit Simeon. He stayed there for two weeks and joined Simeon on his platform to receive instruction.

When Simeon the Stylite died in 459 Daniel inherited the saint's cloak and his lifestyle. He lived on a series of pillars for the next 33 years; the first, which he erected himself just outside Constantinople, provided inadequate protection from the elements and the emperor intervened to supply a platform raised on two joined pillars with a rail and shelter. Daniel refused to descend even for ordination; the archbishop conducted the service at the base of the pillar and ascended by ladder to give the new priest communion. He became famous for prophecy (he foresaw a serious fire in Constantinople in 465), and his sermons attracted vast crowds of listeners. A week before his death Daniel preached his final sermon, and the saint's body was finally brought down, bent and unkempt from his long years of exposure, to be buried at the foot of his pillar.

The following feasts are also celebrated today:
St Damasus I, Pope, a Spaniard: **St Fuscian**, **St Victorinus**, martyrs: **St Gemtian**, martyr.

December 12
SAINT FINNIAN
AD c549

Born and educated in Co Carlow, Ireland, Finnian spent much time in the monasteries of Wales studying under Saints Cadoc and Gildas, and it was in Wales that he took his vows as a monk. On returning to Ireland he founded several monasteries, including those at Aghowle in Co Wicklow and Mugna Sulcain, following the traditional monastic principles of his Welsh teachers.

The most significant of these foundations was Clonard near Kinnegad in Co Meath, which with its central location drew thousands of followers to study there. Finnian died on 12 December, a victim of the "yellow plague" that was sweeping Ireland at the time. His relics remained in a shrine there until it was destroyed in 887. Although he is widely regarded as a bishop there is no clear evidence that Finnian was in fact ordained.

The following feasts are also celebrated today:
St Colman, Abbot in Ireland: **St Columba** or **Columb**, Abbot: **St Corentin**, Bishop of Quimper in the fifth century: **St Cormac**, Abbot of Glendaloch, 659: **St Eadburghe**, Abbess of Thanet, 751.

All possessions of mortals are mortal.
(Latin proverb)

December 13
SAINT ODILIA (Ottilia)
AD c720

Odilia was born at Obernheim, in the Vosges Mountains, the daughter of the Alsatian Lord Adalric. Her father wished to put her to death, despising her as a family disgrace since she had been born blind, but her mother Bereswindis persuaded him to allow her to give the child to a peasant woman who would know nothing of her background.

So Odilia was sent to Baume-les-Dames near Bexançon, and entered the convent there. She was baptized by Bishop St Erhard of Regensburg and during the ceremony, as the bishop touched her eyes with the consecrated oil, she was miraculously able to see. Her brother Hugh arranged for her to return home to be reconciled to her father, but being incensed on hearing of her return he struck his son and killed him. Adalric changed his mind, however, and welcomed his daughter back, replacing his former indifference with extravagant affection, and attempting to arrange for her a suitable and advantageous marriage with a German duke. Odilia fled to avoid the match, wishing to remain a virgin, and her father pursued her with murderous intent. On catching her, however, Adalric was so impressed by her miraculous protection from his anger that he agreed to let her convert his Alsatian castle at Hohenburg (now Odilienburg) into a convent, the abbess of which Odilia became.

Odilia went on to found a second convent at Niedermünster, where she lived until her death. Patron saint of Alsace and the blind.

The following feasts are also celebrated today:
St Adalbert, Bishop of Cambray: **St Anthony Grassi**: **St Lucy**, martyred at Syracuse in 304 by having her eyes plucked out and is often painted with the balls of her eyes in a dish and is invoked for blindness.

December 14
SAINT JOHN OF THE CROSS
AD 1591

Juan de Yepes y Alvarez was born on 24 June in Spanish Old Castile into an impoverished noble family. His father died while he was a child, and his mother moved with John to Medina del Campo, where he attended the school. John was early apprenticed to the silk-making trade, but soon abandoned it to study at the Jesuit college in Medina.

In 1563, he enrolled with the Carmelite order in the town and went on to study theology in Salamanca before being ordained as priest in 1567. On a visit back to Melina he met Teresa of Ávila, who persuaded him to join her reform movement within the Carmelite order, and in 1586 John and four other friars founded the first men's community at Duruelo. John founded and ran a college at Baeza from 1579 to 1581. In 1582, the year of Teresa's death, he became prior at Granada and three years later was appointed provincial of Andalusia, then prior at Segovia. He fell sick and died at Ubeda. He is usually shown in art writing before a crucifix, often illuminated by heavenly light, and sometimes with an eagle holding a pen it its mouth.

The following feasts are also celebrated today:
St **Fingar** and his **Companions**, martyred in Cornwall in 455:
St **Narcissius**, Archbishop of Rheims: St **Spiridion**, native of Cyprus.

December 15
The following feasts are celebrated today:
St **Eusebius**, Bishop of Vercelli, born of a noble family in Sardinia:
St **Florence** or **Flan**, Abbot of Benchor.

December 16
SAINT ADELAIDE
AD 999

The daughter of Rudolf II, King of Upper Burgundy, Adelaide was wedded to Prince Lothair of Italy at the age of 16 as a result of a political agreement between Rudolf and Hugh of Provence, Lothair's father, which had been arranged when she was only two. In 950, however, Lothair died; he may have been murdered by Berengarius, who succeeded him and who tried to force Adelaide to marry his son. She refused and was imprisoned, but when Otto the Great of Germany invaded Berengarius's territory he freed this royal prisoner and took her back to Pavia with him, where they married in 951.

Shortly afterwards he was crowned emperor by Pope John XII in Rome, and he died in 973. For the next 20 years Adelaide faced enmity and opposition from her husband's family. Otto II, son of Otto and Adelaide, succeeded his father, but his Greek wife Theophano disliked her mother-in-law intensely and managed to turn Otto against her. When Theophano herself died in 991 the venerable Adelaide returned, to be invested with the power of regent. She used her new authority to found and restore monasteries in the area, and was much concerned with evangelizing the Slavs. She died at Seltz in Alsace, in the convent which she had founded there. In art she is represented as an empress giving alms or food to the poor, often next to a ship.

The following feasts are also celebrated today:
St **Adalbert**, Bishop of Madgeburg: St **Ado**, Archbishop of Vienne,
875: St **Beanus**, Bishop: St. **Flannan**, Bishop of Killaloe.

December 17
The following feasts are celebrated today:
St Begga, widow, in the seventh century: **St Olympias**, also a widow, called "the glory of widows".

December 18
The following feasts are celebrated today:
St Gatian, first Bishop of Tours in the third century: **St Magnenius**: **St Rufus** and **St Zozimus**, martyrs: **St Winebald**, Abbot, 760.

December 19
The following feast is celebrated today:
St Nemesion, an Egyptian, first accused of theft of which charge he easily cleared himself, but was immediately charged with being a Christian; he was scourged with far more severity than the thieves, and he was then condemned to be beheaded.

December 20
The following feasts are celebrated today:
St Paul, a hermit in the tenth century: **St Philogonius**, trained for the law and equally admired for his eloquence.

December 21
SAINT THOMAS
Apostle

St Thomas, known as "Didymus" or "the twin", was chosen from among the Galilean fishermen to be one of the twelve Apostles whom Jesus chose as the foundation of His Church. St Thomas doubted our Lord's Resurrection, but after Jesus made him place his finger into His wounds, Thomas' incredulity was changed into ardent faith. St Thomas preached the Gospel in the Orient as far as India and there died for the Faith.

The following feast is also celebrated today:
St Edburge, virgin.

December 22
The following feasts are celebrated today:
St Cyril and **St Methodius**, Bishops in the 9th century: **St Ischyrion**, martyr.

December 23
The following feasts are celebrated today:
St Servulus (590), a beggar: **St Victoria**, virgin and martyr.

December 24
The following feasts are celebrated today:
St Thrasilla and **St Emiliana**, two of the three aunts of St Gregory the Great, who became saints.

December 25
The following feasts are celebrated today:
St Eugenia, virgin and martyr.

December 26
SAINT STEPHEN
Martyr – AD c35

Stephen was deacon of the early church in Jerusalem, one of the seven chosen by the apostles to supervise the administration of alms and help in the work of evangelism. Since one of his main functions was to aid the Hellenic widows of the community, it seems more than likely that he was himself a Greek-speaking Jew, and some scholars have speculated that he was born abroad and may have been educated in Alexandria.

Acts record that Stephen performed wonderful miracles after his ordination and that he was an outstanding preacher, whose wisdom was irrefutable. Inevitably he ran into opposition from the Jewish religious leaders.

The elders of the synagogue attempted first to defeat him in debate, and when this proved impossible, they rushed upon Stephen, drove him out of the city and stoned him to death. He is usually represented in art as a deacon with a stone as his emblem, often holding a book or the palm of martyrdom. Patron saint of deacons, invoked against headaches.

The following feasts are also celebrated today:
St Comman, Abbot and founder of the Church of Roscommon: **St Jarlath**, Bishop of Tuam, 540.

What a man is in the sight of God,
so much he is and no more.
(St Francis of Assisi)

December 27
SAINT JOHN THE EVANGELIST
AD c100

A Galilean fisherman who worked with his father Zebedee and his older brother James the Great, John was called from Lake Genesareth along with James by Jesus. He seems to have shared with his brother the fiery temperament that earned them the nickname "Sons of Thunder".

Along with James and Peter, John was present at the healing of Peter's mother-in-law, the raising of Jairus's daughter, the Transfiguration and the agony of Jesus in the Garden Gethsemane. He was sent along with Peter to prepare for the Last Supper, and when the women reported the angel's appearance to them at Christ's tomb it was Peter and John who ran to the garden; the younger and fitter John reached the tomb first but hesitated to enter. John is the only disciple named as being present at the Crucifixion, when Jesus handed his mother into his care.

John's emblem as an evangelist is an eagle, and he is often shown with a cup containing a viper, symbol of the poisoned drink which he was challenged to swallow by a priest of Diana in Ephesus. Patron saint of theologians, writers and all aspects of the book trade.

The following feast is also celebrated today:
St Theodorus, Abbot.

December 28
The following feasts are celebrated today:
St Theodorus, Confessor.

December 29
SAINT THOMAS BECKET (Thomas à Becket)
AD 1170

The child of a wealthy Norman family, whose father Gilbert was a prosperous merchant and sheriff of London, Thomas was educated at Merton Abbey in Surrey and studied law in London before going on to the University of Paris.

The unexpected death of his father, however, meant that his financial situation took a turn for the worse, and he spent some time working as a clerk before attaching himself to the household of Archbishop Theobald of Canterbury in 1141. The archbishop sent him to Rome on several occasions, and then in 1144 to Bologna and Auxerre to study canon law.

Ten years later, having been ordained deacon, he was appointed archdeacon of Canterbury. In this capacity he proved a diplomatic and effective servant for the archbishop in his dealings with the court, and he endeared himself to Henry d'Anjou (later Henry II of England).

Henry elected Thomas chancellor in 1155, the first native Englishman since the Norman conquest to hold such a lofty position. This cordial relationship changed suddenly and completely in 1162 when Henry appointed Thomas archbishop of Canterbury, despite the latter's objections, following the death of Theobald.

Thomas immediately resigned his chancellorship and the day before his consecration was ordained as a priest. He consciously and deliberately changed to an austere regime, adopting a hair shirt and living under strict discipline, determined to carry out properly the job he had not wanted.

In addition to his new ascetic regime, he began to give away vast amounts of money to the poor. All this was immensely irritating to Henry, and the split between the two men worsened when Thomas began to support the interests of the Church over those of the Crown and took upon himself the task of ministering to and improving the spiritual welfare of the king.

Henry was furious: "who will rid me of this turbulent priest!" he stormed to his courtiers. Four of his nobles saw a chance of rendering pleasing service to their sovereign; they visited Becket in the cathedral at Canterbury and murdered him there. The whole of Europe reeled at the news of his death. He was declared a martyr and became a symbol of the freedom and authority of the Church.

Many depictions of Becket survive, most of them showing his death at the hand of the knights before the altar, and this dramatic scene has been immortalised in T S Eliot's play *Murder in the Cathedral*.

The following feasts are also celebrated today:
St Evroul, Abbot, in the sixth century: **St Marcellus**, Abbot.

December 30
The following feasts are celebrated today:
St Maximus, martyred in the seventh century: **St Sabinus**, Bishop of Assisium.

December 31
The following feasts are celebrated today:
St Columba, virgin and martyr: **St Melania**, who lived in the sixth century: **St Sylvester**, Pope, 335.